The South West Way

A Traveller's Companion

For Carla

The South West Way

A Traveller's Companion

Peter Dawson

MACDONALD & CO
LONDON & SYDNEY

Contents

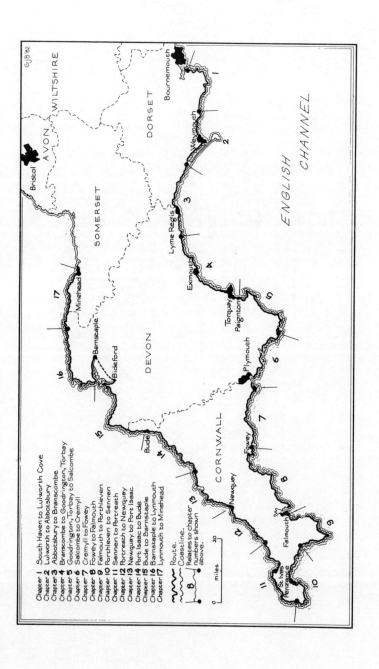

Chapter 1   South Haven to Lulworth Cove
Chapter 2   Lulworth to Abbotsbury
Chapter 3   Abbotsbury to Branscombe
Chapter 4   Branscombe to Goodrington, Torbay
Chapter 5   Goodrington, Torbay to Salcombe
Chapter 6   Salcombe to Cremyll
Chapter 7   Cremyll to Fowey
Chapter 8   Fowey to Falmouth
Chapter 9   Falmouth to Porthleven
Chapter 10   Porthleven to Sennen
Chapter 11   Sennen to Portreath
Chapter 12   Portreath to Newquay
Chapter 13   Newquay to Port Isaac
Chapter 14   Port Isaac to Bude
Chapter 15   Bude to Barnstaple
Chapter 16   Barnstaple to Lynmouth
Chapter 17   Lynmouth to Minehead

Route.
Coastline.
8 Relates to chapter
   numbers shown
   above.

0   miles   20

GJB '82

WILTSHIRE

AVON

Bristol

SOMERSET

DEVON

CORNWALL

St Ives
Penzance

Newquay

Bude

Bideford

Barnstaple

Minehead

Plymouth

Fowey

Falmouth

Torquay
Paignton

Exmouth

Lyme Regis

Weymouth

Bournemouth

DORSET

ENGLISH CHANNEL

11
10
9
8
7
6
5
4
3
2
1
12
13
14
15
16
17

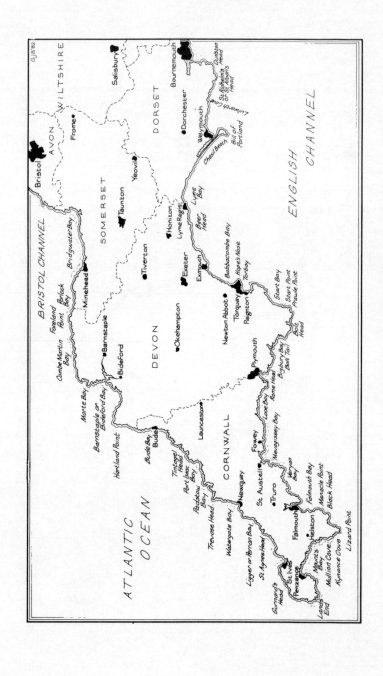

Introduction

The best way to see a country, unless you are pressed for time, is to travel on foot. This book is a companion for those setting out to see one of the world's most beautiful stretches of coastal scenery and, although those who travel on foot will get the most from it, I hope that it will heighten the enjoyment of those misguided souls who insist on using a machine to help them on their way.

Walking is a very complete pleasure and, once tasted, an easy one to become addicted to. The walker is self-sufficient, depending on little but his own strength, resistance, intelligence and a minimum of equipment. Of course degrees of sophistication can be added: technologically advanced equipment, luxury hotels, smart forms of transport to and from the area, exotic regions of the world, but none of this is essential. Walking is one of the rare pleasures which can be enjoyed with little more than the physical and mental attributes we had at birth. And even these need not be extraordinary in any way, for we are free to choose our own pace and the duration of each leg of our journey. The French preface their footpath guides with the maxim: one day's walking, eight day's health. You can argue about the ratio but not about the principle. The more you walk, the healthier you are. How agreeable to stay in shape by striding across some of the finest country the world has to offer, watching the morning-glory awake, shaking the dew from its trumpet-like flower and, in the evening, joyfully weary, seeing an early owl wing its way across a purple sky. The South West Way has been richly endowed by nature and by man: dramatic landscapes, a range of climates, all sorts of plant and wild life, pre-history and history, attractive villages and towns, the sea in all its humours and air which would invigorate a corpse.

THE PATH

The seeds were sown for this coastal footpath in the early 1930s. In 1945 John Dower gave form to the idea in his report The National Parks of England and Wales, and in 1947 the National Parks Committee recommended that there should be a footpath all the way around the coast of England and Wales.

Germination was not swift. The Cornwall coast path was opened in May 1973; South Devon and Dorset in September 1974; and North Devon and Somerset in May 1978. Delay was mainly associated with problems of rights of way; and negotiations are not entirely settled today. Although the path is continuous, it is still not completely coastal and efforts continue to acquire the few outstanding rights. Often it has been the Government itself which has denied or restricted access to various parts of the coast. The path follows the old coastguard path, which coastguards patrolled between their look-outs from their creation in 1822 until just before the outbreak of the First World War. Originally, their task was to look out for the smugglers who infested the coast; now they co-ordinate search and rescue at sea.

Estimates of the length of the path vary, possibly because some authorities choose to omit built-up areas from their calculations – a questionable practice since they have to be negotiated. In 1982 I walked the path from Poole Harbour to Minehead in 19 days and covered 962 kilometres. Estimates vary from 800 to 824 to 884 kilometres. This last is the figure given by the South West Way Association and is probably the best estimate for the official path as it stands today, whereas mine is the distance I travelled.

There are some steep slopes on the path, but the real strenuousness comes from the switch-back nature of the terrain. Unlike walking in the Alps, or any other mountain range for that matter, ascents and descents tend to be grouped closely together on the path and that can be very wearing for someone travelling at speed from one end to the other. However, taken slowly, at the pace of the individual, they should not prevent anyone from completing the path. One spring I met a man of nearly seventy nearing Studland after three month's walk – the first time he had attempted it.

PLANNING AND PREPARATION

This is the longest long distance footpath in the British Isles. Although it will obviously be more satisfying to do the whole of the path at one go, it requires more time than many have at their disposal. It is quite possible to walk the path in several parts and at days, weeks, months or years of interval. On one trip I met a young man bent upon doing all of the long distance footpaths in Britain whose decisions were influenced by the need to get back regularly to pick up his unemployment benefit. The elderly gentleman I mentioned earlier had waited until his retirement in order to be able to do the whole path. You must first decide how much time you have and how far you can manage in that time. I suggest that a person lightly laden can walk at 4 kilometres an hour, walking continuously without halts. Only you will be able to judge your own pace; until you know, use that as your planning figure.

Choose the direction you wish to walk in. I have walked the path both clockwise and anti-clockwise. Although I have walked it often out of season I have never been troubled by the prevailing westerly wind which most writers give as their reason for preferring a Minehead start and anti-clockwise travel. Timing may be out of your control, governed by holiday periods and so on, but you should know that whereas the path is often very much more attractive out of season, the administrative/practical problems are greater. Buses and ferries are less frequent, if not non-existent, and accommodation and refreshment places are often closed. You will be amply repaid for these inconveniences by fewer people and very much more wild-life.

You will need to acquire maps and the SWWA guide for your planning and the journey. Maps are essential even on this path where the sea is a constant reference point and you seldom have to travel more than 1½ kilometres inland to a road. The Ordnance Survey 1:50,000 Landranger series are undoubtedly the best available, although they are expensive. Some walkers find that they can get by on the 1:100,000 Bartholomew's maps, but these are really better for the cyclist than the walker. The SWWA guide has detailed information about the state of the path, temporary diversions, ferries, public transport, accommodation and camping, as well as many useful addresses. Unless you are already an experienced walker, you will also need some specialist advice on your new pursuit. I recommend *Britain at Your Feet*, by David Wickers and Art Pedersen (published in paperback by Hamlyn), which will give you advice on everything from the choice of equipment to the cure of blisters – or, better still, their prevention.

CLOTHING AND EQUIPMENT

The golden rule is buy the best you can afford; if you really can not afford good quality, borrow or hire part or all of your equipment until you can. You will find good advice on the choice of all equipment in *Britain At Your Feet*, mentioned above. You must go to a specialist shop and ask the advice of a knowledgeable assistant; they are quite often ardent walkers themselves. Pamper your feet. Buy the best boots you can. You will not need heavy mountaineering boots with shanked soles, but you will need stout walking boots with vibram soles and leather uppers which come just above your ankle to support it over rough ground. A rucksack, waterproof clothing, wind proof clothing, woollen trousers or breeches, woollen shirts and jerseys, shorts and a swim suit – to make use of the tempting beaches and the fine weather – are other items you will need. A water bottle, a compass, a first aid kit (lots of plaster for your feet), and a knife make up your basic equipment. The specialist shop and *Britain At Your Feet* will give you advice on more specific needs.

ACCOMMODATION AND REFRESHMENT

During the season there is ample accommodation to suit all tastes all the way along the path – hotels of all categories, bed and breakfast places by the hundred, youth hostels, and camping sites. You must always request permission if you want to camp away from recognized sites, and this is often granted. In season it is advisable to book your accommodation in advance. There are generally ample facilities for refreshments on or near the Path, although these too tend to be much more limited out of season and there are some stretches where you are advised to carry whatever you may require in the way of refreshment for the day. These are mentioned in the text and can be seen at a glance on the tables accompanying each chapter. You should always carry a full water bottle, and some high energy emergency rations such as Kendal mint cake, dried fruit, nuts and chocolate, and perhaps some dexedrene or glucose sweets.

TRANSPORT

Many of the ferries are seasonal, so you must pay attention to this when planning your walk. Transport to your starting point poses another problem. If you are walking the whole path, or a considerable part of it, either public transport to the start and from the finish or some kind accomplice who drops you and collects you are indicated. If you are walking for one or two days at a time, either the same methods can be used or you can drive your own car to your finishing point and take public transport or hitch a lift to the start, which will leave you pressed for time as you near the end of your ramble.

WEATHER

A small radio will keep you in touch with general trends. Otherwise newspapers, or telephone bulletins are a useful source and the shipping forecasts should be of great interest as the major dangers for the coastal walker are wind and mist. In both you would be well advised to keep clear of the cliff edge.

HOW TO USE THIS GUIDE

This is a companion to the traveller on the South West Way; it is written from Poole Harbour to Minehead, but it is equally valid in both directions. Each chapter, like ancient Gaul, is divided into three parts: after a short extract to set the scene, the introduction gives a general overview of the section of the path to be dealt with. The guide section takes you over the path in detail, leading you through those places where it is not clear on the ground. This should be studied in conjunction with the latest SWWA guide and your maps. Do not think that you will get by with the waymarking. There are stretches where this is entirely lacking, others where it is deficient or badly maintained. Those responsible could take an example from the excellent standard of waymarking in certain European countries or, much nearer home, from the stretch of this path maintained by the Exmoor National Park. Finally, the gazetteer comments on the places and sights of interest which have usually been highlighted in the guide section. The charts which accompany each chapter are to enable you to plan your walk more easily and contain, at a glance, the information you will find in more detail in the gazetteer.

Obviously it is not possible for a guide of this length to be any more than a genial travelling companion which introduces you to the delights and treasures of the region. You will have to consult more specialized works on those subjects in which you have a particular interest. The geology, which shapes the land and determines the wild life and nature it supports is complex and has been fashioned over millions of years. Since it is so varied, and because this part of the country has been relatively unspoilt by what we think of as progress, birds, plants, insects and beasts are numerous and varied. All of these, together with the history of the South West deserve closer study by those who wish to learn more of them. A book list is included at the end of the book to make this easier.

The South West Way runs through four counties and an exciting variety of scenery. The agricultural land and chalk cliffs of Dorset give way to the resorts and drowned river valleys of South Devon; the starkly beautiful cliffs and granite headlands and smugglers' coves in Cornwall yield to the more rounded cliffs, small bays and austere high moorland of North Devon and Somerset. Within these generalities lie a multitude of textures, tones and details. Landscape, seascape, climate and vegetation interspersed with villages, towns, small ports and historic sites, form a backcloth on which the changing seasons paint their variations. Enjoy this wonderful heritage to the full.

1

South Haven to Lulworth Cove

It was a clear day with little wind stirring, and the view from the downs, one of the most extensive in the country, was unclouded. The eye of any observer who cared for such things swept over the wave-washed town, and the bay beyond, and the Isle, with its pebble bank, lying on the sea to the left of these, like a great crouching animal tethered to the mainland. On the extreme east of the marine horizon, St Aldhelm's Head closed the scene, the sea to the southward of that point glaring like a mirror under the sun. Inland could be seen Badbury Rings where a beacon had been recently erected; and nearer, Rainbarrow, on Egdon Heath, where another stood: further to the left Bulbarrow, where was yet another. Not far from this came Nettlecombe Tout; to the west, Dogberry Hill, and Black'on near to the foreground, the beacon thereon being built of furze faggots thatched with straw, and standing on the spot where the monument now raises its head.

HARDY, Thomas (1840–1928). Novelist and poet. Born Higher Bockhampton near Dorchester. Extract from *The Trumpet Major* (1880).

Introduction

Charm, variety and a minimum of intrusion of modern life characterize this walk from South Haven to Lulworth Cove. The combination of beach and cliff walking and the occasional pretty village to provide contrast make it an ideal walk for those who find kilometres of solid sea beautiful but somewhat monotonous.

7

The path lies through a mixture of open downland, wood, scrub, and agricultural land, but the main interest of the region is its geological variety. The numerous rock types and formations make it a kind of geology text book, especially because these rocky souvenirs of some 350 million years past are easily visible and accessible to the walker who cares about such details. The Tertiary strata, that is, the layer of rock formed most recently, a baby blanket of earth a mere 65 million years old, is mostly chalk at Ballard Down, turning to Wealden Series at Ballard Point, and then converting to Purbeck Beds and Oxford Clay from Swanage all the way to Worbarrow. These terms may be confusing but they are explained later. At Worbarrow the remnants of the Wealden Series (and the Tertiary strata) lie in bands behind this part of the coast, becoming chalky again just before Lulworth Bay.

The effect of this geological variety is expressed in the scenery: sandy beaches alongside arable grasslands, steep rock cliffs terminating woodland and vale. Behind the area known as Studland Bay is a nature reserve occupying 160 hectares and including a well-documented nature trail. Appealing more to the naturalist than the geologist, the variety of flora and fauna here is impressive, alternating between an almost Mediterranean lushness and a Northern austerity.

The Lulworth Ranges, too, offer a rich variety of flowers and plants which have thrived away from the disturbances of tourism and agriculture. The animal population has also derived benefit from this pocket-utopia and if you are lucky you may be greeted by a deer, fox or badger.

Guide

The walk starts at **South Haven Point.** You can get there either by taking the ferry which runs throughout the year from Sandbanks (Bournemouth) or by car, bicycle, or whatever. The path begins at the spot where the ferry docks, in spite of the fact that there is no visible signpost – an omission all the more remarkable because this is the starting point of the longest continuous footpath in the British Isles. Nonetheless, the walker begins his unacclaimed walk along the beach of Shell Bay, continuing in an almost straight line for 5½ kilometres along the firm sand beach of Studland Bay, between

STAGE	CUMUL.	TIME	POOLE TO LULWORTH	TELEPHONE	TRAIN	BUS	FERRY	SHOPS	CAMPING	ACCOMMODATION	REFRESHMENT	CUMUL. DIST. KMS
			POOLE	x	x	x		x	x	x	x	
			SANDBANKS				x					
			SOUTH HAVEN POINT				x					
6½		1:25	STUDLAND	x		x		x		x	x	6½
4	10½	1:	SWANAGE	x		x		x	x	x	x	10½
4	14½	1:	DURLSTON CASTLE			x					x	14½
(5)		(1:15)	(CORFE CASTLE)	x		x					x	
(15)		(3:45)	(WAREHAM)	x		x		x	x	x	x	
(2)		(:30)	(WORTH MATRAVERS)			x					x	
(1)		(:15)	(SWALLAND FARM)							x		
(1¼)		(:20)	(KIMMERIDGE)					x			x	
28¼	42¾	7:	LULWORTH COVE	x		x		x			x	42¾
(1)		(:15)	(WEST LULWORTH)	x		x		x		x	x	

TIMES ARE BASED ON AVERAGE WALKER LIGHTLY LADEN.

NB.
1. STAGE: is the distance between that point and the preceding point.
2. CUMUL.: is the cumulative distance from the beginning of the chapter.
3. TIME: is the time for the stage (between that point and the preceding one) calculated at 4 kilometres per hour – the rate for a lightly loaded person walking without halt.
4. Brackets enclose places not on the Path but easily reached from it, together with distances and times from the Path.
5. CUMULATIVE DISTANCE: is the total distance from South Haven Point.

the dunes of the **Studland Heath Nature Reserve** and the sea. If the winds are not too strong this is an easy walk. To the south one sees the Isle of Wight, and from the limit of the Bay in the west, the walker is watched by a profile of limestone rocks which bear the enigmatic names of Old Harry and Old Harry's Wife.

Just before you reach the pier at the west end of the beach, turn right and climb the steps which lead to the metalled road. Follow the road round to the left and continue past hotel and pub. This is the charming village of **Studland.** At the bottom of the hill cross over the stream, bear right and, almost immediately, off the road to the left, you will see a path marked 'To

Swanage via Old Harry'. Follow this path, which climbs up through trees and scrub before reaching the cliff edge and a high, open well-trodden path. This path leads to **Foreland Point**, across Ballard Down to **Ballard Point**. From Foreland Point, above Old Harry Rocks, and from Ballard Point, the walker is rewarded with a superb view across the whole expanse of Studland Bay to **Poole Harbour** and Bournemouth.

After Ballard Point the path runs steeply down Ballard Cliff towards Swanage. As you start to descend you can see the whole length of the Shingle Beach at Swanage Bay, as well as the sleepy town of **Swanage**. Just before reaching the first bungalows of the Ballard Estate, off the cliffs above the beach, the path crosses a footbridge and at this point you can either take the steps which lead down to the beach and continue into the town or you can stay on the official path, which is well sign-posted, through the Ballard Estate on to the public roads, where you turn left and go down to reach the sea front at the Ocean Bay Cafe. Turn right and follow the sea front, through the town, until you pass the end of the pier, climb up on the footpath which passes seaward of the Grosvenor Hotel. The path leads past the lifeboat station and the shipyards to the coastguard station at **Peveril Point**.

From the Point the path follows the cliff, climbing gently around Durlston Bay, where it turns slightly inland behind a private property called Durlston Wall. Turn left down the steps, cross over the stream and continue up through the scrub and trees on to the cliff top until you arrive at **Durlston Head**, easily identified by **Durlston Castle**, a Victorian castle which looks like a Vauban fort but is a peaceful restaurant, and a large stone globe of the world. The path descends and brings you shortly to **Tilly Whim Caves** – stone quarries disused since 1812 and now closed to visitors – and then passes the first of a pair of tall white posts (marking one nautical mile) to the lighthouse at **Anvil Point**.

The path now climbs through pastures and rough ground, keeping close to the cliffs, fenced sometimes to seaward sometimes to landward. You pass the second nautical mile marker posts and then **Dancing Ledge**, a large rocky shelf below the cliffs but above sea level, just beyond which is a path inland to **Langton Matravers**. Then comes another shelf, **Cannon Cove**, similar to Dancing Ledge with caves in the cliffs about it and an old cannon planted square in its centre pointing out to sea. Continue on to **Seacombe Cliff** where you descend quite sharply into the Combe, the site of old quarry workings. Cross the stream and follow it inland for about 200 metres before turning left up steep steps (the valley path leads to **Worth Matravers**) which climb onto a good farm track and by it, to the left, back on to the cliffs.

You next come to two hills, **East Man** and **West Man**, each with traces of ancient field systems, or lynchets, and in the deep gully between the two the remains of the **Winspit** quarry workings and caves (another path leads inland to Worth Matravers). The path continues along the cliff edge, climbing gently at first and then more steeply past the remains of a war-time wireless station, to **St Aldhelm's Head** with its coast-guard cottages and look-out and a 12th-century chapel.

An alternative route is waymarked inland from just beyond the look-out. This is to avoid risk along the cliff edge in dangerous conditions caused by heavy rainfall or drought. It is a diversion which brings you back on to the path by **Chapman's Pool.**

The main path continues along the cliffs before descending 220 steep steps and carrying on through the broken cliff-fall terrain close to the water's edge. The path is not always easy to follow here, but you cannot get lost as all of the subsidiary paths also lead round to Chapman's Pool. When you reach the boathouses on the shore climb up above them and you will find a path which is waymarked and leads you across the uneven cliff-fall to the gully, which you cross. At low tide you can follow the beach from the boathouses to this point but, except in very dry weather, the mouth of the gully is unpleas-antly muddy. Steps lead up to the far side of the gully and help on the first part of the climb to the top of Houns-tout Cliff, above Egmont Point. A short stretch of cliff-top walking, then steeply down to Egmont Bight, identifiable by its grassy wooded valley, stream, and stout stone wall built above the cliffs. (The valley itself leads inland to the delightful wooded property of Encombe Farm.)

The path is very clear, keeping to the coast as it climbs to the cliff top on the far side and follows the cliff along. Inland you can see the prominent rounded feature of Swyre Head (203 metres) and in the sea below, the start of the Kimmeridge Ledges. You are walking easily along cliffs across good agri-cultural land, and shortly a path leads inland to Swalland Farm, where Mr & Mrs Vearncombe (Tel. 0929 480707) will give you food, shelter and a mass of information about the area past and present. The path goes down and then up to Clavell Tower, the remains of the Clavell family's watch tower built in 1800, before descending steeply by some steps to Gaulter Gap and **Kimmeridge Bay.**

If Lulworth Ranges are closed, turn inland here, for the 20 kilometres or so detour around the ranges to Kimmeridge and Lulworth; if open, make your way around the beach past the coastguard cottages and along a stretch of metalled road to an oil well, Britain's largest onshore well, where you pick up a cliff path and cross the range boundary. The coast path through the ranges crosses about 10 kilometres of fine undulating country. You will need good reserves of breath on this stretch as the slopes are short, sharp and frequent. The path is very well marked throughout and *you must keep to it.*

Go round the small cove, across the curious flat feature Broad Bench, on which there is a disused oil well, and climb up around Hobarrow Bay and Brandy Bay to the grassy upland of Tyneham Cap. Inland you can see the ruins of the deserted village of **Tyneham.** The path follows on along Gad Cliff and then over Gold Down before going steeply down to Worbarrow Tout, a narrow neck of land, where it crosses over to go round **Worbarrow Bay**, a picturesque and popular place for swimmers.

Now you climb again quite steeply to Flower's Barrow, an Iron Age hill fort, descend the steep Halcombe Vale to Arish Mell and then climb steeply once again up to Mupe Bay, with its smugglers caves. From here you can see the ruins of the Jacobean **Lulworth Castle** inland of the path. The path descends steeply and before you reach the range boundary you find a path leading down towards the sea and the **Fossil Forest** (which can be seen from the path). Continue on to the range boundary and cross through it close to the cliffs to round **Lulworth Cove** on a well-trodden path and descend into the village. West Lulworth itself is almost 1 kilometre up the road from the picturesque cove.

Gazetteer

SANDBANKS TO SOUTH HAVEN POINT

On the short trip from Sandbanks to South Haven Point the ferry passes just south of Brownsea Island, which was fortified in the 16th century, during the reign of Henry VIII, to defend Poole Harbour against the French. Later, in the 18th century it was the scene of a massive experiment in agriculture made by Humphrey Stuart of Crichel, an innovative and improving landlord. Later still, in 1907, it was the site of the first scout camp organised by Baden-Powell, founder of the Scout movement. Although the ferry does not call there, the island can be visited by boat from Poole Quay or from Sandbanks everyday from April to September.

The ferry from Sandbanks to South Haven Point runs approximately every 20 minutes from 7a.m. to 11p.m. throughout the year. There may be a break of two weeks in November. Further information may be obtained from the Bournemouth-Swanage Motor Road and Ferry, 6 Floating Bridge, Sandbanks, Poole; Tel. Studland (092 944) 203.

STUDLAND HEATH NATURE RESERVE

Leaving the ferry at South Haven Point the walker sets off along the sands of Shell Bay, named for its rich variety of sea shells, and enters the Studland Heath Nature Reserve. This national nature reserve comprises 160 hectares of dunes, woodland and a freshwater lake called Little Sea. In addition to more than 600 species of flowering plants there is a fascinating variety of birds, insects and reptiles, including the uncommon smooth snake and sand lizard. A well-documented nature trail has been laid out for visitors. The entrance is at Knoll House, a mile out of Studland on the road to South Haven Point.

Pay particular attention to the sand on the beach. Between the dunes and the sea you will walk across patches of 'singing sands'. These are made up of grains of sand all the same size which make a singing noise as they move against each other, your footfall could set them off and drawing a stick across them will do so too.

STUDLAND

The village is recorded in the Domesday Book of 1086 as having salt pans and salt workers as well as a fishing industry. But its history goes back much further, with evidence of Iron Age occupation, as well as five small Bronze Age bowl barrows on Ballard Down, above the village, and the remains of Roman dwellings. St Nicholas Church is described by Pevsner as one of the dozen or so completely Norman village churches in England. Although a complete Norman church, it is not completely Norman as it has some Saxon features. The unusual carvings on the outside of the building, just below the roof line are Norman. In the churchyard, buried side by side, lie the Peninsula War veteran Sgt William Lawrence and his French wife whom he met while serving as a member of the army of occupation in Paris following the signature of the treaty of Paris in 1815. They retired to Studland, where they ran a pub and he wrote his vivid autobiography.

Somewhere beneath the waters of Studland Bay lies the wreck of the San Salvador, one of the ships of Philip of Spain's ill-fated Armada of 1588. It sank after being captured by the English fleet and now rests as a challenge to marine archaeologists. The bay, with its magnificent beach, is a popular holiday place and throughout the year people come to sail, wind-surf, gallop horses or simply walk along the beach listening to its singing sands and observing nature about them. Its southern limit is fixed by The Foreland, off which the two distinctive, weather-worn chalk pillars of Old Harry and Old Harry's Wife, bear stoic witness to passing generations of holiday makers.

Hotels: Manor House Hotel; Tel. Studland (092 944) 288
B & B: Manor Farm; Tel. Studland (092 944) 271
Pub: Bankes Arms; Tel. Studland (some accommodation) (092 944) 225
Bus: To Bournemouth and Swanage

SWANAGE

For more than 150 years Swanage has been a popular seaside resort. The young Princess Victoria visited here in 1835 and, in the days before holidays abroad became almost compulsive, it was an extremely fashionable English resort. Its history goes back to the 9th century when, in 877, King Alfred was given unhoped-for aid in his war against invading Danes by a storm which overwhelmed 120 of the enemy's ships in Swanage Bay, thus depriving them of valuable reinforcements and enabling him to rout the Danish fleet.

In medieval times it became an important port for the export of Purbeck marble, originally much used in ecclesiastical building but, after the Reformation, increasingly used for all manner of secular purposes. Many manor houses were constructed with it and in the 1720s, Defoe comments on the use of Purbeck stone in London for 'paving courtyards, alleys, avenues to houses, kitchens, footways on the sides of high streets and the like'. It became popular again in the 19th century for the construction of new churches and the restoration of existing ones. The importance of Swanage as a port declined, however, with the coming of the railway in 1880, which brought instead the tourists.

Fishing was already an important industry for the town, then no more than a village, in the Middle Ages, and even in the late 17th century the celebrated woman horseback traveller, Celia Fiennes, commented on the excellence of the fish.

The Reverend Andrew Bell, a great educational pioneer, was rector of Swanage after his return from India at the end of the 18th century and, continuing the educational work he had started in Madras, he introduced the system of monitors whereby the older and brighter pupils passed on knowledge to the others.

Bell was also an enthusiastic supporter of Benjamin Festy, a farmer of Downshay Farm near Swanage, who was successfully using lymph from cowpox pustules to inoculate family and friends against smallpox, a disease which was rapidly becoming prevalent in the West Country. It is evident that, although Dr Edward Jenner is generally credited with being the 'Father of Vaccination', Festy preceded him in the use of the process by at least a decade.

All facilities are available at Swanage and accommodation is plentiful in season and adequate throughout the year.

Hotels:	Grosvenor; Tel. Swanage (092 92) 2292
B & B:	The Corner House; Tel. Swanage (092 92) 4410
Buses:	To Dorchester, Weymouth and Bournemouth
Early Closing:	Thursday

CORFE CASTLE

This can be reached by bus from Swanage or on foot from Chapman's Pool, further along the coast. The village has a famous fortress dating from Saxon times. It belonged to the Crown and in 978 Edward the Martyr was murdered here by his step-mother, Queen Aelfthryth. It also served as a prison for Peter the Hermit. At the beginning of the 13th century 20 noblemen were starved to death in its dungeons by King John and Edward II was imprisoned here sometime before his murder early in the 14th century. In the 16th century Elizabeth I gave the castle to Sir Christopher Hatton who then passed it on to Sir John Bankes, Attorney General for Charles I. It was Lady Bankes who, in 1643, defended the castle for the King during a six week siege. Three years later it was under siege again, this time by Fairfax, who went on to capture and dismantle it. The remains of this luckless castle crown a steep hill providing stunning views of the surrounding countryside. Although all that is left of it is ruins, you can still trace the depressing history of this castle from the architectural features of each period from the time of Edgar (959–975) to Henry VII (1485–1509).

WAREHAM

A little further north in the parish church of St Martin, Wareham, is a memorial to T.E. Lawrence, known to the world as 'Lawrence of Arabia'. In the beautiful effigy sculptured by Eric Kennington, Lawrence is shown in full Arab dress. Lawrence is buried a few kilometres away, in Moreton churchyard near Bovington Camp. The soldier and writer died in 1935 as a result of a motorcycle accident.

Clouds Hill, his cottage, with 3 hectares of land, was given to the National Trust by A.W. Lawrence as a memorial to his brother. The cottage, 1½ kilometres north of Bovington Camp, may be visited from April to September.

DURLSTON HEAD

Durlston Castle is rather new as castles go and not really a castle at all. Built in 1890 as a cliff-top restaurant, its main attraction is a terrestial globe in Portland Stone which is 3 metres in diameter and weighs 40 tons. This weighty symbol of dreamy megalomania was a gift to Swanage from a wealthy general contractor who not only gave the world to the town but many other buildings as well. The castle is still a restaurant and refreshments are available during the season.

TILLY WHIM CAVES

The jovial name of these caves does not reflect the reality of this old quarry which dates from the early 19th century. The name in fact comes from the owner, a Mr Tilly, and a hoist or crane which in the local dialect is called a 'whim'. Interesting, if not whimsical in the least, the caves (reached by going along the path beyond the restaurant at Durlston Castle) are similar to those at Winspit, encountered later on.

GEOLOGY AND PALAEONTOLOGY

For the walker with palaeontological inclinations the length of coast from Durlston to Lulworth is a gold mine of Portland Stone, Purbeck Beds and Kimmeridge clay which all form part of the Jurassic system of Mesozoic sedimentary rocks (called the Wealden Series). Even the not-so-down-to-earth walker might find these rocks interesting. About 135 million years old, the Purbeck Beds form the highest part of the Jurassic system and contain a natural encyclopaedia of freshwater and brackish fossils, including those of early mammals. Examples of all three levels of Purbeck Beds can be seen in the 1½ kilometre stretch of coast between Durlston Head and Peveril Point.

DANCING LEDGE

Dancing Ledge is a natural phenomenon and, in spite of its poetic name, was used rather prosaically as a wharf for loading Purbeck stone from the local quarries. The Ledge itself has no talent for either movement or rhythm and derives its name from the effect of the light dancing upon the waters which gently caress it.

CANNON COVE

The cove lies beneath Seacombe Cliff and gets its name from the cannon which sits upon it. No one seems to know just where the cannon came from but in 1786 the East Indiaman 'Halselwell' went down off Seacombe Cliff and of the 250 aboard only 80 survived. Local legend claims that the cannon was a part of the ship's armament and was placed here as a memorial to those lost at sea.

WORTH MATRAVERS

This pretty village is not actually on the coastal path but it can easily be reached by walking on a path from Seacombe Cliff (5 km) or from Winspit Quarry (3 km) further along the way.

The old world charm of Worth Matravers, complete with thatched houses and village church, produces a sense of longing for a return to that most humane place, the small village. The church shares with Studland its name and its architectural value as one of the few remaining Norman churches to have survived in England. It is made of Purbeck stone and green marble which were quarried nearby and it never suffered the alterations and additions which usually happen to village churches. During the Second World War this dreamy little village was the site of one of the country's main radar installations which played an important part in the Battle of Britain.

The village has a good pub, 'The Square and the Compass', called after the tools of the mason's trade now masonic emblems. There is a bus service to Swanage.

WINSPIT QUARRY

The medieval field system of strip lynchets began here in Worth Matravers in the 12th century. Traces of these agricultural tapestries can be seen on the hills of East and West Man, which enclose the Winspit Quarry. The quarry was a source of limestone until the middle of the 20th century. It is now closed, but a happy community of vivid wild flowers and field birds have made a home in the area.

ST ALBAN'S HEAD

This headland is also known as St Aldhelm's Head in honour of the kindly and lively Saint Aldhelm, first Bishop of Sherborne. An enlightened Man of God he travelled far and wide capturing the religious imagination of the masses by singing songs which he composed. His collected religious writings somehow include over 100 riddles, testaments to God and humour, a marriage all too rare in the later days of the church. The chapel here which bears his name is a stout building dating from the late 12th century, some 500 years after the Saint's death in 709. The metre-thick walls and roof are supported by a central pillar with stone arches. The turret in the centre of the roof seems designed to hold a lantern, a light in the night for those at sea. Less poetic but presumably more efficient is the coastguard lookout which stands upon the Head just before the Chapel.

CHAPMAN'S POOL

This peaceful isolated bay sheltered by high cliffs used to be a port for working fishermen. Today the fishing boats, nets and lobster pots in the boathouses belong to the local villagers and are used for pleasure.

KIMMERIDGE

Clavell Tower is not worth going to look at, but as you walk past it you will probably ask yourself 'what is that?' or 'what was that?'. This ruin of a tower was built in 1800, by the Reverend John Richards Clavell, probably as an observatory as there is a rest for a telescope, but possibly simply as a folly. The Clavells first came to Kimmeridge in the early 1600s to exploit the bituminous shale of the Kimmeridge ledges, and the house built by Sir William Clavell in the early 17th century, Smedmere, a few miles inland, testifies to the prosperity of the venture. Looking across the bay, beyond the tower you will see a vision more evocative of Texas and modernity than the Reverend Clavell's Tower – the pumps of Britain's most prolific on-shore oil well, producing 400 barrels a day from that same Kimmeridge shale. Kimmeridge has a post office, a shop, refreshments, and accommodation.

B & B: Kimmeridge Farm; Tel. Corfe Castle (09293) 706
Early
closing: Thursday

LULWORTH RANGES

All the materials of reflection and elements of walking pleasure are on this beautiful and unspoiled – and physically exacting – stretch of the Dorset Coast Path. The main drawback is that they are the firing ranges for the Royal Armoured Corps' Gunnery School and are closed during the week except for the month of August and the first two weeks of September. The ranges are open to walkers on weekends and Bank Holidays but it is advisable to check. A call or a letter to the Range Officer, RAC Gunnery School, Lulworth, Dorset, (Tel. Bindon Abbey (0929) 462721 ext. 824) will tell you when the ranges are open.

If the ranges are closed when you reach this stage of your walk, you will have to make your way, either on foot, hitching, or by taxi for the 20 kilometre detour inland. If you go on foot, you will have to take the roads and paths through East Holme and West Holme around the ranges to the B3071 running south from Wool to West Lulworth. This is the least desirable solution. Normally it is possible to follow the B3070 south west from West Holme to West Lulworth but again this depends on the firing schedule. If you are able to, walk the 6 kilometres from Kimmeridge to Corfe Castle where a bus will take you to Wareham and Wool. You can then walk south on the B3071 to Lulworth Cove. You can visit Corfe Castle and Lawrence's Memorial in Wareham on the way.

TYNEHAM

Until 1943 this village, 2 kilometres inland from Worbarrow, was a pleasant and peaceful place. During the war the villagers were evacuated and the army requisitioned the area and converted it into a military training ground. The inhabitants of the village never returned and now, like its cousin in ruin, Imber, on Salisbury Plain, Tyneham is a ghost town, a grim stage set evoking the memory of war.

LULWORTH CASTLE

The original Lulworth Castle was built in 1146. What stands now is the modern version, built between 1588 and 1641 which was acquired by the Weld family in the middle of the 17th century.

Staunch Roman Catholics and Royalists, the Welds received James I, Charles II and George III at Lulworth, and in 1786 George II gave permission to Thomas Weld to build a church in the grounds, provided that it did not look like a church from the outside. This was the first Roman Catholic Church built in England after the Reformation. In 1830 Charles X, exiled King of France, took refuge at Lulworth Castle as a guest of the Weld family.

In 1929 the Castle was gutted by fire. Restoration was carried out and the family continued to live there. In 1982 they were still an important Dorset family, the Lord Lieutenant of Dorset being Colonel Sir Joseph Weld, OBE, TD.

FOSSIL FOREST

This petrified forest comes just before Lulworth Cove. Signs lead down the steps towards the sea to this fossilized graveyard of trees that lived 200 million years ago.

EAST AND WEST LULWORTH

The name is Saxon for 'Farm of Lulla' and this whole region originally belonged to the Lulworth family. The church in East Lulworth, rebuilt in the 19th century, retains its ancient battlement tower as well as many monuments to the Weld family. West Lulworth, at the head of Lulworth Cove, is much smaller than East Lulworth but both villages attract visitors because of their unspoiled charm.

LULWORTH COVE

The dedicated hammering away of that master sculptor the sea has made Lulworth Cove one of nature's finest works of art. The circular bay enclosed by the chalk cliffs seems to collaborate with the sky to create a patch of blue water even in the greyest weather.

A century ago, that rare and exquisite creature, the Lulworth Skipper, was seen here for the first time. Each year during July and August the delicate brown butterfly returns, in spite of the considerable crowds who also realise that this is one of the most beautiful places on the English coast.

Hotels:	Castle Inn; Tel. West Lulworth (092 941) 311
B & B:	Cromwell House; Tel. West Lulworth (092 941) 253
	Shirley Hotel; Tel. West Lulworth (092 941) 358
	Bishop's Cottage; Tel. West Lulworth (092 941) 268
YHA:	Youth Hostel, School Lane; Tel. West Lulworth (092 941)
Taxi:	Cove House, Tel. West Lulworth (092 941) 468
Buses:	To Bournemouth, Dorchester, Weymouth
Early closing:	Saturday

2

Lulworth to Abbotsbury

The ultimate project in this period of agricultural expansion (17th century) was a far-fetched and ill-considered scheme to drain the Fleet, the area of sea lying between Chesil Beach and the mainland west of Weymouth. This is a long narrow lagoon some 13km long and between 91m and 804m wide. The attempt to drain it was made by Sir George Horsey and others between 1630 and 1646. The legal arrangements, the fact that the organisers called themselves Adventurers, and some of the technical details, recall the temporary draining of the Fenlands of Eastern England and was perhaps suggested by these works. However, the Dorset venture was a complete failure and though a great deal of money and labour was poured into a 'great Dam' and 'divers sluices of stone and Tymber . . . howbeit by some accident and likewise by reason of Stormy windes and tempests the Sea did force or cast upp much Sea Water over and through the gravelly or sandy bank' (i.e. Chesil Beach).

TAYLOR, Christopher (1935–   ). Extract from *Dorset*, in the series *The Making of the English Landscape* published by Hodder and Stoughton, 1970.

Introduction

From Lulworth to Overcombe the path crosses good undulating coastal downland with some sharp gradients, and several stretches of farmland. After Weymouth, Chesil Beach dominates the scenery. You can either walk along it or you can keep to the mainland alongside the Fleet, the stretch of water which separates the two, as far as Langton Herring, where you strike inland across farmland to Abbotsbury. The built-up area of Weymouth and a few small villages break up the coastal walk, offering refreshment, shelter and places of interest to visit.

The land structure is chalk from Lulworth to Osmington Mills, which gives us dramatic broken cliffs, areas of landslip where the sea has successfully sapped them, and fine grassy downland. Purbeck Beds and Oxford Clay take over from Osmington to Abbotsbury, giving a rather duller, less dramatic countryside with lower hills and coastline, and more agricultural land. The long bank of shingle, Chesil Beach, is a rare phenomenon and of great interest to geologists.

Chesil Beach and the Fleet are exciting places for the naturalist. Birds, plants and insects are numerous and varied; although it is precisely lack of variety which is interesting at the Abbotsbury Swannery, home of the largest breeding colony of mute swans in the British Isles. They are not silent, as their name implies, but hiss petulantly if annoyed.

Weymouth has charming relics of faded elegance and some very attractive 18th- and early 19th-century houses. There is also an important Roman site outside the town at Overcombe. The path passes close to or through some attractive villages, and Abbotsbury has several remarkable buildings in addition to its gardens and its swannery.

Guide

Follow the road inland from Lulworth Cove and turn left, before the large car park, to climb back onto the cliffs up a steep path. As you leave the cove, off the path to seaward, you will see Stair Hole, a huge roofless cave hollowed out by the sea, offering you a view of its twisted interior. Climb up, slightly inland, behind Dungy Head and then down, close to the cliffs, towards the striking limestone arch of Durdle Door. The path passes a few metres above the arch, between it and a vast caravan park on top of the cliffs. Continue gently down through pasture, passing Swyre Head, before climbing steeply to Bats Head, a chalk headland with a hole in its base. As you go down and then up at once onto the Warren, you see evidence of ancient field systems traced on both hills. The path climbs on up, with a slight swing inland around the head of a coomb, through agricultural land to White Nothe

DISTANCE		TIME	LULWORTH TO ABBOTSBURY	T E L E P H O N E	T R A I N S	F E R R Y	S H O P S	A C C O M M O D A T I O N	R E F R E S H M E N T	CUMUL. DIST. KMS
STAGE	CUMUL.							C A M P I N G		
			LULWORTH COVE	x		x	x		x x	42¾
8		2:	RINGSTEAD							50¾
3¼	11¼	:50	OSMINGTON MILLS						x x	54
(2)		(:30)	(OSMINGTON)				x		x	
4	15¼	1:	OVERCOMBE	x		x			x	58
2½	17¾	:40	WEYMOUTH	x	x	x		x x	x x	60½
(1)		(:15)	(CHARLESTOWN)				x		x	
10	27¾	2:30	EAST FLEET							70½
			MOONFLEET MANOR					x x	x	
(1½)		(:25)	(LANGTON HERRING)				x		x	
10	37¾	2:30	ABBOTSBURY	x		x	x		x x	80½
(4)		(1:)	(HARDY MONUMENT)							

TIMES ARE BASED ON AVERAGE WALKER LIGHTLY LADEN.

NB.
1. *STAGE: is the distance between that point and the preceding point.*
2. *CUMUL.: is the cumulative distance from the beginning of the chapter.*
3. *TIME: is the time for the stage (between that point and the preceding one) calculated at 4 kilometres per hour – the rate for a lightly loaded person walking without halt.*
4. *Brackets enclose places not on the Path but easily reached from it, together with distances and times from the Path.*
5. *CUMULATIVE DISTANCE: is the total distance from South Haven Point.*

cottages. The start of the White Nothe landslip is visible below to seaward and continues on around Ringstead Bay.

The path continues in front of the cottages and winds down along the edge of the eroding cliffs towards Holworth Farm, where a notice indicates that you should leave the farm to landward. Just after the farm, the metalled road leads left and you take a well-posted, but sometimes indistinct, foot-path across fields, through trees and scrub, down to **Ringstead Bay** and into **Ringstead.** The coastal path continues west from the farm and climbs, crossing two streams by foot-bridge across **Burning Cliff** and descends to join the lower path before Ringstead.

In the village, the path turns left and then right, onto the beach, to pass in front of holiday bungalows. Shortly you climb up around Bran Point, through fields, past some Second World War block houses – opposite which you look down on the remains of the steamer Minx, wrecked in 1929. You then drop down into **Osmington Mills**, where the path describes a dog's leg through the gardens of the picturesque Smuggler's Inn, with its part-thatched roof. (Note that a path leads inland from here, avoiding Weymouth, to West Bexington.) Continue to climb across fields, passing to landward of the first grassy knoll, and to seaward of the next one and its reed-filled, well-fenced pond.

The path continues, inland a little, around Black Head and down towards a holiday camp, whose perimeter fence you skirt to seaward. The path descends quite sharply into a coomb before climbing up round Redcliffe Point and then down towards Bowleaze Cove and a huge Pontins hotel. Cross the River Jordan in front of the hotel and then either follow the road over Furzy Cliff or walk along the beach into **Overcombe** on the edge of Weymouth Bay.

Weymouth can now be reached either by bus or by a 2 kilometre walk along the seafront road. The bus takes you to the statue of George III, from which another bus will take you to **Charlestown**, close to the path to the west of Weymouth, thus enabling you to avoid walking an uninteresting stretch of road.

Otherwise, continue into Weymouth, following the front, along the promenade past George III's statue, to the Town Bridge. Here turn left and walk around Weymouth Harbour along the quay and then along the shore of Portland Harbour to Sandsfoot Castle. From the castle, the coast path leads on around the point – where it crosses the Portland Ferry Bridge road – to Wyke Regis.

At the Ferry Bridge, you again have a choice. The tough, experienced walker may wish to walk the length of **Chesil Beach**, a bank of shingle 28 kilometres long, 20 metres high and 180 metres wide, which runs from Abbotsbury to Portland. It is strenuous walking and once you are on it you must stay on to the end.

The alternative is to continue along the official path. From Ferrybridge it follows the coast along the Fleet, passing through a caravan park, inland around an M.O.D. establishment, past a coastguard look-out and seaward around a military range at Charlestown. When red warning flags indicate firing, carry straight on along the path which cuts across the headland and Tidmoor Point. Go around

Chickerell Hive Point and into **East Fleet**, on Butterstreet Cove.

The path continues through agricultural land, keeping close to the water, with few gradients of any significance. After you enter a sometimes muddy copse take the footbridge across the stream just before **Moonfleet Manor** (an 18th-century house, now a hotel with a bar and restaurant). Go around the hotel property, keeping to the shore. Just beyond the hotel, the path rounds the cultivated headland at Herbury – although it is possible to cut across it – turning left to continue along the coast, where a made-up path leads straight on to **Langton Herring.** Carry on around the headland, cross a metalled road between boat-houses and cottages, go round a large field and you come to a stream at the head of a bay. The path makes a long detour inland here, although attempts continue to have it re-routed along the coast.

The path is well waymarked. Turn inland and follow the wooded banks of the river upstream, over a series of stiles. A fingerpost directs you left across the stream, through two gates and then right along the west bank. You see an old property called Bridge Lane ahead on the left. Enter the field in front of it and head for the corner of the wood (Wyke Wood) on the far side. Waymarks guide you up the eastern (near) perimeter of the wood, across agricultural land, to the far side of a field at the top of the wood. Turn left here and go down on the inside of the hedge and cross over the road. At the far side of the next field, follow waymarks right, over a stile and straight up along a high hedge to a ridge where you are waymarked left past Clayhangar Farm below you. From the ridge you can see Abbotsbury Swannery to seaward, St Catherine's Chapel on its hill ahead and Abbotsbury just inland of it. The path is clearly marked and takes you down along the spur of Linton Hill to meet a metalled road by some farm buildings. Follow the road around to the right, past the fine old tithe barn and into **Abbotsbury.**

Gazetteer

BURNING CLIFF

The whole of this area of cliff overlooking Ringstead Bay burst into flames in 1826 and continued to burn for more than a year. The rapid oxidation of iron pyrites in the oil shales of the Kimmeridge Beds, the substance of these cliffs, caused the blaze and fuelled the persistent fire.

At Burning Cliff a path leads through the White Nothe landslip. This is the legendary smugglers' escape route described in **Moonfleet** by J. Meade Faulkner, but it is said to be dangerous for walkers today. Both Burning Cliff and White Nothe Cliff and now National Trust properties. They were acquired in 1968 with funds from Enterprise Neptune, set up to protect the coastline of Britain as part of the National Heritage.

RINGSTEAD

Nothing remains of this deserted seaside village. Lumpy, grassy mounds mask its bricks and stones and mark its site. It was abandoned – along with many others – in the 14th or 15th century. According to Christopher Taylor in his book on Dorset in the series 'The Making of The English Landscape', this desertion is mainly in the chalk lands of the county and therefore cannot be attributed to the retreat from the marginal lands common elsewhere at this time. He thinks that the plague (which entered the country in 1348 through the port of Melcombe Regis) was the principal cause.

OSMINGTON MILLS

The path winds through the grounds of the picturesque, half-thatched, Smuggler's Inn, whose name reflects the nature of one of Dorset's most profitable industries – smuggling and evading the Excise men – which Thomas Hardy refers to often in his writings. The inn was one of the many mills which used to abound in Dorset. The Domesday Book records no less than 276 of them in the county in 1086. Its use as a smugglers' retreat was only a side-line. The village is very small but offers accommodation and refreshment.

Hotels: Smuggler's Inn; Tel. Preston (0305) 833125
            Osmington Mills Hotel; Tel. Preston (0305)
            832398

OVERCOMBE

The village is virtually a suburb of Weymouth now and not very interesting. The remains of a Romano-Celtic temple were discovered in 1843, just off the road at Jordan Hill above the village. It dates from the 4th century and there is a Roman villa a few hundred metres from it. First and second century vessels have been found in a pre-Roman cemetery, also nearby. All of which suggests that the place was more important in olden times than it is today. Telephone, refreshments, shop and bus service to Weymouth.

WEYMOUTH AND MELCOMBE REGIS

Facing each other across the mouth of the River Wey, these towns were founded as ports in the mid 13th century. They succeeded Radipole, a port since Roman times, further inland at the tip of Radipole Lake. The new ports flourished in the 14th century and became very important in the export of wool. But prosperity brought unwelcome recognition, and the French raided them frequently. If the French were unwelcome, their visitor of 1348 was even more so; it was through Melcombe Regis that refugees from the Black Death brought the Plague to England.

Henry VIII recognized the value of the sheltered anchorage provided by the Bill of Portland and in 1540 he built the castles of Portland and Sandsfoot to protect the bay. These were further links in the chain he was constructing from Kent to Cornwall to protect his blessed Isle from invasion by the quarrelsome French. Sandsfoot is now in ruins but Portland Castle still stands.

There was always great rivalry between the two ports until Elizabeth I joined them by Royal Charter in 1571. However, the removal of the wool staple to Poole had already triggered their decline.

It was only in the mid 18th century that the towns began their climb back to popularity and importance. The Duke of Gloucester built a residence in Melcombe, Gloucester House, which today forms part of the Gloucester Hotel, and George III, following his example, stayed in Weymouth in 1789 and was a regular visitor and patron until about 1811. His statue stands proudly in the main square beside the sea front, presiding over its tarnished elegance. The great revival of the town as a resort started then and it expanded outward from the small medieval settlements, particularly on the north (or Melcombe) side of the river. Today Weymouth is a flourishing port, a busy terminal for ferry services to the Channel Islands, and one of England's busiest holiday resorts, with every facility for the traveller.

Hotels:	Ingleton, Greenhill; Tel. Weymouth (0305) 785804
Early closing:	Wednesday
Tourist information:	Tel. Weymouth (0305) 785747

CHESIL BEACH

This is a unique shingle bank which runs from Portland in the east to West Bay near Bridport in the west. Twenty-eight kilometres long, 180 metres wide, and 20 metres high at Portland, it gradually decreases in width and height until it reaches Abbotsbury 20 kilometres away, where it merges with the shore. At this point it is 155 metres wide and 7 metres high. At the same time, the shingle which composes it has diminished from veritable 'boulders', 7½ centimetres in diameter to pebbles the size of a pea. No one can explain this phenomenon which is not seen on other beaches. The bank has been created by the action of the sea over thousands of years, helped from time to time by freak storms like the Great Storm of 1852, which gave the bank its beach. The bank has caused the loss of many ships, and in the early 19th century, a ship of 500 tons was actually blown right over it into the Fleet behind. It has been a boon to the plunderers of Dorset; in 1495 alone six military transport ships were wrecked there. Today the bank constitutes a long, tiring, boring trudge, but a place of great interest to the naturalist and the fisherman.

EAST FLEET

This curious village is small and quite unspoilt by modern building. A great storm in 1824 killed many of its inhabitants, wrecked houses, and destroyed part of its church. The few houses that survive are very pretty and the remains of the church, dating from the 17th century, are worth a lingering glance as you pass.

MOONFLEET MANOR

Right on the path, this 18th-century manor house was made famous as the setting for J. Meade Faulkner's novel, *Moonfleet*, published in 1898. It is now a hotel, open throughout the year, which provides a comfortable alternative stopping place to Weymouth. The hotel incorporates an (undistinguished) restaurant and a pub, the Mohun Arms. Tel. Weymouth (0305) 786948.

LANGTON HERRING

This attractive Dorset village, referred to as 'Longton' in the Domesday Book, is only a few minutes detour (1½ kilometres) off the path and has a public house and restaurant, The Elm Tree (Tel. 030587 257), which offers shelter, refreshment and repose to those for whom Abbotsbury still seems a little distant. There is also a bus service to Abbotsbury.

ABBOTSBURY

This is where The Fleet, the brackish lagoon enclosed by Chesil Beach between here and Portland, comes to a head, and it is here that the famous Abbotsbury Swannery was established in the 14th century. The Fleet, Chesil Beach and the swannery are now part of a nature reserve. The swannery can be visited daily from May to September, and visitors are sure to see literally hundreds of the mute swans, which are its principal residents, and other birds. Mute swans are large, fluffy, white birds, whose orange beaks have a black tip and a black knob near the head. They are not quite silent; all make a hissing noise when disturbed and some even manage a feeble squeak. Swans used to be prized as a luxury food and were strictly controlled by the Crown, but now they are sought more for their decorative qualities than for their meat. The gardens are also worth a visit, as they have a sub-tropical air about them and contain 7,000 plants, many of which are unusual in Britain.

Abbotsbury itself was the site of a Benedictine Monastery, founded by Urk, or Ork, under King Canute in the first quarter of the 11th century. It later became St. Peter's Abbey and reached the height of its influence in the Middle Ages when the Great Tithe Barn was built. This barn is the only part of the Abbey which survives. Eighty-four metres long and thatched with reed, it is the biggest tithe barn in Britain and a beautiful example of medieval architecture.

At the time of the Reformation in 1539 the Abbey was taken from the Church and granted to Sir Giles Strangeways, and although their home was razed in the Civil War in 1655, it is this family who own most of the village today. The Strangeways Estate sees to the upkeep of the village, preserving its tranquil, undisturbed, coherent character, its old-fashioned shops, well-conserved buildings, English cottage gardens, and even some dying crafts such as a blacksmith and a thatcher.

Near the Tithe Barn is the church of St Peter, which is mainly 16th-century but has some earlier features. It, too, bears the shot-wound scars of the Civil War. A little way off, on Chapel Hill, stands a 14th-century chapel dedicated to St Catherine and possibly built as a beacon for sailors. You can visit the chapel and from it you have a commanding view of the surrounding countryside. The slopes of the hill carry traces of Bronze Age agricultural workings. Abbotsbury has shops, accommodation and refreshment.

Hotel:	Ilchester Arms; Tel. Abbotsbury (030587) 243
Buses:	Bridgport, Weymouth
Early closing:	Thursday

HARDY MONUMENT

Four kilometres north-east of Abbotsbury, on Black Down, is the 25 metre tower erected in 1846 as a memorial to Vice Admiral Sir Thomas Masterman Hardy, Flag-Captain of H.M.S. Victory at the Battle of Trafalgar and Nelson's life-long friend. The National Trust acquired the ¾ hectare site in 1938. It overlooks the village of Portesham, where Hardy lived most of his life.

3

Abbotsbury to Branscombe

After securing accommodations, and ordering a dinner at one of the inns, the next thing to be done was unquestionably to walk directly down to the sea. They were come too late in the year for any amusement or variety which Lyme, as a public place, might offer; the rooms were shut up, the lodgers almost all gone, scarcely any family but of the residents left — and, as there is nothing to admire in the buildings themselves, the remarkable situation of the town, the principal street almost hurrying into the water, the walk to the Cobb, skirting round the pleasant little bay, which in the season is animated with bathing machines and company, the Cobb itself, its old wonders and new improvements, with the very beautiful line of cliffs stretching out to the east of the town, are what the stranger's eye will seek; and a very strange stranger it must be, who does not see charms in the immediate environs of Lyme, to make him wish to know it better. The scenes in its neighbourhood, Charmouth with its high grounds and extensive sweeps of country, and still more its sweet retired bay, backed by dark cliffs, where fragments of low rock amongst the sands make it the happiest spot for watching the flow of the tide, for sitting in unwearied contemplation; — the woody varieties of the cheerful village of Up Lyme, and, above all, Pinny with its green chasms between romantic rocks, where the scattered forest trees and orchards of luxuriant growth declare that many a generation must have passed away since the first partial falling of the cliff prepared the ground for such a state, where a scene so wonderful and so lovely is exhibited, as may more than equal any of the resembling scenes of the far-famed Isle of Wight: these places must be visited, and visited again, to make the worth of Lyme understood.

AUSTEN, Jane (1775–1817). Extract from *Persuasion*. She visited Lyme Regis in 1804 and wrote the novel in 1815–16. It was published posthumously in 1818.

Introduction

You have to make some fairly stiff climbs and descents on this stretch which includes the two highest points on the south coast, Golden Cap and Thorncombe Beacon. In addition, both the long continuation of Chesil Beach and the difficult going of the East Devon landslips provide a challenge to the walker. But several kilometres of good, undulating cliff walking, and some fine sea and inland views help you to forget these minor inconveniences.

The unique formation of Chesil Beach dominates the first few kilometres of the walk, its pebbles getting uniformly and gradually smaller as we go west. From Abbotsbury to the other side of Burton Bradstock, the land structure is corn-brash, inferior oolite, a few hundred metres of Purbeck Beds, and Oxford Clay around Bexington. At West Bay, we meet the Lias, which continue on to Lyme Regis, with cretaceous rocks from there to Branscombe – apart from some new red sandstone around Seaton and isolated chalk outcrops at Beer. Because of the numerous landslips, most of this part of the path is very rewarding for geologists and fossil hunters. It was around Lyme Regis that some of the most important British fossil finds were made.

The same landslips provide rich rewards for naturalists. Certain areas have remained undisturbed by man for centuries. Plant and insect life has developed naturally and unhindered, and the landslip between Lyme Regis and Seaton offers a protected habitat to a great variety of animals and birds. Chesil Beach and Burton Mere are both areas of interest to the ornithologist.

Indications of prehistoric and historic settlements repeatedly come into view: medieval field systems, Iron Age forest and traces of more recent history. Although there are several attractive villages and towns, both on and off the path, with buildings, trades and commerces of interest, the path is little disturbed by urban development.

| DISTANCE | | TIME | ABBOTSBURY TO BRANSCOMBE | TELEPHONE | TRAIN | BUS | FERRY | SHOPS | CAMPING | ACCOMMODATION | REFRESHMENT | CUMUL. DIST. KMS |
STAGE	CUMUL.											
			ABBOTSBURY	x	x	x				x	x	80½
6	6	1:30	WEST BEXINGTON								x	86½
6	12	1:30	BURTON BRADSTOCK			x		x	x	x	x	92½
3	15	:45	WEST BAY	x	x			x	x	x	x	95½
(4)		(1:)	(BRIDPORT)	x	x			x	x	x		
(¾)		(:15)	(EYPE)		x				x	x		
5	20	1:15	SEATOWN							x	x	100½
6½	26½	1:40	CHARMOUTH	x	x			x	x	x	x	107
2½	29	:40	LYME REGIS	x	x			x	x	x	x	109½
9½	38½	2:25	SEATON	x	x			x	x	x	x	119
1½	40	:25	BEER	x	x			x	x	x	x	120½
4½	44½	1:10	BRANSCOMBE	x	x			x	x	x	x	125

TIMES ARE BASED ON AVERAGE WALKER LIGHTLY LADEN.

NB.
1. *STAGE: is the distance between that point and the preceding point.*
2. *CUMUL.: is the cumulative distance from the beginning of the chapter.*
3. *TIME: is the time for the stage (between that point and the preceding one) calculated at 4 kilometres per hour – the rate for a lightly loaded person walking without halt.*
4. *Brackets enclose places not on the Path but easily reached from it, together with distances and times from the Path.*
5. *CUMULATIVE DISTANCE: is the total distance from South Haven Point.*

Guide

You can leave Abbotsbury either by the foot-path from the centre of the town, signed at first to St Catherine's Chapel and then swinging right to pass north and west of the hill, south of the town, or you can pass through the town and take the well-made track to the left at the western limit of Abbotsbury, where the B3157 climbs off to the right. This second path joins the first after about 500 metres and continues as a farm track, around a hill with evidence of ancient cultivation, to rejoin Chesil Beach by a car park.

The path now runs behind the shingle of Chesil Beach

(Cogden Beach, Burton Beach) for about 9 kilometres to Burton Cliff. You pass a coastguard look-out and, inland, the buildings of Castle Farm, with the mound of Abbotsbury Castle beyond it. Then you pass in front of a few houses where a road goes inland to West Bexington. Two kilometres further on you reach **Burton Mere**, a marshy, reed-filled, inland water, rich in birdlife. You must pass inland of this. Error here will oblige you to flail along the shingle of the beach for quite a way. Another 3 kilometres and you pass a turning inland, leading to **Burton Bradstock**. The coastal path continues on through a caravan park, close to the sea and, leaving the caravans, dips down behind the beach before climbing up onto the ochre coloured Burton Cliff and a short stretch of good, open, grassy cliff-top walking. Go steeply down off the cliff towards another caravan park and a river. To cross the river, either make a detour upstream to cross it on a foot-bridge and then come back through the caravans to the path, or wade across the stream where it spreads out towards the sea on the beach. It is then at its shallowest.

Climb up onto East Cliff, on the far side of the small bay, and walk along the cliff top to seaward of the golf course. Here you see the urban mass of **Bridport** inland. Follow the path down off the cliff and turn inland across a car park, then left on the main steet of **West Bay** around the well-protected 14th-century harbour, formerly Bridport Harbour, and back onto the sea front.

The direct path on to the cliffs has been closed because of erosion. Where the land starts to rise, turn right up a private road (public right of way) and then take the fourth turning on the left, which leads back on to the cliffs and the coast path. Continue to climb up on to West Cliff, down to the caravans of Eype (pronounced 'Eep') Mouth, across a car park and up the other side, to begin the steep climb to **Thorncombe Beacon**. There is more evidence of erosion here, with some of it so recent that fences are still to be seen stretched out over empty gaps where the cliffs have fallen away. The path undulates across the head of several coombs to a wooden seat with a guardrail at the top. This is Thorncombe Beacon. Dip down after the beacon and up on to Dog House Hill, Ridge Cliff and then down into Seatown, with its large caravan park and the Anchor Inn by the water's edge. Cross the River Winniford on the beach, where it suddenly disappears beneath the pebbles.

Now start the climb up **Golden Cap** on the far side. Climb along the cliffs and then across fields to make the final steep ascent by a series of hairpin bends from landward of the summit. This is the highest point on the South Coast, 191 metres. Inland lie the remains of the 13th-century chapel of St Gabriel.

From Golden Cap you climb steeply down to **St Gabriel's Mouth**, where you cross the stream on a foot-bridge. Climb up around the landslip and, by the cliffs, to Stonebarrow Hill. Go down around the landslip of Cain's Folly to the River Char, which you cross by a foot-bridge. Then turn right, up Lower Sea Lane, into **Charmouth**.

Considerable cliff erosion has occurred between Charmouth and Lyme Regis which has entailed some re-siting of the path, using roads and paths for some of the way. An alternative, when the tide is out, is to walk the 2 kilometres or so along the beach. But beware, high tide reaches the Lyme Regis end first.

Otherwise, go up Lower Sea Lane and turn left on to the main road and then, after 800 metres or so, left along Old Lyme Hill. A path leads off this to the cliffs above **Black Ven**, a National Trust nature reserve. Go on around the perimeter of the golf course to Timber Hill, from which a track leads down to the main road. Turn left, and steeply down into **Lyme Regis**.

Go down on to the sea front and follow it round to the Cobb, the ancient harbour dating from the 14th century. Cross the car park above it and climb steeply up steps and then across fields out of Dorset and into Devon. A track then takes you to landward of Underhill Farm and into the **Landslip** which continues for 7 of the 11 kilometres to Seaton. This is stiff walking over broken ground and you must keep to the path, as much of this is nature reserve.

The path climbs out of the landslip over Haven Cliff and along a lane which takes you to Axe Cliff Golf Club. Cross the fairway, go round the club house and down the drive. Turn left on to the road and follow it to the bridge over the River Axe, which you cross. Then turn left again on to the sea front at **Seaton**.

At the western end of the sea front the path climbs at first and then after about 800 metres dips down into Beer. Take the main street and then, opposite the coastguard cottages, turn along Little Lane, from which you climb up onto Beer Head, the most westerly chalk cliff in Britain. Pass to seaward of the coastguard look-out. Now you have the choice of walking through the Hooken Landslip, from which the footpath emerges through a caravan park on the way to Great Seaside and Branscombe Mouth, or climbing over Hooken Cliffs and joining the lower path just beyond the caravans. From Branscombe Mouth you can either take the road, or a path up the valley into **Branscombe** village, about ¾ kilometre away.

Gazetteer

WEST BEXINGTON

Just off the coast path, this small village has a good pub, The Manor Hotel, offering hearty meals or simple lunchtime snacks in its cellar bar and comfortable overnight accommodation. Tel. Abbotsbury (030587) 220.

BURTON BRADSTOCK

One of Dorset's most charming villages, it has records which go back to Saxon times. The Domesday Book shows it as having no fewer than eight mills and a flock of 800 sheep in 1086. A church is also recorded but the present church of St Mary dates from the 14th or 15th century. Like many Dorset towns or villages, it had a flourishing textile industry in the 17th and 18th centuries, spinning locally grown flax for ropes and fishermen's nets. Today its attractive cottages and houses and its three pubs are reward enough for the traveller who makes the short detour inland.

Hotel: Bay View Hotel; Tel. Burton Bradstock (030889) 205

Pubs: Dove, Anchor, Three Horseshoes

WEST BAY

Attempts were first made to construct a harbour here in 1274, but rough weather and stormy seas frustrated repeated efforts. A satisfactory harbour was not built until 1740, and even that had to be reconstructed in 1824. It was called Bridport Harbour and used for the export of ropes and nets made in Bridport. The harbour is no longer dredged and is used only by a few fishing boats and pleasure craft. There are shops, refreshments, and accommodation.

Hotel: Haddon House; Tel. West Bay (03083) 23626
B&B: Bridport Arms; Tel. West Bay (03083) 22994
Bus: To Bridport

BRIDPORT

Situated just over 3 kilometres inland of the path, Bridport is an important town. Pevsner describes it as 'one of the best towns in Dorset and for a continuously sustained urban feeling probably the best of all'. He attributes this to the three unusually broad main streets – 'their broadness the result historically of Bridport's medieval prosperity', coupled with the Georgian development of the 18th and 19th centuries.

King Alfred fortified the town against the Danish invaders and it is one of only four Boroughs listed in the Domesday Book. Hemp and flax flourished in the rich soil of the Marshwood Vale and these basic commodities, coupled with Bridport's proximity to the sea, determined the industry for which the town was to become renowned: rope and net manufacture. In 1213 King John ordered 'to be made at Bridport, night and day, as many ropes for ships both large and small as they could and twisted yarns for cordage'. By the 16th century, by virtue of an act of Parliament of 1530 authorizing the manufacture, Bridport had acquired a virtual monopoly of this trade.

During the turbulent years of the mid 17th century, the town, in common with many others in Dorset, was a centre of Royalist activity and in 1651 gave fleeting shelter to the young Prince Charles during his attempt to flee the country after the Battle of Worcester. It was one of the centres of trial and execution for the infamous Judge Jeffreys' 'Bloody Assizes', following the Monmouth Rebellion of 1685.

Bridport was, however, too far inland to be a satisfactory port and West Bay remained Bridport's harbour until the railway came to take away its trade in 1884. Today Bridport and West Bay are popular holiday resorts, and Bridport's rope- and net-making industry still thrives, though its raw materials, many of them man-made fibres, are all imported. The harbour at West Bay, the Georgian Town Hall in Bridport, as well as many private dwellings have traversed the centuries unspoilt and are worth a visit.

Hotel: Greyhound, East Street; Tel. Bridport (0308) 22944

B&B: Gurtopps; Tel. Bridport (0308) 22068
YHA: West Rivers House, West Allington;
         Tel. Bridport (0308) 22655
Buses: Lyme Regis, Dorchester, Weymouth

GOLDEN CAP ESTATE

This National Trust property comprises about 800 hectares of hill, cliff, farmland, undercliff and beach, including 8 kilometres of coast between Eypemouth and Charmouth. It has all been acquired within the last 20 years, save for Golden Cap itself (11 hectares), which was given to the Trust by Lt. Col. H.J.G. Weld in 1936.

The Welds are an important family in the history of Dorset. Humphrey came to Lulworth Castle (and completed the building of it) in the reign of James I. Being devout Roman Catholics, they were strong supporters of the Royalist cause. In 1830, Thomas Weld was the first English Cardinal to be created by the Pope since the Reformation, and in 1837 his brother, Joseph, became the first Catholic to be appointed High Sheriff of Dorset for 300 years. His great-grandson, Colonel Joseph Weld OBE is the present Lord Lieutenant of the County.

At 191 metres, Golden Cap is the highest point on the South Coast. Seen in the setting sun, as the yellow Jurassic limestone reflects the golden rays, you understand the fine aptness of its name, the softness of its contours. Inland off the path are the remains of St Gabriel's Chapel, which once stood sentinel over St Gabriel's Mouth, the valley leading north towards Morcombe Lake.

BLACK VEN

This wild expanse of gorse and bramble between the cliff and the sea is now a Nature Reserve with no public access. Black Ven Marls, upon which Lyme Regis is built, are shaley rocks given to spontaneous combustion like those of Burning Cliff. The area is rich in ammonite fossils, and it was here, in 1811, that 12-year-old Mary Anning, daughter of a Lyme Regis carpenter, found the Ichthyosaurus which is now in the Natural History Museum in London. Fired by the discovery, the young archaeologist went on to find a plesiosaurus and, in 1828, the first example of a pterodactyl to be found in Britain. The famous Charmouth geologist, James Harrison

(1819–1864), who discovered the fossil of the armoured dinosaur, Scelidosaurus Harrisoni, had a great respect for Mary Anning's intelligence and expertise. Black Ven is still a rewarding hunting ground for the geologist and the naturalist.

CHARMOUTH

Lyme Regis, Bridport and Charmouth have, since the Middle Ages, been the three most important towns on the West Dorset Coast and are, even today, the most popular resorts.

Saxon burial mounds and other traces of early settlement indicate that Charmouth existed at least as early as the 8th century. In the 9th century it was the site of battles between the Saxons and Viking invaders.

During the Civil War in the 1640s, together with the two towns already mentioned, it supported the Parliamentary cause. It is hardly surprising, therefore, that in the renewed Civil War after the execution of Charles I his son, recognized as Charles II by the Royalists, should have received something less than understanding treatment. Fleeing south after his defeat at the Battle of Worcester in 1651, he reached Charmouth, where a local skipper, Stephen Limbury, agreed to take him to France for £60. Limbury's wife, however, suspecting something was afoot, locked her husband in his bedroom, thus preventing him from keeping his rendezvous with Prince Charles. Coincidentally, the parson Bartholomew Wesley, great-great-grandfather of Charles Wesley, assisted in Prince Charles' escape to Bridport. He took no action when the ostler at the Queen's Armes, where Prince Charles was hiding, reported his suspicions to him.

Today the town, situated on the busy A35 main road, has some attractive buildings, but a great deal of less attractive sprawling modern development. It is a popular holiday centre.

Hotel: Queen's Armes, The Street; Tel. Charmouth (0297) 60339

B&B: Mrs Forsey, Sunrise, Arminster Road; Tel. Charmouth (0297) 60561.

Buses: Lyme Regis, Bridgport, Dorchester

LYME REGIS

Lyme was mentioned in the Domesday Book as trading in salt

and fish, and was given its title by Royal Charter of Edward I in 1284, when it was made 'a free Borough with the liberties of Londoners and the right to set up a merchant guild'.

Towards the end of the 13th century it was donating a fair amount of money to Edward I to help finance his wars. Only a few years later, during the Hundred Years War (1337–1453), together with Poole and Wareham, it provided 26 ships manned by 479 men for the Crecy expedition of 1346.

In the 16th century a Lyme Regis man, Arthur Gregory, (a secret agent and an expert in forcing the seal of a letter undetected), produced the evidence of Mary Queen of Scots' complicity in the Babington Plot which led to her trial and execution. This, of course, ultimately led Philip II of Spain to send his Armada against Britain in 1588. When the Spanish fleet sailed up the Channel, two ships from Lyme Regis turned out to assist the Royal warships in repelling the Spaniards. Almost a century later, Lyme Regis was the scene of the start of the ill-fated Monmouth Rebellion. Charles I refused to debar his Catholic brother, James, from the throne and nominate the eldest of his illegitimate children, the Protestant Duke of Monmouth, as his successor. Thus, when James II succeeded Charles in 1685, Monmouth returned from exile in Holland to raise a Protestant rebellion in the West Country. He landed at Lyme Regis, where anti-Catholic dissenters were numerous, and within three days raised a force of 1200 men. The rebellion was short-lived. Within a month, following his defeat at the Battle of Sedgemoor, Monmouth was captured, tried and publicly executed on Tower Hill.

Lyme Regis owes its very existence to the Cobb, a large breakwater constructed soon after 1284 and forming a natural harbour which enabled the recently created Free Borough to become a port of some importance.

A document dated 1378 states that in 1331 the town 'was well built and inhabited by . . . rich and powerful merchants owning fifteen great ships and forty boats'. By 1378, the town was 'for the most part destroyed and wasted by the sea and those merchants except six or eight have died or withdrawn, the Cobb . . . having been swept away last Martinmass by the sea, stopping all navigation'.

Since those turbulent times, Lyme Regis has become a tranquil, orderly resort. Its heyday was probably in the early 19th century, when Jane Austen was a visitor. She featured the Cobb in her novel, *Persuasion*.

Owing to repeated damage to the Cobb by the sea, storms,

enemy raids and other disasters, the importance of Lyme Regis as a port diminished and, by the 18th century, it had been transformed into a Regency watering place. It is as a seaside resort that it flourishes today.

Walking around it, you will see many reminders of an elegant past. One can easily conjure up the spirit of its powerful days when great wooden ships of war and merchantmen snuggled in its harbour. A visit to the museum in the Guildhall will provide more tangible fuel to such imaginings.

Hotel:	Alexandra Hotel; Tel. Lyme Regis (02974) 2010
B&B:	Angel Inn; Tel. Lyme Regis (02974) 3267
Early closing:	Thursday
Tourist Information:	Tel. Lyme Regis (02974) 2138

DOWLANDS LANDSLIP

If you are out late in the evening and very lucky you might hear the song of a nightingale here. This nature reserve, rich in fossils, plants, flowers, and birds, is one of its rare breeding grounds. The landslip, stretching 8 kilometres between Lyme Regis and Seaton, is just what it says – land which has slipped. The collapse is thought to have been caused by water trickling through the pervious limestone down to the impervious clay, where it rested and provoked the slip.

The most famous of the landslips, which still occur, was at Christmas 1839, when a great chunk of land at Dowlands collapsed, taking with it fields, crops, orchards, cottages and all. Eight million tons of rock and earth foundered, leaving a chasm 200–400 metres wide and 800 metres long. The President of the Geological Society happened to be staying nearby and so was on hand to document the incident thoroughly.

This spot is a naturalist's paradise because the vegetation has been allowed to develop quite undisturbed by man, and geologists will enjoy the huge number of fossils waiting to be discovered in the fractured rock. If you wish to visit parts of the nature reserve not on the marked path, you must obtain permission from the Nature Conservancy Office in Taunton.

SEATON

Seaton may have been a Roman port but was certainly a port in medieval times, as it sent two ships and 25 sailors to the siege of Calais in 1346. It was a busy port in pre-Norman days and records confirm the repeated re-building of the harbour. In the 16th century the Erle family of Bindon spent a fortune trying to improve it.

In 1825 Telford made a survey for a proposed ship canal from the Axe to the Bristol Channel. A copper bolt in the wall of Axmouth church was placed there in 1837 in the course of a survey to determine the difference between the levels of the Bristol and the English Channels. Had the canal been constructed, Seaton/Axmouth might have become an important port. Instead, the arrival of the railway in 1867 put paid to its days as a commercial port, and in 1877 a toll bridge was built which effectively cut what had been the harbour off from the sea. The bridge, one of the first concrete bridges to be constructed in the world, remained a toll bridge for 30 years until Saunders Stephens, the Lord of the Manor, paid £2,000 to free it from toll.

One of the most renowned smugglers in the West Country is buried in the graveyard of the 14th-century church. Thomas Rattenbury was one of many who used Seaton as a centre of smuggling operations in the 17th and 18th centuries.

Today Seaton is a popular but quiet seaside resort with a good beach and an annual Arts Festival. A private electric tramway, which used to belong to British Rail, runs from Seaton to Colyford and Colyton. The town has all facilities.

Hotel:	Bay Hotel; Tel. Seaton (0297) 20073
B&B:	St. Margaret's Guest House, 5 Seafield Road; Tel. Seaton (0297) 20462
Early closing:	Thursday
Buses:	(summer only) Sidmouth, Axminster

BEER

Just beyond Seaton, Beer too had its smuggler, Jack Rattenbury, born there in 1778. He gained fame as the 'Rob Roy of the West' and, after an adventurous life in his chosen trade, settled down in Beer to a peaceful retirement, became a fisherman and published his *Memoirs of a Smuggler* in 1837.

Beer did have a more respectable side and was renowned for its lace. The lace for Queen Victoria's wedding dress was made there, as well as for Queen Alexandra and Princess Alice. It was also a busy fishing village and its quarry, for Beer Stone, was known to the Romans. The stone has the peculiar quality of being so soft when first quarried that it can be cut with a saw. Today it is a quiet, unspoilt former fishing village with all facilities.

Hotel: Dolphin Hotel; Tel. Seaton (0297) 20068
B&B: Weston House; Tel. Seaton (0297) 22248
YHA: Bovey Combe, Townsend; Tel. Beer (0297) 20296
Buses: (summer only) Sidmouth, Seaton, Axminster

BRANSCOMBE

This is a pre-Saxon settlement and one of the most attractive villages in South Devon. The name is thought to be a corruption of St Brendan the Voyager, who had a chapel in Seaton. The charming church is dedicated to the 7th-century Saints, Winfred and Branwallader, and in it you will find a memorial to Joan Wadham with her two husbands and 20 children, one of whom, Nicholas Wadham, founded Wadham College at Oxford in 1610.

The manor belonged to King Alfred during his reign and was later given by King Athelstan to the monastery which became Exeter Cathedral in 995. Church Living, opposite the church, has parts dating back to the 13th century.

The village contains many picturesque buildings and its shops have a timeless air about them. Although the blacksmith's forge, built in 1580, is no longer in operation, other shops look just as old and still carry on their daily commerce. The village has all facilities.

Hotel: The Mason's Arms; Tel. Branscombe (029780) 300
B&B: Mill Farm; Tel. Branscombe (029780) 277
Buses: (summer only) Sidmouth, Seaton, Axminster

4

Branscombe to Goodrington

Exmouth, lying three miles to the eastward of Dawlish, on that side of the river Ex, is by no means liable to the criticism which I have just ventured to throw out on the latter place. It is a town of some extent; and, therefore, neither simplicity, nor picturesque beauty is expected in it. The houses may be grouped into any form that fancy suggests, without the builder incurring the censure of having spoiled the scene by incongruous archi-tecture.

The variety and grandeur of the view which the houses near the shore command, is seldom equalled. Old Ocean opens his heaving bosom to the south, and the Ex comes sweeping down in a broad sheet of water, from the opposite point. This estuary, sprinkled with shipping, inclosed between hills, which are ornamented with groves and mansions, castles and cities, presents, at full tide, and under a calm sky, the picture of an Italian lake. Limited in time, I could only visit, by a distant view, scenes which promise such gratification on a closer inspection — Topsham, and the beautiful country around it; Exeter and its venerable cathedral; the bold, broad, commanding summit of Hall-Down; and the magnificent seat and grounds of Manhead, which ornament its eastern declivity. Powderham-castle is immediately opposite to me, but I do not regret my inability to visit it, since its situation is low, and the grounds about it are uninteresting. Besides, I have no passion for magnificence, unless it be united with a little taste; and should therefore receive no sort of pleasure in contemplating such gew-gaws as a silver grate plaistered over with gold, and three window-curtains, on each of which has been lavished the enormous sum of seven hundred guineas!!!

WARNER, Rev. Richard (1763–1857). Divine and antiquary. *A Walk Through Some of the Western Counties of England* (1800). Re-issued in 1809 as *A Walk Through Somerset, Devon and Part of Cornwall.*

Introduction

After the uncomplicated journey from Poole, this part of the coast introduces the problem of crossing an estuary – in a small way at Budleigh Salterton and Teignmouth, more seriously at Exmouth, where the Starcross Ferry is only seasonal. You will also need to negotiate the built-up area of Torbay, where almost 35 kilometres of coast have sunk beneath concrete, brick and steel. In general, however, this stretch provides good coastal walking with one or two fine views inland of unspoilt English countryside: lush green pastures, dark woods, gentle hills and valleys with charming towns and villages set amid them. There are a couple of fairly steep slopes in the first 10 kilometres after Branscombe but otherwise no very taxing walking.

Although Devonian slates and shale distinguish Kilmorie flats on the headland before Torbay, the geological structure of this area is almost exclusively new red sandstone. The beach at Budleigh Salterton is a favourite for pebble hunters, and a couple of kilometres further on the area below the cliffs, known as The Floors, harbours many different birds. Dawlish Warren is a nature reserve for salt-water flora and birds.

Evidence of pre-historic man continues, with traces of ancient field systems visible almost in Torquay itself. Buildings, ports, early railway architecture and even the remains of Brunel's expensive experiment, the Atmospheric Railway, are to be seen along the way. Interesting also are the small seaside resorts, some of which, like Sidmouth, retain much of the character which first made them fashionable watering places.

Guide

From Branscombe Mouth, climb landward around the long grey house, 'The Lookout', around Captain Horton's copse and up on to a well marked path. This path runs below the

STAGE	CUMUL.	TIME	BRANSCOMBE TO GOODRINGTON (TORBAY)	TELEPHONE	TRAIN	BUS	FERRY	SHOPS	CAMPING	ACCOMMODATION	REFRESHMENT	CUMUL. DIST. KMS
			BRANSCOMBE						x	x	x	125
8	8	2:	SIDMOUTH	x		x		x	x	x	x	133
(3)		(:45)	(SIDBURY)									
(10)		(2:30)	(OTTERY ST MARY)									
3¼	11¼	:50	LADRAM BAY HOLIDAY CAMP						x		x	144¼
(½)		(:10)	(OTTERTON)									
7¼	18½	1:50	BUDLEIGH SALTERTON	x		x		x	x	x	x	161½
(2)		(:30)	(EAST BUDLEIGH)									
6½	25	1:40	SANDY BAY								x	168
3¼	28¼	:50	EXMOUTH	x	x	x	x	x	x	x	x	171¼
(16)		(4:)	(EXETER)	x	x	x		x	x	x		
			STARCROSS				x		x		x	
½	28¾	:10	COCKWOOD			x					x	
2	30¾	:30	DAWLISH WARREN		x	x			x	x	x	173¾
3¼	34	:50	DAWLISH	x	x	x		x	x	x		177
1¾	35¾	:25	HOLCOMBE			x					x	178¾
2½	38¼	:40	TEIGNMOUTH	x	x	x	x	x	x	x	x	181¼
			SHALDON	x			x	x	x	x		
(2½)		:40	(STOKE IN TEIGNHEAD)									
(5)		(1:15)	(HACCOMBE)									
4	42¼	1:	MAIDENCOMBE	x		x			x	x	x	185¼
1½	43¾	:25	WATCOMBE									186¾
1½	45¼	:25	BABBACOMBE	x		x	x				x	188¼
			ODDICOMBE									
15	60¼	3:45	TORQUAY	x	x	x			x	x	x	203¼
			PAIGNTON									
			GOODRINGTON									

TIMES ARE BASED ON AVERAGE WALKER LIGHTLY LADEN.

NB.

1. STAGE: is the distance between that point and the preceding point.

2. CUMUL.: is the cumulative distance from the beginning of the chapter.

3. TIME: is the time for the stage (between that point and the preceding one) calculated at 4 kilometres per hour – the rate for a lightly loaded person walking without halt.

4. Brackets enclose places not on the Path but easily reached from it, together with distances and times from the Path.

5. CUMULATIVE DISTANCE: is the total distance from South Haven Point.

shoulder of the cliff to landward, through trees, with Branscombe village – the church suddenly visible – straggling up the valley below. The often muddy track becomes a farm track between stout walls, and where the track bends sharply right, leave it, striking out diagonally across the field ahead and on the left, towards Coxe's Cliff and the coast. Notice the important fortifications of an Iron Age fort to seaward. The path winds on, irregularly marked, but generally following the line of the cliff, which shows considerable and curious evidence of erosion, with whole slabs of fields breaking away although still cultivated. The path climbs up to Weston Cliff and then goes smartly down to Weston Mouth.

Continue along the pebble beach for a few metres and then climb inland, through woods, around mounds which are the spoil heaps of many years lime-burning, around the head of a coomb, descending first then climbing back towards the coast and Dunscombe Cliff. From here, go steeply down to **Salcombe Mouth**, turning inland to cross the river on a foot-bridge and then back seawards. Climb up the other side on to Salcombe Hill Cliff above Chapman's Rocks and down, gently at first, then quite steeply and finally by steps to the bridge across the River Sid, and **Sidmouth.**

Walk along the attractive sea front and, opposite the entrance to Peak House, up the hill on the broad grass slope to seaward of the road. At the top, take to the road again and just round the bend, after Peak Cottage, turn left off the road to climb up through woods and gorse towards Windgate. Go down and up again through woods to High Peak, and then down steeply through woods which look not unlike the Black Forest, to Ladram Bay and its austere holiday camp.

Cross the stream bridge and climb across the field ahead of you, towards the coast. The path now keeps to seaward, close to the cliffs, across farm lands of pasture and cultivated vegetables, before dropping down towards the River Otter. Turn inland along its bank and cross it by the road bridge a kilometre further on. Once across, come back along its bank towards the sea and turn right on to the sea front at **Budleigh Salterton.**

Continue along the seafront. At the western end a path leads up, through gorse and pinewoods, along the perimeter of West Down Golf Course to West Down Beacon. Below, to seaward, are **The Floors**. The path goes down quite steeply now, crossing a stream on a foot-bridge above Littleham Cove, and cutting across Straight Point, a rifle range, close to the perimeter wire. Continue through the caravans of the Sandy Bay Holiday Park before climbing up again on to the High Land of Orcombe, National Trust property. Go down around Orcombe Point, with its coastguard look-out, and past Orcombe Rocks to the road which leads you into **Exmouth**.

From May to September, there is a ferry to take you to Starcross. Otherwise, you will have to go by bus or train to Exeter and on again to **Dawlish Warren** on the other side of the estuary.

From the ferry, you must walk 3 kilometres along the road, through Cockwood to Dawlish Warren, where the path recommences, although it is incomplete until Holcombe. The route continues along the main road to Dawlish, Holcombe and Teignmouth. However, it is possible to turn left in the centre of Dawlish Warren, take a foot-bridge across the railway and walk along the promenade beside it, or along the beach if the tide permits, to the far side of **Dawlish**, crossing over the line on to the main road by a foot-bridge as the railway disappears into a tunnel before Old Maid Rocks.

Continue along the road to **Holcombe** and cross over the railway where it emerges from another tunnel before Parson and Clerk Headland. Walk along the promenade or the beach – if the tide permits – to Teignmouth, where you rejoin the road. Pass the pier and walk on to the ferry which, throughout the year, will take you across the mouth of the River Teign to **Shaldon**.

Turn left and walk along the road until it turns sharp right about 700 metres from the ferry, where you carry straight on along a path which climbs over fields on to the cliffs around Bundle Head and down towards **Labrador Bay**. Just before the bay, the path goes inland around a private property. It then climbs again, continuing along the coast, often in woods or between hedges, past Herring Cove, Mackerel Cove and Blackaller's Cove to **Maidencombe**, where it runs along the road for a few metres before resuming its course along the cliffs. It goes past Shackley Bench and Bell Rock, down through the Valley of the Rocks, past Watcombe, up again on to the cliffs and down past Petit Tor Point into **Oddicombe**. It is possible to travel right the way across the Torbay built-up area by public transport.

From Oddicombe you continue at sea level around Long Quarry Point, past **Babbacombe** and up off Babbacombe Beach on to Walls Hill and Babbacombe Down. Pass behind Anstey's Cove, down steps to the road and, after about 100 metres, cross Anstey's Cove car park to Bishop's Walk, which takes you around Black Head. The path now crosses the road and follows it south, above it, inland, and on to Ilsham Marine Drive, which it more or less follows, passing Hope's Nose and Thatcher Rock to a path which goes down left to a car park at the beginning of Meadfoot Sea Road. Take this path around Meadfoot Beach and then turn up a path through woodland on to Daddyhole Plain behind Daddyhole Cove. This leads through the Rock End Estate and eventually brings you out beside the Imperial Hotel, **Torquay**. From here to Goodrington, you follow the sea front as closely as possible, with much road, promenade and beach walking through Torquay and **Paignton** and a pleasant path over Hollicombe Head.

Gazetteer

SALCOMBE REGIS

This village is a few hundred metres off the path, by a good track from the bridge at Salcombe Mouth, and has an interesting church. The pillars and font are transitional Norman, the chancel door is Norman and other parts are Early English. In the chancel itself you can see an unusual panel dated 1695, which bears an inscription in English, Greek, Hebrew and Latin.

SIDMOUTH

Another South Coast port whose origins are difficult to date precisely. Just to the west, on High Peak, there are the remains of an Iron Age camp and it is known that the town sent three ships and 62 men to the siege of Calais in 1346. Risdon says that in the late 17th century it was 'one of the chiefest fisher towns in this shire and serveth much provision unto the eastern parts, wherein her principal maintenance consists'. That is its early history.

By the turn of the 18th century the town had found its true vocation as a seaside resort and many of the buildings which lend it charm and dignity today date from that period. The town is rich in Regency and early Victorian houses. In 1819 the Duke and Duchess of Kent brought their baby daughter, later Queen Victoria, to stay here, setting a fashion followed by many of the nobility. Hints of this respectability linger and the town is still a resort popular with the elderly. It has a pretty example of a Victorian sea-front and good shops.

Hotel: Westcliff Hotel, Manor Road; Tel. Sidmouth (03955) 3252

B&B: Hilltop, Ascerton Road; Tel. Sidmouth (03955) 77413

Early closing: Thursday

Buses: Seaton, Lyme Regis, Exmouth, Budleigh, Salterton

SIDBURY

Situated just north of Sidmouth, still on the River Sid, Sidbury has a church with a Saxon crypt. An unusual gunpowder store-room over the porch was used at the time of the Civil War.

OTTERY ST MARY

Rather farther north and slightly west of Sidmouth (10 kilometres on the B3176), this small town has a good example of an Early English church, which has survived practically unaltered. A college was founded there by Grandisson in 1335, and the North Aisle was added by Cicely, Countess of Dorset, in 1520. Cadhay Manor House, built in 1550 by John Haydon, is open to the public.

The town also has strong literary connections. Coleridge was born there in 1772, and Thackeray used to spend his holidays there. He even adopted the town, which he called Clavering St Mary, for his novel *Pendennis* (in which Exeter became 'Chatteris' and Sidmouth, 'Baymouth').

OTTERTON

Half a kilometer from the path, on a foot-path inland from Ladram Bay or Smallstones Point, this village was part of a manor given by William the Conqueror to the monastery of St Michel in Normandy. The Benedictine Priory was a cell of that monastery and its remains are close to the church.

BUDLEIGH SALTERTON

Long before the 13th century this was a fishing port and salt-working centre. Neither exists today. The town is now a quiet seaside resort and a popular retirement place. Sir John Millais made the beach famous as a setting for his painting 'The Boyhood of Raleigh'.

Hotel:	Rose Mullion Hotel, Cliff Road, Budleigh Salterton; Tel. Budleigh Salterton (03954) 2288
B&B:	White Cottage, 25 East Budleigh Road; Tel. Budleigh Salterton (03954) 3574
Early closing:	Thursday
Buses:	Exeter, Exmouth, Sidmouth

EAST BUDLEIGH

Only half an hour's walk from the path, north of Budleigh Salterton, lies East Budleigh, the birthplace of Sir Walter Raleigh, the man who introduced the potato to England. He was born in Hayes Barton Farmhouse in 1552. The farmhouse, which is open to the public, is of Tudor origin and has a most unusual beam, 25 metres long, which runs the length of five rooms. The church has 60 or so very fine carved bench ends which were probably executed by sailors returned from the sea as an act of thanks for their survival. The tomb of Raleigh's first wife, Joan Drake, is also in the church. The vicarage is full of secret hiding places, which lend force to the legend that it served as a shelter for smuggling parsons.

EXMOUTH

Exmouth has a considerable history, both as a commercial and as a military port. Known as Axenmouth in Saxon times, its foundation is very ancient and there was already a harbour here in Roman times. In 1346 the town sent no less than 10 ships and 193 men to the Siege of Calais, and in 1588 it sent ships against the Spanish Armada.

In the 17th century the town was heavily engaged in the Newfoundland cod trade and in the 18th century it increased its commercial activity by exporting wool to Portugal and Holland. The Newfoundland trade is an interesting example of the development of international trade in general. It developed into a triangular affair: salt and manufactured goods were carried to Newfoundland, salted cod from Newfoundland to Portugal and the Mediterranean, and wine and fruit from the Mediterranean to Exmouth. Another three-cornered trade link developed with the export of manufactured goods from Exmouth to West Africa, slaves to the West Indies and sugar and rum back to Exmouth.

In the 19th century Exmouth had a sizeable fishing fleet, but this gradually lost importance in favour of Brixham, which was nearer the fishing grounds. Exmouth also had a shipbuilding business capable of building ships of up to 400 tons, but a disastrous fire in 1880 resulted in the transfer of this business to Dartmouth.

By the mid 18th century Exmouth was already starting to develop as a pleasure resort and the many elegant 18th- and 19th-century buildings which survive bear witness to this. Lady Nelson and Lady Byron both lived there in Georgian houses on the fashionable Beacon.

In 1798 two sisters, the Misses Parminter, built a curious 16-sided, almost circular house, which has diamond-shaped windows and is modelled on a church in Ravenna in Italy. Inside, the gallery is decorated with a shell and feather motif, and the building, built as a non-conformist chapel, is still used for inter-denominational services. Called 'A La Ronde', it is situated in Summer Lane and open to the public on Sundays throughout the year and daily between Easter and October. 'Point in View' is another cottage 'orné', which was built in 1811 as a chapel. It is surrounded by dwellings for 'four deserving spinsters'.

Apart from general sight-seeing in the old parts of the town, it is worth visiting the Steam and Countryside Museum, which houses old agricultural equipment and working steam engines. Also on display there are shire horses, Shetland ponies and other farmyard animals. Another curiosity is the Model Railway Exhibition – a must for children of all ages – which has a scenic lay-out for the model trains, including marshalling yards and a model dock. Both of these are open daily from May to September.

Hotel:	The Barn Hotel, Foxholes; Tel. Exmouth (03952) 74411
B&B:	Bicton Inn; Tel. Exmouth (03952) 72589
Bus:	To Exeter and Budleigh Salterton
Rail:	To Exeter

Ferry: Normally daily May/September but check first;
            Tel. Exmouth (03952) 72589

(When the Ferry is not running, you will have to travel around
the Estuary through Exeter on foot or by public transport.)

EXETER

The cathedral city of Exeter is the county town of Devon and
has a history which goes back over 2,000 years. In the 12th
century it was the fourth most important city in England.

The Ancient Britons knew it as Caer-Isc, city of the water;
the Romans as Isca et Legio Secunda Augusta, the name of
the legion which garrisoned it. In Saxon times it became
Exancester and thus, through the distortion of time, Exeter. It
was first granted a Charter during the reign of Henry I
(1100–1135).

The city was fought over repeatedly. Vespasian in the 1st
century, Penda of Mercia in the 7th, the Danes in the 9th (in
894 AD the Danes used 250 ships in the attack but were
repelled by King Alfred), the Cornish Britons in the 10th – all
attacked it. Athelstan, who reigned from 925–940 recaptured
it from the bellicose Cornishmen, re-walled it and gave it the
status of a Mint Town. In the 11th century William I wrested it
from King Harold's mother, Githa, (the old girl held out for 18
days before the city was taken). In the 12th century King
Stephen (1135–1154) captured it from Matilda, and in 1497
Perkin Warbeck (who had landed at Whitsand Bay) tried to
grab it. However, he was driven off by Henry VII and later
executed. During the Civil War the city was briefly in parliamentary hands but was taken by Sir John Buckley. It became
the Royalist headquarters for the south-west until its re-
capture by Fairfax in 1646, when, as a way of drawing the city's
teeth, Rougemont Castle, built by William the Conqueror,
was dismantled.

Until 1290 the city was an important port as it could take
quite large ships, but then Countess Wear, wife of the Earl of
Devon, built a weir across the Exe, just above Topsham,
which prevented ships from reaching Exeter. Topsham then
became the port for the town, and goods had to be carried to it
overland. Despite repeated demands for its removal, the weir
remained until 1539, when an Act of Parliament authorized its
destruction.

In 1564 a canal was constructed (opened in 1566), which ran

for about 8 kilometres beside the river. Its locks are the earliest examples in the world of the 'Pound Lock' (first envisaged by Leonardo da Vinci), by which vessels are raised or lowered between different levels. At Double Locks, 2 or 3 kilometres from Exeter, the lock is unusually of turf instead of masonry, and the balance beams of the gates came from the main mast of HMS Exeter, removed after the Battle of the River Plate. Today the canal is used mainly by yachts and other pleasure craft.

Only parts of Rougemont Castle exist today, but the cathedral of St Peter and St Mary, around which Exeter grew, still dominates the city, to which the see of Devon and Cornwall was removed in 1050. There used to be a Benedictine monastery, founded by Athelstan in 932, on the site. Bishop Warlewast built the cathedral in 1132 and it was rebuilt and extended during the following seventy years. Only the twin towers and part of the walls of this early building, remain, the rest is 13th- and 14th-century.

There are many other churches, chapels and buildings which deserve your attention, but special mention must be made of St Nicholas's Priory (open Tuesday to Saturday), which was built to incorporate Athelstan's Benedictine monastery and mint; St Katherine's Priory, the Benedictine nunnery of Polscoe, founded in 1150; the medieval Guildhall, built in 1468–70, but enlarged and completed in 1592–4; the Customs' House, built in 1681; and the underground passages, which can be visited and which were used to supply water to the city until the introduction of piped water.

The Maritime Museum has a collection of 75 boats from all over the world, some of them quite famous, and the Rougemont and Royal Albert Memorial Museums and the Topsham Museum should also be visited.

Tourist Information: Tel. Exeter (0392) 72434

STARCROSS

A notable place for two reasons. It is the home of the oldest yacht club in England (possibly in the world) – the Starcross Yacht Club, based at Powderham nearby – and it has the last vestiges of Isambard Kingdom Brunel's expensive and unsuccessful undertaking, the Atmospheric Railway. This was intended to operate on atmospheric pressure. Pumping houses, situated at intervals along the track, created a vacuum in a pipe which lay between the tracks. The vacuum acted on a piston in the pipe which was connected to the train above, thus pulling the piston (and the train) along. The piston was also pushed from behind by air rushing into the pipe and creating momentum. Leather was used to seal the slot in the pipe through which the piston was connected to the train. To make this air-tight, grease was applied to it. However, the grease appealed to rats, the rats ate the grease and the leather, hence the failure of the project, the loss of £426,000 invested, and the introduction of a conventional locomotive on the line from Exeter to Plymouth. All that remains is the red sandstone pumping station at Starcross (now a warehouse) and a few bits of the original broad rails, used as a fence near the building.

There is a pub in the village and a bus stop at Lockwood, half a kilometre south.

Train: To Exeter and Torbay

DAWLISH

A fishing village recorded in the Domesday Book as Doelis or Doules, Dawlish became a small 'watering place' or seaside resort in Regency times. Both Jane Austen and Charles Dickens were frequent visitors and some attractive Regency and early Victorian houses, which they must have known, still stand today. The railway station, designed by Brunel, has survived unaltered. The village is still a popular small resort.

Hotel: Lamorna Hotel; Tel. Dawlish (0626) 863365
B&B: Barton Grange; Tel. Dawlish (0626) 862242
Trains: To Exeter and Torbay
Buses: To Newton Abbot and Exeter
Tourist
Information: Tel. Dawlish (0626) 863589

TEIGNMOUTH

Both town and port are old. The town's seal dates back to Ethelred the Unready (1002) and it is referred to in a Charter of Edward the Confessor in 1044. The Domesday Book records 24 salt workers in the town in 1086 and it sent 7 ships and 120 men to the Siege of Calais in 1346. It seems to have attracted fire: the Danes burnt it in 790 and 1001, and in 1338 and 1690 the French did so too. In spite of the fires, the town prospered.

In the 18th and 19th centuries a considerable trade developed in the export of granite, which was brought from Dartmoor on a unique tramway which ran on granite rails. Some of these rails can still be seen. The New Quay was built in the 1820s to handle the Hay Tor granite used (amongst other things) for building London Bridge – the bridge which now stands in the Arizona Desert.

Ball clay was shipped from Teignmouth to the potteries of Staffordshire (via Merseyside) from 1743. Today most of it is shipped, still from Teignmouth, to the Continent for industrial purposes.

Teignmouth was one of the first resorts to be developed on the Devon coast. John Keats lived there with his dying brother and completed 'Endymion' there in 1818, Jane Austen and Fanny Burney are also known to have visited the town.

Its fine sandy beach and its opportunities for offshore and deep-sea fishing make it a popular resort for families and fishermen.

Hotel: Ivy House, Sea Front; Tel. Teignmouth (06267) 2735

B&B: Regia Hotel, The Harbour; Tel. Teignmouth (06267) 5915

Bus: To Torbay, Exeter, Newton Abbot

Ferry: Teignmouth – Shaldon, all-year service; Tel. Teignmouth (06267) 6271

Early closing: Thursday

Tourist Information: Tel. Teignmouth (06267) 6271

STOKEINTEIGNHEAD

One kilometre west of the path, after crossing the River Teign, lies the village of Stokeinteignhead. The church is medieval and has a clerical brass of 1375 and a magnificent carved wood screen of the same period.

HACCOMBE

About 2 kilometres west, beyond Stokeinteignhead, the village has a very old church, mainly decorated English in style. Two families, the Haccombs and Carews, were successively Lords of the Manor, and the church has many monuments to members of both. On the door of the church are two horse-shoes, which were nailed there to commemorate a wild wager by Haccomb that Carew could not swim on horse-back across the Teign Estuary. He could; he did; he won – but no-one knows what he won.

LABRADOR BAY

The Bay got its name from Captain Trapp, a Labrador trader, who built a house above the Bay in the 18th century. The house no longer exists but it used to be of great use to smugglers and sheltered at least one French spy.

MAIDENCOMBE

The village is attractive because it has remained unspoilt; picturesque because of its thatched cottages and pub. Rudyard Kipling lived there briefly and mentions it in his autobiography. The village has shops, post office and buses.

WATCOMBE

It was here that Brunel, the great 19th-century engineer, chose to build the mansion which was to be his home when he retired. He died before it was completed.

KENT'S CAVERN

This is just off the path, inland of Anstey's Cove, at Wellswood, and it is a very important Palaeolithic site. As early as 1745 W. Morton wrote of being conducted around this labyrinth of limestone caves by the light of candles held in slotted sticks by 'two ancient females and not in the most comely of their years'.

Exploration of the cavern between 1825 and 1829 convinced the Roman Catholic priest, J. MacEnery, that man had existed for hundreds and thousands of years longer than current teaching supposed. This discovery was so at odds with the whole cosmology of his Church and of natural science as it was then understood that he did not have the courage to publish his findings.

Between 1865 and 1880 a noted scientific investigator,

William Pengelly from Looe, carried out a complete and systematic excavation of the site and fully confirmed MacEnery's findings. He discovered over 1300 man-worked flints and many other implements, together with the bones of long-extinct animals, such as the Cave Bear, Sabre-toothed Tiger, Woolly Rhinoceros and Mammoth. Much of what he found is on display in the Torquay Natural History Museum.

Nowadays, the cavern is a popular tourist attraction. Electric light has made candles unnecessary and has given rise to another curious phenomenon: a hart's tongue fern has grown up under each light bulb. They were not planted by man and it is believed that water carried their spores as it seeped through the porous limestone above. It is strange that they flourish never having seen daylight or experienced normal climatic conditions outside.

BABBACOMBE

Babbacombe was the scene of the brutal murder of old Miss Keyse in 1884. She was found with her throat cut and her skull fractured, after a fire. Her footman was found guilty of the murder and sentenced to death. His infamy turned to fame as John 'Babbaccombe' Lee, the man they couldn't hang. Three times they tried, three times the gallows refused to function, and the Home Secretary commuted his sentence to life imprisonment. He was released in 1907, married, and died in the United States of America in 1933.

TORBAY

In 1968, Torquay, Paignton and Brixham were amalgamated to form Devon's largest holiday resort, stretching for almost 35 kilometres along the coast. It now has a resident population of more than 100,000, and this is greatly increased at peak holiday periods.

In 1119, St Norbert founded an order known as the Premonstratensians at Premontre, near Laon in Northern France, and in 1196, William Brewer, Lord of the Manor of Torre, founded an Abbey of the Order on the shores of Torbay. King John granted the monks fishing rights over the bay in 1200, but the monastery was dissolved at the time of the Reformation and is used as an art gallery today.

The 16th-century chronicler, Leland, referred to 'a peere and socour for boats in the bottom of Torre Prior' and at about the same time a smuggler was caught with 'thirty hogges-heddes of wine in a cellar in Torbay and sugars in quantities not known'. A quay was built in the 16th century but the harbour itself was not constructed until 1750. It was extended in the early 19th century, with the construction of the South Pier in 1800, the Inner Harbour in 1806, and the Outer Harbour between 1867 and 1870.

In spite of all this activity and investment, the 19th century saw the decline of Torbay as a fishing port, its principal activity since the time of King John, in favour of Brixham, where new trawlers found a safer anchorage. By the mid 19th century both the ship-building industry and the trade in timber imports from Canada had also died.

However, Torbay had been developing a new industry since the time of the Napoleonic Wars, when the British Fleet used Torbay as a safe anchorage from which to harry the French. This industry was tourism. Torbay became one of the principal genteel watering places on the south coast. Both its climate and its beautiful setting were ideal for this. At first it was patronized by naval officers and their families (Napoleon, who saw it as a prisoner from the Bellerephon, compared it to Port Ferrajo in Elba), and it was soon adopted by the gentry, the nobility and the literary establishment of the 19th century.

The Duchess of Sutherland lived in Sutherland Towers and entertained Princess Alexandra of Wales there. German princes and Russian archdukes took up residence. Elizabeth Barrett Browning and Charles Kingsley lived there, Lord Lytton died there, and Disraeli was a frequent visitor. More recently, that great modern playwrght, Sean O'Casey, made it his home.

Paignton was an older foundation. A Saxon named Paega built a church there in the 6th century, but even that was built on the site of a Bronze Age settlement. The present church is largely Norman with some 15th-century additions. Fishing was one of the town's earliest industries, and even today Paignton fishermen have the right to dry their nets on the green. In the 17th century Paignton was heavily involved in the development of the Newfoundland fishing industry.

It was also important as a commercial port: coal and culm (anthracite dust) were brought in, and cider and the famous Paignton cabbages were shipped out. The transition from port to resort began in 1880 when a wily speculator from the Midlands, encouraged by Torbay's increasing and fashionable popularity, bought up land and started to develop it.

Hotels:	Imperial, Parkhill Road; Tel. Torquay (0803) 24301
	Mount Nessing Hotel; Tel. Torquay (0803) 22970
B&B:	Glenmore Guest House, Chatsworth Road; Tel. Torquay (0803) 27930
Bus:	To Exeter
Trains:	To Exeter, London
Early closing:	Wednesday
Tourist Information:	Tel. Torquay (0803) 27428

5

Goodrington to Salcombe

*Brixham is haunted and dominated, and let us hope it always
will be, by the memory of the most splendid fleet of little ships
that ever sailed the seas; the Brixham Sailing Trawlers. . . .*

*Brixham was of old a fishing port, besides being a commer-
cial port of some significance too. In the early 19th century
Brixham developed the first great trawling fleet in the
world. . . .*

*The largest of the Brixham smacks were called Dandies, the
medium class Bumble-bees and the smallest Hookers. A
Dandie might cost, to build, £1000. The general custom was to
divide the catch into shares, the ship getting one, the gear
another, the Captain and each man one and there were
generally two men beside the skipper. The skipper, who was
generally the owner too, might hope to make about a pound a
day, the fishermen four shillings, but of course this varied
enormously according to the catch. There was many a week in
which the ships couldn't put to sea at all because of the weather,
and then captain, owner and crew got nothing. There was no
'national insurance'. On the other hand, sometimes they struck
it rich.*

SEYMOUR, John. Author of travel books. Extract from *The
Companion Guide to The Coast of South West England*
published by Collins, 1974.

Introduction

Too much road walking makes this an unsatisfactory stretch of
the path. The worst parts are from Man Sands to Kingswear
and from Stoke Fleming to Torcross. The urban areas of

Goodrington, Brixham and Dartmouth, in spite of their charm, can be pretty tedious to walk through, and although rich in wildlife, Slapton Sands is still long and monotonous. On the credit side, there are some enchanting coastal stretches between Hallsands and Portlemouth.

Practically the whole of this area is composed of Devonian shale and slate. An exception is the large headland between Hallsands and East Portlemouth, which is New Red Sandstone, and Berry Head has a lime-stone sub-strata which determines the plant life which grows there. Slapton Sands and the raised beach to the East of Prawle Point are both natural features worthy of attention.

Slapton Ley is a nature reserve, and there are others at Start Point and Berry Head, a country park. Prawle Point is a rewarding view point for ornithologists on the look out for migrating birds, and butterfly enthusiasts find their rewards in summer between Hallsands and Portlemouth.

Of the places you pass through on this part of the route Dartmouth and Salcombe have the most varied history and architecture, but Kingswear, Stoke Fleming, Slapton, and Portlemouth all have buildings or stories which will capture your imagination.

Guide

The path leads south from Goodrington, landward of the railway line, round Saltern Cove. It passes under the railway at Broad Sands, follows the bay close to the shore, and then climbs up across the grassy headland past Elberry Farm, around Elberry Cove. From there you continue along a straight grassy stretch, beside the golf course, around Fishcombe Point and down to Churston Cove. You then cross the Cove and climb up between two holiday camps, and down into **Brixham**.

Follow the road round past the harbour, the long breakwater and the coastguard station to Shoalstone Point, where you pick up the path again. This leads you to **Berry Head** (a country park) and its lighthouse, round the Head, across Berry Head Common and close to the cliff edge, past a holiday camp, around Durl Head. The path now descends through scrub to St Mary's Bay, then climbs up around it towards Sharkham Point. Carry on up to Southdown Cliff and go down

STAGE	CUMUL.	TIME	GOODRINGTON (TORBAY) TO SALCOMBE	TELEPHONE	TRAIN	BUS	FERRY	SHOPS	CAMPING	ACCOMMODATION	REFRESHMENT	CUMUL. DIST. KMS
			GOODRINGTON	x	x	x		x	x	x	x	203¼
5	5	1:15	BRIXHAM	x		x		x	x	x	x	208¼
2	7	:30	BERRY HEAD								x	210¼
10	17	2:30	KINGSWEAR	x	x	x	x	x		x	x	220¼
			DARTMOUTH	x		x	x	x	x	x	x	
5	22	1:15	STOKE FLEMING	x		x		x			x	225¼
1	23	:15	BLACKPOOL SANDS	x		x					x	226¼
1¾	24¾	:30	STREETE	x		x			x	x	x	228
3	27¾	:45	SLAPTON							x	x	231
3¼	31	:50	TORCROSS	x		x		x		x	x	234¼
1½	32½	:25	BEESANDS	x		x				x	x	235¾
1½	34	:25	HALLSANDS									237¼
(1)		(:15)	(EAST PRAWLE)	x			x		x		x	
13½	47½	3:25	EAST PORTLEMOUTH				x		x	x		250¾
			SALCOMBE	x		x	x	x	x	x	x	

TIMES ARE BASED ON AVERAGE WALKER LIGHTLY LADEN.

NB.
1. STAGE: is the distance between that point and the preceding point.
2. CUMUL.: is the cumulative distance from the beginning of the chapter.
3. TIME: is the time for the stage (between that point and the preceding one) calculated at 4 kilometres per hour – the rate for a lightly loaded person walking without halt.
4. Brackets enclose places not on the Path but easily reached from it, together with distances and times from the Path.
5. CUMULATIVE DISTANCE: is the total distance from South Haven Point.

by a good path to the southern limit of Man Sands, where the path is interrupted.

At this point you have a two-hour walk inland, along a track at first, then along country lanes, past Woodhuish Farm, along Scabbacombe Lane and left past Kingston to Coleton. Turn right to pass Brownstone Farm and Higher Farm, from which you take a footpath down across the head of Mill Bay Cove to Home Farm. Continue up along the coast road around One Gun Point to the Lower Ferry landing stage in **Kingswear**. The ferry operates throughout the year across the

River Dart to **Dartmouth**. (In summer one operates to the Castle.)

Turn left along the road out of Dartmouth towards the Castle. Just beyond it the path turns down to Blackstone Point, climbs up around Compass Cove, down towards Willow Cove, up past the coastguard look-out at Coombe Point, and along behind Warren Cove. It then turns inland to a National Trust car park. From here the path continues along the road to **Stoke Fleming**, Blackpool Sands, Streete and all the way along **Slapton Sands** (about 10 kilometres) to **Torcross**. It is possible to take a bus from Dartmouth or Stoke Fleming to Torcross.

When the tide is out you can walk along the beach from Torcross to Hallsands. Otherwise climb the steps (marked 'footpath') which lead up where the main road turns sharply inland, pass the hotel and climb onto the cliff path. The path goes inland to avoid a disused slate quarry and then drops back down to the coast at Sunnydale. It then follows the road past a large caravan park through **Beesands** and continues as a coastal path to **Hallsands**.

Pass in front of the houses and climb up seaward of the Hallsands Hotel and Mildmay Cottages following signs. The path continues as an undulating high cliff path across well-fenced agricultural land, with an unusual number of dry stone walls, until it reaches the car park and the metalled drive leading to the lighthouse at **Start Point**. Take this drive, go round the Point (a nature reserve), and down to pass above Foxhole Cove, round above Raven's Cove, down to Peartree Point, up around Mattiscombe (pronounced 'Matchcombe') Beach and down to Lannacombe Beach.

Cross over the road and the bridge across the stream, and climb up the track. Go inland slightly around the coomb at Woodcombe Sand, past Stinking Cove, and past old green-houses and scruffy gardens which look pretty in spring. The path continues close to the coast across worked farm land, in and out of fields, past Gorah Rocks, Horseley Cove and Langerstone Point to **Prawle Point**, the southernmost point in Devon.

From Prawle Point the path descends to go round Macely Cove. It then climbs up over Gammon Head, down to the coomb before Pig's Nose, around Deckler's Cliff, down into another coomb and up to the Gara Rock Hotel. Continue around the coast, below Portlemouth Down, over Rickham Common, and follow the estuary into Mill Bay. From here the road takes you the remaining kilometre along the shore to the **Portlemouth** Ferry. The ferry runs throughout the year and takes only a few minutes to reach **Salcombe**.

Gazetteer

BRIXHAM

The name is a corruption of Byri or Byrig, the Saxon word for castle or fortification, which gives a clue to the length of Brixham's history. For most of the town's long existence it has been a fishing port and it was here in the 19th century that deep sea trawlers were invented. This innovation was so successful that the fleet outgrew both the port and the fishing grounds of Lyme Bay. The trawlers ventured farther and farther afield, at first around Land's End to the Irish Sea and then up-channel, through the straits of Dover into the North Sea.

This inevitably led to an exodus of boats and people, and Brixham fishermen and their families became the founding fathers of the fishing ports all along the East Coast. The fishing industries of Lowestoft, Great Yarmouth, Boston, Grimsby, Hull and Scarborough were all started by Brixham fishermen. The price of this fishing pioneering was Brixham's own decline into a kind of deep-sea obscurity. By 1928 barely 2000 tons of fish were landed here while in a port like Hull nearly 100,000 tons were recorded.

Brixham's luckless history was not confined to its fishing industry. In the 18th century this port was heavily engaged in the three-cornered trade with Newfoundland and the Mediterranean. By the 19th century nearly 200 Brixham-registered schooners were trading throughout the world. With the arrival of that useful monster the railway Brixham suffered another blow, as this cheaper and more efficient means of transporting goods to major ports took over.

Temporary salvation came when in the middle of the 19th century iron ore was discovered near the town, and the paint which was manufactured from it was shipped throughout the world. When new processes were developed for the manufacture of paint, the iron-ore mines, at their peak nine in number, also became an industrial casualty.

In spite of its discouraging history Brixham has maintained a dreamy optimism. In 1960 a new fish dock with ice-making plants, cold-stores and all the apparatus of modern fishing ports was constructed here. For all their salty determination, however, Brixham's citizens are more likely to find a future in the less romantic industry of tourism.

William of Orange, whose statue presides in stony state over the inner harbour, landed here on 5 November 1688 to claim the English throne. The harbour was too small to hold his 670 ships, and his 30,000 men had to disembark in relays. William became King of England the following year, and, although he died in 1702, acts of violence are still carried on in his name on Ulster's strife-torn streets. Admittedly this has little to do with Brixham, but it is worth pondering who the Ulster Protestants would have chosen as their champion had William not stepped ashore here.

In 1824 Henry Francis Lyte became the first vicar of All Saint's church in Brixham. The church itself is fairly unremarkable, but twice a day, at 12 noon and 8 p.m., the carrillon plays Abide with Me and Praise my Soul the King of Heaven, two of the Reverend Lyte's most famous hymns. Windmill Hill, or Philip's Cavern, was discovered in 1858. It is very similar in form and in the contents found when it was opened to Kent's Cavern at Babbacombe, which has already been described. It is just south of Brixham harbour. Brixham has all facilities.

Hotel:	Quayside Hotel, King Street; Tel. Brixham (08045) 3357
B&B:	Smuggler's Haunt, Church Hill; Tel. Brixham (08045) 3050
YHA:	Youth Hostel, Galmpton; Tel. Brixham (08045) 842444
Bus:	To Torbay, Newton Abbot and Kingswear
Early closing:	Wednesday
Tourist Information:	Tel. Brixham (08045) 2861

BERRY HEAD

The name comes, like Brixham, from the Saxon for fort; and the place seems to be littered with them. There is an Iron Age cliff fort and remains of fortifications against the French, thrown up in the 16th, 17th, and 18th centuries. The most recent ones were built at the time of the Napoleonic wars, early in the 19th century. The site is superb. It commands and protects the whole of the safe anchorage of Torbay. The head and the common land behind is scheduled as a country park and noted for its birds. Gannets, fulmars, kittiwakes, guillemots and other sea birds live or visit there, and many interesting grasses and plants grow on the limestone soil. An official guide book is available during the season from the kiosk in the car park.

MAN SANDS AND LIME BURNING

The remains of many lime kilns suggest that ships used to unload coal here to burn the lime quarried at Berry Head. Quarried lime was burnt to make quicklime, a product used in numerous industries, among them iron and steel, agriculture, building, coal mining, chemicals, pharmacy, cosmetics, tanning, wire drawing and sewage treatment. Essential as it was to so many processes, it remained a very low-value commodity and not worth the cost of lengthy transport. Thus, the burning plants were located as close to the quarries as possible.

KINGSWEAR

The fortunes of this small town have long been inseparable from those of its more important neighbour Dartmouth. Nevertheless, it is independently famous for its crabs and lobsters.

You may visit the gardens of Kingswear Court Lodge and see Kingswear Castle, built, with Dartmouth Castle opposite, in about 1491 as a defence against the French.

Kingswear is the terminus for the Torbay Steam Railway, which runs from Paignton in the summer months. The town has all facilities.

Hotel:	Redoubt; Tel. Kingswear (080425) 295
Bus:	To Torbay
Train:	To Paignton
Ferry:	All year, frequent service; Tel. Kingswear (080425) 342
Early closing:	Wednesday

DARTMOUTH

The Saxons called it Ludhill, but it has been an important harbour and port since the Romans occupied it. Its history has been turbulent right up to the Second World War, and it has a remarkable place in British naval history.

The town was burnt by the French at the end of the 12th century, repelled an invasion by them in 1404, and was burnt by them again shortly afterwards. During the Civil War it declared for Parliament, fell after four weeks of siege to Prince Rupert in 1643, and was recaptured for Parliament by Fairfax in 1646. Heavy bombing damaged the town considerably in the Second World War, but it still managed to remain a haven for the Royal Navy. On D Day, 33,000 American troops were despatched in 485 ships from Dartmouth to the beaches of Normandy.

In 1190 Richard the Lionheart (Richard 1) assembled 100 ships in the harbour for his Crusade to the Holy Land, one of those incredible adventures of Christian chivalry, a blend of piety and man's thirst for exploration, plunder and war. In 1346 Dartmouth sent the third largest contingent to the British fleet at the siege of Calais – 31 ships and 757 men. Chaucer's shipman, Sir John Hawley – shipowner, pirate, privateer, Lord Mayor and benefactor of the town – came from Dartmouth. He died in 1408 and his memorial brass is in St Saviour's church.

Sir Walter Raleigh, Sir Humphrey Gilbert, and the navigator John Davis all had close links with the town. Sir Humphrey Gilbert, the distinguished explorer and coloniser, was born at Greenaway House in 1537 (more recently the home of the late Agatha Christie). He claimed Newfoundland for the Queen, discovered the Gilbert Sound and was drowned when his ship, the Squirrel, sank while returning from Newfoundland in 1583.

John Davis, protégé of Sir Humphrey Gilbert, was born at Sandridge House, between Dartmouth and Stoke Gabriel. In 1585 he sailed to the Arctic for the first time in search of the North West passage. He repeated his voyage in 1586 and 1587, discovering the Davis Strait between Greenland and Baffin Island in Canada. He also traded with the Eskimos. Later he transferred his attention to the Southern Hemisphere. On one of those voyages, in 1592, he discovered the Falkland Islands.

The pioneer of the steam engine, Thomas Newcomen, was born in Dartmouth in 1663. Visiting the Cornish tin mines he decided that there had to be more efficient ways to work a pump than straight horse power, and he produced his first steam engine in 1712 after ten years' research. It incorporated the important innovations of the internal condensing jet and automatic valve gear, which led to the internal combustion engine. One of his engines is displayed in Newcomen House. Now operated electrically, the engine dates from 1725, and was working on a canal under its own steam until 1913.

The Castle was completed directly opposite Kingswear Castle in about 1494. In emergencies a chain was stretched between the two to close the river mouth. This was the first castle in England to be equipped with gun platforms and ports (the ports are the original ones). Above the Castle stand the ruins of one built in 1380, refortified and renamed Gallant's Bower during the Civil War. It is now National Trust property.

St Petroc's church is close to the Castle. It was built in 1641 on the site of a cell where the Saint lived until his death in 594. St Saviour's church is near the estuary. Although mainly early to mid 17th century, parts of it are much earlier. The carved stone pulpit, the rood screen, and the main door are its best features.

The Royal Naval College, usually just called Dartmouth, was designed by Sir Aston Webb and was completed in 1905. It replaced the sailing ship Britannia, which had been moored in the Dart as training ship for Naval officers since 1863. The Dartmouth town museum has a rich collection of local and maritime history and is open daily.

Hotel:	Royal Castle Hotel, 11 The Quay; Tel. Dartmouth (08043) 2397
B&B:	Townstall Farm; Tel. Dartmouth (08043) 2300
YHA:	The Parish Hall, Streete, Dartmouth
Bus:	To Plymouth, Kingsbridge, Totnes and Torcross
Ferry:	To Kingswear, all year, frequent service.
Early closing:	Wednesday
Tourist Information:	The Quay; Tel. Dartmouth (08043) 2281

STOKE FLEMING

St Peter's church, unchanged since the 14th century, contains two of the earliest and the best brasses in Devon. They commemorate John Corp, who died c. 1361, and his wife, daughter, or granddaughter, who died in 1391.

George Parker Bidder (1806–1876), 'the Calculating Boy' or 'the Human Calculator', lived in the village for a number of years. A century and a half before computers were invented this mathematical genius was doing complicated calculations instantaneously in his head. He became a civil engineer and worked with George and Robert Stephenson on a number of projects. These included the Victoria Docks in London, and the construction of the first swing-bridge in the world, on the Norwich to Lowestoft railway.

The village is on the bus route from Dartmouth to Kingsbridge and has shops and refreshments.

BLACKPOOL SANDS

The French landed on this sandy beach from Brittany in 1404 but were driven off by the locals helped by Dartmouth men. Then, in 1470, Richard Neville, Earl of Warwick (the Kingmaker) landed here, forcing Edward IV to flee to Flanders. Edward returned in 1471, and in April of that year Warwick was out-generalled and killed at the Battle of Barnet.

SLAPTON AND SLAPTON BEACH

Slapton, just off the path, has a 14th-century church, St James', and the ruins of a college, founded in 1372 as a chantry by Richard de Brien, one of the first Knights of the Garter.

The village and 12,000 hectares of surrounding land were evacuated in 1943 and used as a training ground by American forces preparing for the D Day landings in Normandy. The area at the time virtually became a battle ground, as live ammunition was used for training, but the only reminder of the period is the statue on Slapton Beach, unveiled by General Grunther in 1954, as a gesture of thanks from the American forces to the local population.

Slapton Ley, the largest freshwater lake in Devon, is a private nature reserve, leased to the Field Studies Council. Nature trail booklets are available from the Centre at Slapton, and visitors can join the guided walks which take place between June and September. The Field Studies Centre receives thousands of students each year.

Inn:	Tower Inn, Slapton; Tel. Kingsbridge (0548) 580216
YHA:	Youth Hostel, The Parish Hall, Streete, Dartmouth
Bus:	To Dartmouth, Kingsbridge

TORCROSS

This is another fishing village which enjoyed a period of prosperity while trading with Newfoundland. The local fishermen kept Newfoundland dogs which they trained to swim out to meet incoming boats and bring their ropes ashore, thus allowing the fishermen to remain dry. It was the most easterly of the pilchard villages. The path leaves the road and the Dartmouth/Kingsbridge bus route here. There are shopping facilities, refreshments, and accommodation.

Hotel:	Torcross Hotel; Tel. Torcross (054858) 206
B&B:	Cove Guest House; Tel. Torcross (054858) 448
Bus:	To Kingsbridge and Dartmouth
Early closing:	Saturday

HALLSANDS

The fishing village which stood here is in ruins, the victim of ignorant dredging. Shingle was dredged from the beach to build Devonport Dockyard at the turn of the century. This so undermined the structure of Hallsands that, during a ferocious storm in 1917, the whole village collapsed into the sea. Only one house was spared. Nature has completed the work of man's negligence and few traces of the village remain.

START POINT

Steart is the Saxon word for tail – so the head started life as a tail. The area is a nature reserve, a resting place for a variety of migrant birds in spring and autumn. The lighthouse warns shipping of the infamous Blackstone Rock, on which many ships have been wrecked. During a storm in March 1891, four ships were wrecked in a single night and 47 men lost their lives.

PRAWLE POINT

Not far from Start Point, Prawle Point is just as treacherous to sailors as its neighbour. Two tea clippers were lost there, in 1868 and 1873, turning the sea a pungent leafy brown. When a fruit ship went down here, the lemons turned the sea into a field of buttercups, and the local price of lemons fell sharply: for weeks they were selling all along the coast at a mere 6 pence for 50. In 1892 the steam ship Maria ran onto the rocks there, and the heavy seas and vicious rocks smashed the year-old ship to pieces. A more cheerful event was the capture off the Point of the huge French warship Cleopatra. The tiny British ship HMS Nymph overpowered the crew and took the ship as prize in 1793.

EAST PORTLEMOUTH

In the Middle Ages East Portlemouth was more important than Salcombe, sending 5 ships and 19 men to the Siege of Calais in 1346, against Salcombe's none.

The church is called St Winwalloe, after the saint who was driven out of Wales by the English in the 6th century. He fled to Brittany and founded a monastery at Landevennec, which also had a branch at Landewennack in Cornwall. The churchyard is filled with the sad graves of sailors. Inside the church the screen has paintings depicting the lives of the Saints.

The village has a post office store, and the Gara Rock Hotel (Tel. (05884) 2342) is on the path, outside the village. There is a frequent ferry service all year. For information call Bradford (0274) 32104.

SALCOMBE

This is the most southerly of Devon's resorts and has a climate Mediterranean enough to allow oranges and lemons to grow outside. Salcombe was a port from very early times but its development was restricted by the bar opposite Sharp Tor to the south. Tennyson was inspired by it to write his poem 'Crossing The Bar' while staying at Salcombe with the historian J.A. Froude.

Fort Charles, now a ruin on a rock off North Sands beach, was built by Henry VIII as harbour defence. It was known as the Bulwark. In the Civil War it was strengthened and garrisoned by the King, and withstood two Roundhead sieges –

including one which lasted four months – before surrendering to Parliament on honourable terms.

In the 19th century, more than 300 ships were launched from Salcombe's yards in one five-year period alone. The Steam Age ended that, as yards grew up near the industrial centres, close to sources of iron and coal. Salcombe never completely surrendered to steam, however, and yachts are still built here. The lagoon-like estuary is the largest yachting centre in Britain.

In season visitors outnumber locals by almost ten to one, and most of the old boathouses or warehouses down by the quay have been turned into flats or boutiques, while many of the workers' houses have become chic holiday homes for the rich.

Hotel:	Marine Hotel, Cliff Road; Tel. Salcombe (054884) 2251
B&B:	Harbour Lights, Devon Road; Tel. Salcombe (054884) 2765
YHA:	Youth Hostel, Overbecks, Sharpitor; Tel. Salcombe (054884) 2856
Bus:	To Plymouth and Kingsbridge
Early closing:	Thursday
Tourist Information:	Market Street; Tel. Salcombe (054884) 2736

6

Salcombe to Cremyll

CROSSING THE BAR

Sunset and evening star,
  And one clear call for me!
And may there be no moaning of the bar,
  When I put out to sea,

But such a tide as moving seems asleep,
  Too full for sound and foam,
When that which drew from out the boundless deep
  Turns again home.

Twilight and evening bell,
  And after that the dark!
And may there by no sadness of farewell,
  When I embark;

For tho' from out our bourne of Time and Place
  The flood may bear me far,
I hope to see my Pilot face to face
  When I have crost the bar.

TENNYSON, Alfred, Lord (1809–92). The poem is said to have been inspired by a rough passage over the bar at Salcombe in the yacht *Sunbeam* when staying with the historian J.A. Froude.

Introduction

Planning this section demands special care as there are three rivers and the large urban area of Plymouth to cross. Once clear of Salcombe and its small holiday satellites of North and

South Sands, the path soon becomes a fine open cliff path rising gently to Bolt Head. From Bolt Head to Bolt Tail the scenery is spectacular: high cliffs, open views and a rocky, indented shoreline. Several steep climbs up and down may daunt the faint-hearted, but no one should be defeated by them, provided that the weaker ones have patience.

Beyond Bolt Tail, after the Hopes, the walk to Bantham is easier and on it you will meet the first river crossing. After Bigbury on Sea there is a strenuous walk of 3½ kilometres to Beacon Point and an easy walk to Wonwell ('wonnel'), where there is no bridge or ferry across the river Erme. You must either wade across it or make a lengthy detour. Then, after a brief swing inland, there is a steep section to Beacon Hill and a pleasant cliff-top walk to Noss Mayo/Newton Ferrers. (At either of these you are once more at the mercy of seasonal ferries, and you may choose instead to take a bus to Plymouth.) Once across the river Yealm, however, there is a pleasant walk through Wembury to Wembury Point, and the route then gets rather built up as far as Turnchapel, where Plymouth interrupts the official path.

The rock is metamorphic mica and schist from Salcombe to Hope. From Bolt Tail on it is Devonian sandstones and shale, which make for variety in the shape of the coastline, the nature of the land and the vegetation and wild life it supports.

The nature reserve at Wembury, and the coast about it, are noted for their birds. Great Mew Stone, off the Point, is a breeding ground for sea birds, as is Stoke Point, Burgh Island and the coast from Bolt Tail to Salcombe. The several estuaries attract a range of species of wader. The Yealm and the Erme are haunts of the avocet with its unusual turned-up beak, and butterflies abound on the wilder parts of this stretch of coast.

The well-preserved Iron Age cliff fort on Bolt Tail is the oldest evidence of man you will see; Salcombe, in its picturesque and peaceful setting, is the prettiest. Inner Hope is still a charming collection of buildings. Outer Hope, though more developed, has some pretty cottages. The church at Stoke Point and that at Wembury deserve a visit and there is a lot to be seen around Plymouth.

| DISTANCE | | TIME | SALCOMBE TO CREMYLL | TELEPHONE | TRAIN | BUS | FERRY | SHOPS | CAMPING | ACCOMMODATION | REFRESHMENT | CUMUL. DIST. KMS |
STAGE	CUMUL.											
			SALCOMBE	x		x	x	x	x	x	x	250¾
7¼	7¼	1:50	PORT LIGHT HOTEL							x	x	258
3	10¼	:45	INNER HOPE, OUTER HOPE	x		x		x		x	x	261
1½	11¾	:25	THURLESTON	x		x		x		x	x	262½
3¼	15	:50	BANTHAM	x			x	x		x	x	265¾
2¼	17¼	:35	BIGBURY-ON-SEA	x		x		x	x	x	x	268
(1)		(:15)	(RINGMORE)	x						x	x	
(3)		(:45)	(KINGSTON)									
4	21¼	1:	MOUTHCOMBE	x							x	272
6	27¼	1:30	STOKE HOUSE	x				x			x	276
9	36¼	2:15	NOSS MAYO	x		x	x	x			x	287
			NEWTON FERRERS	x		x	x	x	x	x	x	
3¼	39½	:50	WEMBURY	x		x		x		x	x	290¼
2½	42	:40	HEYBROOK BAY			x					x	292¾
12	54	3:	PLYMOUTH — STONEHOUSE	x	x	x	x	x	x	x	x	304¾

TIMES ARE BASED ON AVERAGE WALKER LIGHTLY LADEN.

NB.

1. *STAGE: is the distance between that point and the preceding point.*
2. *CUMUL.: is the cumulative distance from the beginning of the chapter.*
3. *TIME: is the time for the stage (between that point and the preceding one) calculated at 4 kilometres per hour – the rate for a lightly loaded person walking without halt.*
4. *Brackets enclose places not on the Path but easily reached from it, together with distances and times from the Path.*
5. *CUMULATIVE DISTANCE: is the total distance from South Haven Point.*

Guide

Take the road out of Salcombe, seaward along the estuary to North Sands, on to South Sands and up into the National Trust property of Sharpitor. The path continues through woods at first and then emerges on open cliff around Sharp Tor, climbs down into the coomb above Starehole Bay and up over Bolt Head just inland of the antiquated coastguard look-out. Then, after a steep descent to Off Cove, it crosses the Warren, passes Steeple Cove with its coastguard look-out and down into the coomb by Stannings Cove. With Ham Stone just out to sea, it will take you steeply down into the coomb above Soar Mill Cove, up again over Cathole Cliff, above Lantern Rock, and over West Cliff past the radio masts on **Bolberry Down** and the Port Light Hotel. After Ferny Hole Point and Hugh's Hole you will then come to **Bolt Tail**.

Walk around the Point and down in to Inner Hope and Outer Hope, then up on to the cliffs again and across Great Ledge, with Thurlestone Rock in the sea below. Follow the path around the bay and out to Warren Point. Continue on along the coast, seaward of Thurlestone and its golf course, until you arrive at **Bantham**. The ferry across the Avon operates in season on request (ask for Mr Cater at the thatched boat house in Bantham; Tel. 054857 359). If the ferry is not running you can wade the river at low tide. Otherwise you must make a 12 kilometre detour inland (a path follows the estuary) to cross by bridge from Bridge End to Aveton Gifford and back along the west bank to the sea. Very great care must be exercised when wading the river. The starting point is close to the boat house, and it must only be attempted at low tide and in good conditions. If in doubt it is best to take local advice. If the tide is low when you arrive on the west bank walk left, along the sands, to Bigbury on Sea. If the tide is high, walk up the path towards Mount Folly and left along the B3392 for about 1½ kilometres into **Bigbury on Sea**. Burgh Island lies just off shore. The path continues westward along the shore, past Challaborough, up over the cliff around Toby's Point, down towards Ayrmer Cove, over the next headland to Westcombe Beach and up very steeply close to the cliffs, seaward of the Scabbiscombe Estate perimeter fence. Go around **Hoist Point**, dip once more and go up around above Meddrick Rocks, then down around Beacon Point and Fernycombe Point to **Wonwell Beach**.

You now have to cross the river Erme, where there is no bridge or ferry. You can wade across for about an hour either side of low tide. To do so use the ford leading to the Mothecombe road, visible on the far bank.

Once across follow the road through Mothecombe, bearing left where the road forks right to Holbeton and turn left when, one kilometre out of the village, the road bends sharply to the right. Go along the farm road for 300 metres and then take the footpath to rejoin the coast path at Bugle Hole.

Turn right along the coast, down into Gull Cove and up around St Anchorite's Rock. The path then takes you to Carswell Cove, past an old quarry by Wadham rocks and up around Beacon Hill, where you pick up a track which takes you past Stoke House around **Stoke Point** and along a good track, 'Nine Mile Drive', seaward of the coastguard look-out. Carry on above Netton Island, Hillsea Point and Blackstone Point, pass seaward of Warren Cottage, over the Warren and around Gara Point and Mouthstone Point into **Noss Mayo**.

The ferry may not be running across the river Yealm to Warren Point. Call the operators to find out; Tel. 0752 872210. If there is none you can catch a bus to Billacombe and Plymouth and then another back to pick up the path at Wembury.

From the ferry at Warren Point climb up and walk along the cliffs, on National Trust property, around Season Point, past Blackstone Rocks and down to **Wembury**. Leaving the town inland, pass behind the beach and climb up on to the cliffs again to go around Wembury Point, with Great Mew Stone to seaward and the Naval establishment, HMS Cambridge, inland. The path crosses the range danger area, but if the ranges are in use you will be diverted through the grounds of the establishment itself and back on to the cliffs.

Following the cliffs, you now pass Heybrook Bay, with Renny Rocks and Shag Stone in the sea below you, and Andurn Point to **Bovisand Bay**. Climb up again to pass over Staddon Point and, seaward of the golf course, to Staddon Heights, where you meet the road which takes you around Jennycliff Bay and into Turnchapel. Here you can take a No. 7 bus, outside the guard room of HMS Mountbatten, to Plymouth and a No. 26 from the centre of **Plymouth** to Admiral's Head, where you catch the ferry for **Cremyll**.

Gazetteer

SHARPITOR

The modern house, which was willed to the National Trust with 3 hectares of land by Otto Overbeck in 1937, is now a youth hostel and a museum. The house and gardens, which have many shrubs and roses on display, are open throughout the year.

BOLT HEAD

There is a cavern on Bolt Head called Bull's Hole. A black bull disappeared into it once, was lost for a week and then re-emerged, its coat completely snow white. Proof that even bulls worry.

SOAR MILL COVE

The foundations of the mill and the course of the mill leet, which brought water down to power the mill, are still visible, but the mill itself has gone.

In April 1936 the famous four-masted Finnish steel ship, Herzogin Cecile, struck Ham Stone, off the cove. She ran aground in thick fog, bound for Ipswich. This was one of the few remaining ships to have competed in the great grain race from Australia to England, which she won for eight years in succession. She was refloated and beached in Starehole Cove for shelter, but a month later broke her back, broke up and finally disappeared in 1939.

A little further on, by the Lantern Rock, you can see the boilers of the Janet Rowe, wrecked in 1913.

BOLBERRY DOWN

The cliffs are dangerous here, and rock falls are common. Successive landslips have revealed many caves, one of which is called Ralph's Hole after the smuggler who took refuge there in the 18th century.

BOLT TAIL

A large Iron Age cliff fort crowns this headland busy with sea birds and wild flowers. In the cove below the 90 gun frigate HMS Ramilles was lost in 1760 with 708 of her 734 man crew, and the cove was re-named after her to commemorate the disaster. She was only one of many ships these rocks have claimed. In 1907 the liner Jebba, homeward bound from Sierra Leone with 155 passengers and crew, ran aground also in dense fog. The Hope Cove lifeboat was unable to help, so two local men, Isaac Jarvis and John Argeat scrambled down the 65 metre cliffs in total darkness, rigged up a bosun's chair and saved all those on board, thereby winning the Albert medal for their bravery.

OUTER HOPE, INNER HOPE

Both were fishing villages trading in lobsters and pilchards. There was a time when local boats produced £7,000 worth of pilchards a year, and the whole population was engaged in oil-extraction and salting the fish for export. Now that lobsters are very scarce and the pilchard industry has fallen away to nothing, the villages exist mainly on tourism. Nevertheless, Inner Hope remains unspoilt and is a good example of a small, mid-19th century village – but it does get crowded in season. The villages have most facilities, including a post office.

Hotel:	Lantern Lodge Hotel; Tel. Galmpton (0548) 561280
B&B:	Hope and Anchor Inn; Tel. Galmpton (0548) 561294
Bus:	To Kingsbridge and Salcombe
Early closing:	Wednesday

THURLESTONE

The name means 'holed stone', and the holed stone it comes from stands on the shore of Bigbury Bay. The village is picturesque and very old. Its 14th-century church was rebuilt in the 17th century, but the red sand-stone font is Norman. The village has a post office and store.

Hotel:	Heron House Hotel; Thurlestone (0548) 561308
Bus:	To Kingsbridge
Early closing:	Thursday

BIGBURY

This village, a little inland of the path, has an ancient church which was substantially rebuilt in Victorian times. There is a 14th-century brass to Sir William Bigbury, and an unusual lectern, carved by Thomas Prideaux as a present from Bishop Oldham of Exeter (1505–1519), which has the body of an owl and the head of an eagle. Next door to the church is Bigbury Court, an 18th-century mansion built on the site of a much earlier house, some of whose outbuildings remain.

BIGBURY ON SEA

This is not a very attractive village, but it does have many of the facilities a walker might need: refreshments, shops, accommodation, and a post office.

Hotel: Henley; Tel. Bigbury on Sea (054881) 240
B&B: High View, Warren Road; Tel. Bigbury on Sea (054881) 283
Buses: seasonal

RINGMORE

R.C. Sherrif wrote *Journey's End*, his play about the First World War, in the pub of the same name here. The circular church, All Hallows, is unusual for Devon, and like many churches played a part in the Civil War. A loyal Royalist parson, William Lane, set up a battery of cannon near Aveton Gifford (to the north west) to deter the Roundheads. When he ran out of ammunition he spiked the guns and rolled them into the river. He then hid in a secret room in the church tower, leaving only when he was pardoned.

Inn: Journey's End, Ringmore; Tel. Bigbury on Sea (054881) 205

HOIST POINT

This was named when the locals grew potatoes on the common land round about, just above Westcombe Beach. They used to hoist seaweed up from the beach for use as fertilizer.

KINGSTON

The village is a good 5 kilometres inland of the path and can be reached by footpath from Westcombe Beach or Wonwell Beach. For those not deterred by this extra walk, there is a fine pre-perpendicular church, St James, and Wonwell Court, a Georgian-fronted mansion, parts of which date from the 16th and 17th centuries.

WONWELL BEACH

The few cottages are in ruins. One of them, the pilot's house, used to be painted white, as a marker for shipping, and the pilot was paid extra for the inconvenience caused by the white paint. His job was to guide ships up river to Clyng Mill or Ermington where, prior to 1851, there were wool factories.

There is neither bridge nor ferry across the mouth of the river Erme. The choice therefore lies between a 16 kilometre detour to cross the river on the A379 at Sequers Bridge, or wading across. This is possible only for one hour either side of low water. But great caution is necessary, especially in bad weather. The South West Way Association booklet has detailed instructions.

MOTHECOMBE

This is a completely unspoilt village belonging to the Flete Estate. Refreshments are available in the old school.

STOKE POINT

You come to the partly restored ruins of St Peter the Poor Fisherman's church on the beach just before the Point. The roof collapsed in the 1860s, and the church was allowed to become a ruin. However, the roof has now been partially repaired and both church and church yard have been tidied up. It used to be the church of Noss Mayo, and in the south-east corner is the tomb stone of a pirate.

Rowden Farm, just inland of Stoke Point, is a good example of a purpose-built mid-Victorian farmhouse and is still a prosperous well-run farm today. Refreshments are available near Stoke House.

NOSS MAYO

This hamlet of medieval origin was owned by Lord Revelstoke, who in the mid-19th century had 'Nine Mile Drive' cut by local fishermen short of work.

There is a post office, a village store and two pubs. Buses run to Newton Ferrers and Plymouth. The ferry leaves from a point on the road about 800 metres short of the village, and crosses either to Newton Ferrers or to the far side of the estuary. It is seasonal, and when it is not running you must walk or ride to Newton Ferrers and go on to Plymouth by bus, as there is no other way of crossing the Yealm.

NEWTON FERRERS

The church of the Holy Cross at Newton Ferrers is mainly 15th century, but some parts are two centuries older. Out of season the way westward is broken here as the ferry across the Yealm (the same that serves Noss Mayo) is seasonal. The village has shops, a post office, a bank, refreshments and accommodation.

Hotel:	River Yealm Hotel; Tel. Newton Ferrers (0752) 872491
B&B:	Briar Hill Farm; Tel. Newton Ferrers (0752) 872252
Buses:	To Plymouth and Noss Mayo
Ferry:	Seasonal only; Tel. Newton Ferrers (0752) 872210

WEMBURY

The village was recorded as Weigenbeorge in the Anglo Saxon Chronicle, and the Danes were defeated here in 851. The church of St Werburgh faces out to sea, which is unusual, and is 15th century except for a 14th-century tower. There are two interesting monuments in the church – one to Sir John Hele, who died in 1608, and his family; the other to Lady Narborough, who died 70 years later. Sir John Hele is also commemorated in the Hele Almshouses in the village, which were built in 1682. Other buildings of interest are Langdon Court, an Elizabethan mansion built in 1577, and Wembury Manor, built in 1591, whose chapel dates from 1682. The village has a post office, stores and refreshments in the Mill Teashop, run by the National Trust.

B&B:	10 Hawthorne Park Road; Tel. Wembury (0752) 863038
Bus:	To Plymouth.

GREAT MEW STONE

This lies off Wembury Point and is in the danger zone of the live firing ranges of HMS Cambridge. In 1744 Magistrates ordered a man to be banished to the rock in punishment for an offence of which they had found him guilty. He took his wife and family with him, and when he returned to the main-land his daughter remained on the island, married, and raised three children there. In the 19th century Samuel Wakenham settled there as warrener, looking after the rabbits for the landlord. In those days rabbit meat was a delicacy, and their skins were sought for clothing. The remains of a cottage stand on the island, but it is uninhabited once more, and the rock now belongs to the Ministry of Defence.

BOVISAND HARBOUR AND FORT

The harbour was built between 1816 and 1824 to enable ships to be provisioned without having to go into Plymouth Dock. A reservoir was built up the valley and fresh water piped direct to the ships. Bovisand Fort is the best preserved of the Palmerston forts. It was built in the 19th century to defend Plymouth from attacks by the French, who were constantly casting expansionist eyes across the English Channel.

THE BREAKWATER

This was one of the most remarkable engineering feats of its time, and even now remains impressive. First suggested by Earl St Vincent in 1806, to protect Plymouth sound's superb anchorage from southerly gales, construction of the breakwater was started under John Rennie in 1812 and completed in 1841. It is 1570 metres long, 40 metres wide at its base and 4.6 metres wide at the top. It contains 4 million tons of Oreston limestone and 3 million tons of dressed granite. Built on existing shoals, it encloses an area of over 450 hectares. The channels on either side of it are each 12 metres deep and over 800 metres wide. There is a fort behind the breakwater to protect it, which draws its fresh water supply from its own artesian well.

SALTRAM

Saltram House, its contents, and 60 hectares of land were given to the National Trust in 1957 by the Treasury, who had accepted them in payment of death duties. There was a dwelling on the site as early as 1218, probably connected with the salt workings in the river Plym. Although the present house, ordered by John and Lady Catherine Parker in the 1750s, incorporates some parts of its Tudor predecessor it is pure 18th century, and one of the finest examples of Robert

Adam's work. Not only the structure of the house but the decoration and much of the original furniture were designed by him, to create a coherent and harmonious whole. The salon and the dining room (completed in 1768) are outstanding. The portrait painter Sir Joshua Reynolds lived nearby, and 14 of his works hang in the house. In addition to a disused 18th-century chapel, the grounds contain a summer house, known as Fanny's Bower, and an orangery, both in the style of the house.

PLYMOUTH

The record of continuous settlement of the estuaries of the Tamar and the Plym starts with the entry for Sutone in the Domesday Book, where it is noted as a fishing village on the shore of what we call Sutton Pool. But there is much evidence of earlier settlements. Traces of Paleolithic man and of Bronze Age and Saxon occupation have been found in caves at Cattedown and Oreston.

By the middle of the 13th century the village, then known as Sutton Prior and Sutton Valetort, had prospered and grown. By 1252 it was a market centre, with a fleet of 300 ships. Edward I used it as a naval base and, in the spring of 1279, sailed from there to France with a fleet of 325 ships.

The French attacked in 1338, but were repelled by the Earl of Devon, and eight years later, the future Plymouth mustered 26 ships and 603 men for the siege of Calais. In 1350 and 1377 the French attacked for the second and third times, burning part of the town on the last occasion. Another assault followed in 1400 and they again tried to burn the town in 1403, again without success. Although the following years were peaceful, the decision was taken in 1439 to fortify the town's defences. In the same year the Burghers applied for a charter of incorporation and it became the first municipal corporation to be created by Act of Parliament. In recognition of this it was called the King's town of Plymouth.

The port grew in importance. Margaret of Anjou landed there in 1471, Katherine of Aragon in 1500. In 1584 Sir Francis Drake had waterworks constructed (a sign of considerable importance for the times) and water was drawn from Dartmoor, 40 kilometres away. Four years later the English fleet assembled there to engage and ultimately scatter the Spanish Armada.

Plymouth became a starting point for many important

voyages. William Hawkins made the first of three voyages from Plymouth in 1528; Drake left in 1577 to sail around the world; Sir Walter Raleigh sailed to America in 1606 to found the colony of Virginia and introduce tobacco smoking to the world; and it was from Plymouth that the Pilgrim Fathers set sail in the Mayflower in 1620.

The town declared for Parliament in the Civil War and subsequently withstood three months siege by the King's forces. William of Orange's fleet took refuge here after landing their Prince, and future King, at Brixham in 1688. Two years later the construction of the great naval dockyard started, in the Hamoaze, and the area became known as Plymouth Dock.

By the 19th century Plymouth Dock was threatening to outstrip Plymouth in size, and a third small area, Stonehouse, was growing up between them. In 1823 Plymouth Dock changed its name to Devonport and, aided by the coming of the railway, which greatly facilitated the development of trade, all three sites expanded rapidly. Eventually, in 1914, all three were incorporated as the town of Plymouth, which became a city in 1928 and was given a Lord Mayor in 1935. The centre of the city was almost totally destroyed by German bombs in 1941 but has been rebuilt as a modern city centre.

The Citadel on the Hoe was built by Charles II in 1666, on the site of a fort built in 1592. There had been a castle near there since the early 15th century and part of one rounded bastion still stands. The Citadel formed one of the double ring of Palmerston forts, constructed in the 19th century as a defence against a possible French invasion under Napoleon III. There were 9 forts in the inner ring and 22 in the outer. Drake's Island was originally fortified as part of these defences and later became a prison. Today it serves more usefully as an adventure training centre, giving courses in sailing, climbing, expeditions, and marine biology.

The City art gallery and museum and the Marine Biological Association Aquarium under the Citadel are both worth a visit. If you have the energy (it won't take much), a walk through the docks and the Barbican (the old city), can be an intriguing experience, and the view from the Hoe is one of the best of its kind in England. The City has all facilities: trains, buses, airport, shops, post offices, banks, refreshments and accommodation.

Hotel:	Astor Hotel, 14 Elliott Street, The Hoe; Tel. Plymouth (0752) 25511
B&B:	Kynance Hotel, 111/113 Citadel Road, The Hoe; Tel. Plymouth (0752) 266821
YHA:	Youth Hostel, Belmont House, Devonport Road, Stoke; Tel. Plymouth (0752) 52189
Ferry:	All year Stonehouse – Cremyll; Tel. Millbrook 202. (Take No. 26 bus from city centre to ferry point.)
Tourist Information:	Tel. Plymouth (0752) 264849

EDDYSTONE LIGHT

The first Eddystone light was built by Sir James Winstanley in 1698. Made of wood and iron, it was destroyed, together with its builder, in a tremendous storm in 1703. The next one, also of wood, was destroyed by fire from its own light in 1755. The third, built of granite, had its foundations undermined by the sea and was dismantled in 1881; part of it was re-erected and now stands on the Hoe. The present lighthouse, the fourth, was built by Sir James Douglas for Trinity House and was put into service in 1882. Whether because of its troubled history, or because of its remoteness – 20 kilometres out to sea, a lonely situation for the poor keeper in the olden days – it is the most famous of Britain's lighthouses.

ISAMBARD KINGDOM BRUNEL

Several examples of his work have cropped up on the journey west. He did much to modernize the Westcountry by his work on the railways and in civil engineering of all sorts. There is a short stretch of his broad-gauge railway line in Sutton Pool, and it is generally now agreed that this would have been a far more satisfactory standard gauge for the railways.

The original Millbay Docks were almost entirely designed by him, but perhaps his most attractive design was the Royal Albert Bridge, which carries the railway in a gentle curve from Plymouth into Cornwall across the river Tamar at Saltash. Opened in 1859, it was originally designed as a timber viaduct. But the Admiralty required greater width and height, and Brunel therefore designed a suspension bridge with two spans of 140 metres, using chains designed for the Clifton suspension bridge. His finest and most impressive engineering achievement, it is also almost his last, as he died just after its completion, aged 53.

ANTHONY HOUSE, TORPOINT

Take the Torpoint ferry from Devonport if you wish to visit this house; it is worth the diversion. It was built for Sir William Carew on the banks of the Lynher, between 1711 and 1721. The Carews had owned the land since the 15th century and this replaced an earlier house. The central block is of silver grey Pentewan stone and the wings are of warm red brick. The house was given to the National Trust in 1961 by the present occupant, Sir William Carew Pole, who has also given a considerable amount of land including the park to the Trust. Nearby, there is another of the Palmerston forts.

CREMYLL

Celia Fiennes, writing in 1698, described the ferry crossing to Cremyll: 'It was at least an hour going over, almost a mile, and notwithstanding there was five men rowing and I set my men to row also, I do believe we made not a step of way for almost a quarter of an hour, but blessed be God, I came safely over at last.'

The journey is quicker now, and there is less uncertainty about arriving, but in bad weather it can still be a pretty bleak crossing. There are a couple of pubs in Cremyll, shops, a cafe and a taxi service – all busily patronised by sailors.

7

Cremyll to Fowey

Thence to Millbrooke two miles and went all along by the water, and had the full view of the dockyards. Here I entered into Cornwall, and so passed over many very steep, stony hills, though here I had some two or three miles of exceeding good way on the downs, and then I came to the steep precipices — great rocky hills. Ever and anon I came down to the sea and rode by its side on the sand, then mounted up again on the hills, which carried me almost in sight of the South Sea. Sometimes I was in lanes full of rows of trees, and then I came down a very steep, stony hill to Lonn (Looe) 13 miles, and here I crossed a little arm of the sea on a bridge of 14 arches. This is a pretty big seaport, a great many little houses all of stone, and steep hill much worse and three times as long as Dean Clapper hill, and so I continued up and down hill. Here, indeed, I met with more enclosed ground, and so had more lanes and a deeper clay road, which by the rain the night before had made it very dirty and full of water in many places; in the road there are many holes and sloughs wherever there is clay ground, and when by rains they are filled with water, it is difficult to shun danger.

FIENNES, Celia (1662–1741). *Through England on a Side Saddle* (1695).

Introduction

Parkland, cliffs and unavoidable roads make the walk to Fowey a very mixed affair. After a stately promenade through Mount Edgecumbe's parkland there are over 20 kilometres of almost unrelieved road walking from Polhawn Cove to Looe. From West Looe there is footpath again, running through mainly unspoilt cliff country, to Polruan and Fowey. There are one or two gradients to test your legs between Looe and Polperro, but it is enjoyable walking nonetheless. This is not a physically exacting stretch of path, and the two estuaries, at Looe and at Fowey, are easily crossed.

The underlying rocks are Lower Devonian, giving a countryside which is an undramatic mixture of agricultural land, woodland, scrub, low cliffs and generally indifferent beaches. Whitsand Bay is an exception; it has a fine sandy beach nearly 5 kilometres long. The Fowey estuary is one of the typical Cornish rias, formed when the sea, swelled by the waters of the disappearing Ice Age, washed back up deeply chiselled river valleys.

These valleys are treasure-filled hunting grounds for marine biologists, ornithologists and botanists. In spring the short woodland stretches are speckled with early flowers, and late spring or early autumn are the best seasons for walking on this part of the coast. The area is thick with people in summer and on fine week-ends, and wildlife is far more abundant in spring and autumn.

Polperro is the prettiest place you visit on this stretch. It is a perfect, picture-book-pretty, natural port, which reached its limits in the 19th century and which has not been spoiled by modern building. Parts of Looe and Fowey are also agreeable to wander through, but all of these places become uncomfortably crowded in the high holiday season.

Guide

A No. 26 bus will bring you to Admiral's Head, Stonehouse, and the ferry to **Cremyll**. The path starts at the ferry terminal, goes inland slightly and then bears sharp left towards the coast. It follows a good path through the **Mount Edgcumbe** park, passing inland of the lake, close to the house, then back to the coast, past Raveness Point, through woods past Redding Point and **Picklecombe Point**, where it bends inland to avoid the houses. It comes back to the coast on a well-made track, which it follows, leaving the woods shortly before Hooe Lake Point lighthouse. Pass the lighthouse and continue along the coast past Cavehole Point to emerge after 3 kilometres in **Kingsand**. Walk through the village, and the contiguous **Cawsand**, and continue around the coast on the road, through woods, to Penlee Point.

STAGE	CUMUL.	TIME	CREMYLL TO FOWEY	TELEPHONE	TRAIN	BUS	FERRY	SHOPS	CAMPING	ACCOMMODATION	REFRESHMENT	CUMUL. DIST. KMS
			CREMYLL	x		x	x				x	304¾
1½	1½	:25	MOUNT EDGECUMBE								x	306¼
(1)		(:15)	(MAKER)			x						
4	5½	1:	KINGSAND, CAWSAND	x		x		x		x	x	310¼
9	14½	2:15	FREATHY	x		x		x				319¼
5½	20	1:25	PORTWRINKLE	x		x				x	x	324¾
5	25	1:15	DOWNDERRY	x		x		x		x	x	329¾
1	26	:15	SEATON	x		x		x		x	x	330¾
2	28	:30	MURRAYTON									332¾
2	30	:30	MILLENDREATH BEACH	x				x			x	334¾
2	32	:30	LOOE	x	x	x		x		x	x	336¾
6	38	1:30	TALLAND BARTON	x					x	x	x	342¾
2	40	:30	POLPERRO	x		x		x	x	x	x	343¾
(1)		(:15)	(LANSALLOS)	x								
(½)		(:10)	(LANTEGLOS)									
10	50	2:30	POLRUAN	x		x	x	x	x	x	x	354¾
			FOWEY	x		x	x	x	x	x	x	

TIMES ARE BASED ON AVERAGE WALKER LIGHTLY LADEN.

NB.
1. STAGE: is the distance between that point and the preceding point.
2. CUMUL.: is the cumulative distance from the beginning of the chapter.
3. TIME: is the time for the stage (between that point and the preceding one) calculated at 4 kilometres per hour – the rate for a lightly loaded person walking without halt.
4. Brackets enclose places not on the Path but easily reached from it, together with distances and times from the Path.
5. CUMULATIVE DISTANCE: is the total distance from South Haven Point.

You now leave the metalled road and follow the coast on a wide grassy path. This takes you past the coastguard station, and on to **Rame Head** with its ruined chapel and its magnificent views. Carry on past Queener Point and inland of the old fort at Polhawn Cove.

Here the path takes to the road again almost all the way to Portwrinkle, nearly 10 kilometres away. If the tide is out, it is possible to walk from Polhawn Cove to Portwrinkle along the rocks and the beach. Otherwise, follow the road, through Tregonhawk and **Freathy**, and inland of the rifle ranges on Tregantle Cliff. Take care to look for and take the path which leads off to the left, about 1 kilometre before **Crafthole**. This crosses Trethill Cliffs, passing seaward of the golf course and rejoining the road at the entrance to **Portwrinkle**.

The road leads you through the village and, just after Cargloth Farm where the road bends round to the right, the path leaves it to the left, crosses Batten Cliffs for 1¼ kilometres, then rejoins the road, to take you into **Downderry** and **Seaton**. At low tide it is possible to walk along the beach from Downderry to Seaton.

Behind the beach in Seaton, cross the bridge over the stream and turn sharp left. Continue along this metalled road for over 1 kilometre until, on an upward gradient, you see the coast path signed up through woods to the left. Climb first by very well-made steps and then by a windy path up through trees and bushes to the cliff top, before descending to the right along the coast. The path now continues, well marked and with solid stiles, undulating across the face of the cliffs past **Murrayton**, over the National Trust property of Bodigga cliff and down to **Millendreath Beach** and its holiday village.

Cross over behind the beach on the road, which you follow round through the villas and chalets to Plaidy, another collection of holiday villas. Cross the estate on Plaidy Park Road, which ends in a 'T' junction. There you turn left, back towards the sea for a few metres and then, in front of the grandiose circular entrance to a house called Dove Rock, right on to a track which takes you along the cliffs to **Looe**.

Descend the narrow streets of East Looe and turn right inland up the main street to emerge by the pretty harbour. Cross the bridge into West Looe and turn left to go down the western side of the harbour. Continue along the road to Hannafore Point, past grand hotels and the coastguard station opposite **Looe Island**. Where the road ends in a cul de sac go through a kissing gate into a field and on to the coast path.

Just inland here are the remains of the ancient chapel of **Lamanna**. The path follows the coast through fields around Portnadler Bay. To the east, Looe (or St George's) Island dominates the sea view. Climb up through bracken and gorse, over a stream which plunges down a narrow rocky cleft to the shore, then on up, more steeply, through the gorse and bracken of the National Trust property of Hendersick with Bridge Rocks and Hore Stone in the sea below.

The path goes up and down, sometimes fenced to seaward, sometimes to landward, always above the shore, seldom way-marked but always easy to follow. Where you have a choice it is normally advisable to take the lower transverse path, provided that it does not head directly towards the sea. Go seaward of the hill concealing **Talland Barton** church, and down on to a metalled road by the Smuggler's Rest Cafe. Turn left and left again along the road into **Talland Bay**.

Cross the stream on a small foot bridge behind the beach, turn left up a steep metalled track marked 'cul de sac', and almost immediately left off it onto the waymarked coast path. You come out on to metalled road again for a few metres, before forking slightly left on to the coast path on which you enter the National Trust property of Talland's Cliff. Go around Downend Point, with its memorial to the men of Talland and Polperro killed in the 1914–18 War, continue along the well-defined path above the coast, across the National Trust property of the Warren and down the narrow, steep streets into picturesque **Polperro**.

You cannot cross the harbour mouth so continue round, through the village, crossing over the Roman bridge behind the harbour and coming back along its western side. Just past the Blue Peter pub the coast path is signed up steps on the right. Climb up on to the cliff path and, once clear of the houses, keep left following National Trust signs for Chapel Cliff.

The path continues above the shore, climbing up around the small headland by Larrick Rocks, around Color's Cove, and up over Blackybale Point. Here you get a clear view of the lunar landscape of china clay spoil heaps to the west. Go sharply down the other side of the Point past Penslake Cove. There you pass a large white obelisk marine marker, before descending to cross a footbridge.

Climb up, past a rock bearing the National Trust sign for Lansallos Cliff, which you climb over before going down round Parson's Cove to West Coombe.

Here you cross the stream and climb up across the headland of Sandheap Point, taking care not to descend seawards. Then cross another stream, above Palace Cove, by a footbridge, and go on up around the western end of Lantivet Bay, past a disused watch house, to walk around Pencarrow Head.

Descend slightly and then go up around the higher cliffs of Lantic Bay, down the far side of Blackbottle Rock, past a white marker post and seaward of a coastguard look-out. Go diagonally inland across a field and leave it by way of a ridiculous stile which obliges you to take off your rucksack. On the road once more, turn right and then left and go down into **Polruan**, to the harbour, for the frequent all-year ferry to **Fowey**.

Gazetteer

MOUNT EDGCUMBE

The original house was built in the mid 16th century for Sir Richard Edgcumbe, Comptroller of the King's Household under King Henry VIII. Obviously his own pocket was quite deep, for he built an imposing Tudor mansion in red sandstone around a large central hall set off by a row of Doric columns. It was completely destroyed during the blitz on Plymouth in 1941 but was rebuilt in 1952. Even in the 19th century the locals were allowed into the park on one day each week, and quite often Lord Mount Edgcumbe chose Saturday to enable workers from the dockyards to benefit. Cornwall County Council acquired the house and grounds in 1970 and the public can visit the house in season and the grounds at any time.

PICKLECOMBE POINT

The fort was built in the early 19th century to protect the entrance to the estuary, already of considerable strategic commercial and military importance. Hawkins Battery and Grenville Fort, named after the two great sailors, are just a little farther West.

MAKER

The church of St Julian is about 1 kilometre off the path, on the western boundary of Mount Edgcumbe Park. It has a very ornate west tower, a Norman font and several monuments to the Mount Edgcumbe family. There are good views to the other side of the promontory from the church.

KINGSAND AND CAWSAND

These twin villages were in separate counties until 1844 –

Kingsand in Devon and Cawsand in Cornwall. With the realignment of the county boundary they both ended up in Cornwall and are today, for all practical purposes, one community. They are unspoilt fishing villages, noted in the past for smuggling and for their safe anchorage. Before the building of Plymouth breakwater, the fleet used to lie in Cawsand Bay safe from southerly gales. The villages were then both busy and prosperous, as it was more convenient to victual the ships from them than to fetch supplies by sea from Plymouth. As well as smuggling and victualling the fleet, the villages did have another legitimate and profitable activity: they took part in the best years of the pilchard fishing industry.

Nelson and Lady Hamilton often stayed at the Ship Inn, and there is a house known as Lady Emma's Cottage near Picklecombe Point. During the 18th century Cawsand was one of the busiest smuggling centres in the south west. Harry Carter, the smuggler of Prussia Cove, of whom more later, was captured off Cawsand, escaped, and swam ashore there, to be found exhausted by his brother.

Facilities are limited but there are refreshments, accommodation, shops, a telephone and a bus service to Cremyll and Torpoint.

Hotel: Criterion Hotel, Cawsand Bay; Tel. Plymouth (0752) 822244

B&B: Halfway House Inn, Cawsand; Tel. Plymouth (0752) 822279

RAME HEAD

There is the site of an Iron Age promontory fort on the Head and a beautiful chapel dedicated to St Michael. The chapel was first licensed for mass in 1397 but was rebuilt in 1882 by the Earl of Mount Edgcumbe. It also served as a beacon for shipping, and payments for lighting are recorded as early as 1488.

The church of St Germanus in Rame, slightly inland of the Head, has a chancel and a nave dating from 1259 but the remainder of it is mainly 15th-century.

FREATHY

This small seaside village is of little interest but does have a shop, a bus to Torpoint and a public call box.

TREGANTLE FORT

This fort, together with that of Anthony to the north, was an indispensable part of Plymouth's western defences. Without these forts the Maker – the whole of that crab's claw of land from Crafthole eastwards – would have been an ideal approach and launching ground for an attack on Plymouth and its harbour.

PORTWRINKLE

Once a fishing port, the village is today almost entirely given over to tourists and holiday homes. The Whitesands Bay Hotel, or rather the building it occupies, used to stand at Torpoint. It was built by Lord Graves in a rather dull neo-Elizabethan style with a symmetrical facade. Although it is easy to see why it might have been pulled down, it is hard to imagine why anyone should have gone to the trouble of re-erecting it at Portwrinkle.

Hotel: Whitesands Bay hotel; Tel. Portwrinkle (0503) 20276

Bus: Torpoint, Plymouth

DOWNDERRY

A simple, undistinguished village, whose string of holiday villas and bungalows lines the coast road like bunting. It has a bus service to Looe and Plymouth, village stores and a post office.

Hotel: Wide Sea; Tel. Downderry (05035) 240

SEATON

Another small resort with facilities for refreshments, shopping and accommodation. A bus service runs to Looe and Plymouth.

B&B: Blue Haven Guest House; Tel. Downderry (05035) 310

MURRAYTON

Just beyond Seaton and close to the path is the monkey

sanctuary at Murrayton. This is a collection of Brazilian woolly monkeys who have taken to the woods of southern Cornwall like apes to the Amazon jungle. They live virtually in the wild in a large system of interconnecting cages and they are free to escape when they wish. None of them has.

MILLENDREATH BEACH

This a purpose built holiday village. Refreshments and a shop are available in season.

LOOE

East and West Looe, on opposite sides of the Looe estuary, were separate towns until 1832. They were each granted a charter by Henry III in the 13th century. Both were important fishing and trading ports from medieval times and achieved a certain notoriety as centres for smuggling in the 18th and 19th centuries.

In Edward III's reign East Looe was, after Fowey, the most important port in Cornwall. In 1337 it sent 12 ships and 249 men with him to the Hundred Years War and in 1346 sent 20 ships and 315 men to the siege of Calais. In the 18th and 19th centuries it grew in importance both as a fishing port and as a port for the export of granite from the quarries around Liskeard. From here granite was shipped for the new Westminster Bridge, for the Embankment and for the base of the Albert Memorial in London. Today, although Looe is still important as a mackerel fishing port, much of the town's income is earned from tourism and from the development of game fishing. Amateurs come from miles away to fish Blue Mako and Porbeagle sharks, dicing with danger under the fatherly supervision of the wily Looe fishermen.

Some 14th-century details still survive in East Looe church but it was greatly rebuilt in the 19th century. The church of St Nicholas in West Looe was endowed before 1330, was used as a town hall after the Reformation and, later, as a school. It was considerably rebuilt in the 1850s and the unusual arcade was constructed from the timbers of a wrecked ship.

Looe is less unsavoury than it was when the 19th-century guide writers found it. Then the pretty, narrow cobbled streets, much of its charm today, doubled as open sewers, which conspired with the stench of fish to make the place quite unpalatable.

Hotel: Hannafore Point Hotel, Marine Drive; Tel.
                 Looe (05036) 3273
B&B: The Ship, East Looe; Tel. Looe (05036) 3124
Early
closing: Thursday
Tourist
Information: Tel. Looe (05036) 2072
Bus: Plymouth, St Austell, Seaton, Liskeard
Train: Plymouth, London

LOOE (or ST GEORGE'S) ISLAND

The island looks like a large steamed pudding turned untidily into the sea off Hannafore Point. Two monks lived there in the 12th century and there are traces of a chapel or a chantry dedicated to St George, which is where the island gets its other name. It was later used by smugglers who found that the island's many caves suited their purpose admirably.

LAMANNA

On the mainland opposite the island are the partly excavated remains of a Benedictine Priory. The chapel of Lamanna, Celtic in origin but enlarged in the 13th and 15th centuries, was part of it.

NAUTICAL MILEPOSTS

There are several measured nautical miles along the south coast and you can see the first pair of markers for this one on the cliffs above Looe Island. The pair marking the other end are on the cliffs above Talland Bay. They are used by the Royal Navy for speed trials.

TALLAND BARTON

The tower of this 13th-century church plays hide-and-seek with you over the brow of the hill, inland of the path, as you approach Talland Bay. It has an unusual tower, detached from the body of the church, the path between it and its church covered by a wagon-roofed porch dating from the late 15th or early 16th century. The builder was obviously influenced by the Italian campanile style.

POLPERRO

This is another ancient fishing port; Leyland described it bluntly in the 16th century as a 'fishar tonne with a peere'. Until the tourists found the town, Polperro's lifeblood was fishing and smuggling. Even the smuggling was carried out 'honestly'. It was so institutionalized that the smugglers had their own banker: they used to entrust their money to Zephaniah Job who would then make advances to them for their trips across the Channel. The town has a smuggler's museum which has a certain curiosity value.

Rough weather has repeatedly harassed the harbour, which has frequently been badly damaged. The piers were injured in 1774 and again in 1817, and in 1824 they were almost completely destroyed. The damage occurred so often that a public fund was set up in 1887 to pay for the repairs. It still exists today: there are collecting boxes in the town and the visitor is asked to contribute to the upkeep of the port.

The town really is unspoilt. Crooked cottages, all brightly painted and well kept, crowd cheerfully about the narrow cobbled streets which wind up and down on either side of the romantic little harbour. Choose your time well; go there out of season if you can or, if not, out of the tourist rush hours.

Hotel:	Crumplehorn Mill; Tel. Polperro (0503) 72348
B&B:	Mill House Hotel; Tel. Polperro (0503) 72362
Early closing:	Saturday
Buses:	Lode, Plymouth

LANSALLOS

The beautiful 15th-century church of St Ildierna is worth the kilometre detour inland behind Lantivet Bay: it has some magnificent 15th- and 16th-century benches and carved bench ends. There is a public telephone, a few houses and little else in the tiny hamlet.

LANTEGLOS

St Willow's is another small church just off the path. Built in the late 13th century, it was appropriated to the hospital of St John at Bridgewater in 1284. The church contains 15th- and 16th-century monuments to the Bohun family, who had seats at nearby Bodinnick and at Boconnoc to the north.

POLRUAN

Punches Cross, an old wooden cross on a rock to the east of the river mouth, marks the spot at which Jesus is supposed to have landed, when a boy, with his uncle Joseph of Arimathea. He walked to St Saviour's chapel at the top of the hill and from there to Glastonbury. The chapel, which certainly existed when Christ was a boy, was rebuilt in 1488 by Sir Richard Edgcumbe, but is now a ruin. The town is a very ancient one and returned two members to Parliament in the reign of Edward III.

B&B: Florizel Guest House; Tel. Polruan (072687) 208

Ferry: All year, frequent. For information call Par (072681) 3472

Buses: Lode, Plymouth

FOWEY

This has always been one of the most important sea and fishing ports in the West Country. The Earl of Montaigne owned it at the time of the Norman Conquest, and its men and ships were serving causes or the country from the very earliest times.

In the 11th and 12th centuries it sent ships to the crusades. In 1303 there were eight Fowey ships engaged in the Bordeaux wine trade and others were trading throughout the known world. Nineteen ships and 547 men were sent against the French in 1337; 29 ships and 720 men against the Scots in 1343; and in 1346 Fowey provided 47 ships and 770 men for the Siege of Calais – a number only exceeded by Yarmouth.

The port acquired an unenviable reputation as a base for pirates and privateers. So much so that, in the middle of the 15th century, Edward IV denounced it for these activities and deprived it of its ships, handing them over to Dartmouth as an example against piracy. Just prior to this, in the reign of Henry VI, the French had landed there, massacred some of the inhabitants and set fire to the town. Following on this earlier tragedy, Edward's action was a severe set-back to the town's prosperity.

However, Fowey recovered, and when Henry VIII was building his coastal defences he constructed St Catherine's Fort on the rocks at the harbour entrance, near the site of the medieval chapel of St Catherine whose beacon was a welcome guide to sailors. Edward IV had previously ordered a block-house to be built on either side of the estuary so that a chain could be stretched between them to close the harbour mouth – although it was never quite clear whether he wanted to keep the privateers in or keep the enemy out.

During the Civil War Fowey was held by the Parliamentary forces under the Earl of Essex, who was driven out in 1644, and fled by sea to Plymouth. In 1646 Fairfax re-occupied the town for Cromwell and made his headquarters in the Ship Inn.

From the middle of the 18th century Fowey became one of the principal ports for the shipping of china clay and the harbour was constantly being enlarged and deepened. By the 1870s ships of up to 10,000 tons could be accommodated and they can still be seen loading at Fowey's quays today. This trade vies with tourism as the main revenue earner for the community.

Place, the home of the Treffry family, is a Tudor house which was restored in the first half of the 19th century. The original house was called Cune (or Crown) Court and was probably a royal residence for the Kings of Cornwall. 'Place' is the Cornish word for palace. The church of St Nicholas is earlier than most Cornish churches, having been re-dedicated in 1336. Many 14th-century details can still be seen, although the church was added to in the 15th and 16th centuries. The 18th-century town hall incorporates part of what might have been a 14th-century chapel. It stands at the bend in the long, crooked street which is the oldest part of Fowey. The town has all facilities.

Hotel:	Riverside Hotel, Passage Street; Tel. Fowey (072683) 2275
B&B:	Harbour View; Tel. Fowey (072683) 3545
YHA:	Youth Hostel, Penquite House, Golant; Tel. Fowey (072683) 3507
Bus:	To Par and St Austell
Early closing:	Thursday
Tourist Information:	Albert Quay; Tel. Fowey (072683) 3320

8

Fowey to Falmouth

My Dear Hodgson, — Before this reaches you, Hobhouse, two officers' wives, three children, two waiting-maids, ditto subalterns for the troops, three Portuguese esquires and domestics, in all nineteen souls, will have sailed in the Lisbon packet, with the noble Captain Kidd, a gallant commander as ever smuggled an anker of right Nantz.

We are going to Lisbon first, because the Malta packet has sailed, d'ye see? — from Lisbon to Gibraltar, Malta, Constantinople, and 'all that', as Orator Henley said, when he put the Church, and 'all that', in danger.

This town of Falmouth, as you will partly conjecture, is no great ways from the sea. It is defended on the seaside by twin castles, St Mawes and Pendennis, extremely well calculated for annoying everybody except an enemy. St Mawes is garrisoned by an able-bodied person of four-score, a widower. He has the whole command and sole management of six most unmanageable pieces of ordnance, admirably adapted for the destruction of Pendennis, a like tower of strength on the opposite side of the Channel. We have seen St Mawes, but Pendennis they will not let us behold, save at a distance, because Hobhouse and I are suspected of having already taken St Mawes by a coup de main.

The town contains many Quakers and salt fish — the oysters have a taste of copper, owing to the soil of a mining country — the women (blessed be the Corporation therefor!) are flogged at the cart's tail when they pick and steal, as happened to one of the fair sex yesterday noon. She was pertinacious in her behaviour, and damned the mayor.

This is all I know of Falmouth.

BYRON, Lord (1788–1824). Extract from a letter dated 2 July 1809.

Introduction

Daphne du Maurier lived and wrote at Menabilly, close to Fowey on the Gribben Peninsular, sharing her love of Cornwall with those who read her sensitive, descriptive books. The first 8 kilometres, which cross her country, are enjoyable open walking and take you as far as Par. You then have to put up with an unsightly industrial complex in Par and a lot of road walking until you clear Mevagissey. Then open country, high cliffs – Nare Head and Dodman Point both rise above 100 metres – and the odd village make up the landscape you walk through all the way to Place or St Mawes, where you take the ferry for Falmouth.

Devonian rocks run on under your feet: Lower Devonian to just before Mevagissey and Middle Devonian to Falmouth. These, we know, are a jumble of different slates, grits, limestones and sandstones. The landscape clearly shows the effect of such a structure – the softer rocks worn away to form coves and bays while the harder masses still stand as headlands. Thus, Nare Head is formed of igneous rock and Black Head of greenstone. Dodman Point, which is made of the softer grey slate, owes it survival to the deep waters which surround it and which have protected it from erosion. Apart from the collection of river mouths which join the sea at Plymouth, the estuary at Falmouth, called Carrick Roads, is the most impressive ria on the south west coast.

You now enter an area of micro-climates which favour unusual plant and flower growth, many of which have been brought from abroad by sailors. Polridmouth Cove, for example, has almost sub-tropical flora, and you will be surprised by the variety and the abundance of flowers, shrubs and trees in spring, summer and autumn. Man's presence, on the other hand, discourages wildlife, which is rare near houses and roads; but in the open country you will see many sea birds and, near rivers, waders as you walk along.

The Tudor castles at Falmouth and St Mawes, the port of Falmouth with its maritime history stretching back into the mists of time and Charlestown, which played so great a part in the development of the china clay industry, are all fascinating places to visit. And both Caerhayes Castle and Mevagissey reward the walker who has time to sight-see.

Guide

Turn left on leaving the ferry and walk out of Fowey on the road, with the estuary on your left, around Readymoney Cove and up through the woods at the far side of the beach, to cut across the headland past the National Trust remains of St Catherine's Castle. Continue along the cliff edge around above Coombe Hawne and, shortly, down through woods to the attractive bay of **Polridmouth** ('pridmouth').

Cross over the stream, between the lake and the beach, and climb up on to the National Trust property of Gribbin Head, passing across it inland of the red and white striped navigational marker post. Go around Platt Bay and Little Gribbin, along the cliff tops and down through woods to **Polkerris**.

The path passes behind the Rashleigh Arms in Polkerris and climbs back on to the cliffs. At Little Hell it turns almost due north to go around the eastern edge of Par Sands and continues on to the main road. Turn left along the main road for about 1 kilometre, past an enormous caravan site which lies to seaward, under a railway bridge, into **Par**. There you turn left to cross back under the railway again and right, past the harbour and – following the perimeter fence of the china clay works – out on to Spit Point.

Continue along the cliff edge, around Fishing Point, past the Golf course, Crinnis Beach, and the modern entertainment centre at Carlyon Bay. Cross over the Casino road and continue along the cliff leaving the Carlyon Hotel to landward. Pass landward of the coast guard look-out, around Landrion Point and across Apple Tree Point, down into **Charlestown**. Continue along the coast, past little Polmear Island, up past Duporth Holiday Camp, across Carrickowel Point and down through trees into **Porthpean**.

Keeping close to the beach, climb up out of Porthpean across Phoebe's Point and inland across a field to pass inland of Castle Gotha Farm, between it and the prehistoric campsite after which it is named. Go through three kissing gates to a road leading down into Trenarren. Carry straight on until you reach a cottage by the beach. Turn right, over a stream along a path which climbs inland until it joins the road. Turn left and follow the road down steeply into **Pentewan**.

Go through the village on the road, over the bridge and turn left at the 'T' junction. The path follows the road, past the huge caravan site, until the road bends sharp right. The path

STAGE	CUMUL.	TIME	FOWEY TO FALMOUTH	TELEPHONE	TRAINS	BUS	FERRY	SHOPS	CAMPING	ACCOMMODATION	REFRESHMENT	CUMUL. DIST. KMS
			FOWEY	x		x	x	x	x	x	x	354¾
(½)		(:10)	(MENABILLY)									
7	7	1:45	POLKERRIS	x							x	361¾
2¾	9¾	:40	PAR	x	x	x		x	x	x	x	371½
2½	11¼	:40	CARLYON BAY			x				x	x	374
2	13¼	:30	CHARLESTOWN	x	x						x	376
6	19¼	1:30	PENTEWAN	x					x		x	382
3	22¼	:45	MEVAGISSEY	x		x		x	x	x	x	385
2	24¼	:30	PORT MELLON	x							x	387
4	28¼	1:	GORRAN HAVEN	x		x		x		x	x	391
8	36¼	2:	PORTHLUNEY COVE									399
3	39¼	:45	PORTHOLLAND COVE	x					x			402
3	42½	:45	PORTLOE	x		x		x	x	x	x	405
(2½)		(:40)	(VERYAN)			x						
9	51½	2:15	PORTSCATHO	x				x	x	x	x	414
8	59½	2:	ST ANTHONY	x								422
11	70½	2:45	ST MAWES	x		x	x	x		x	x	433
(13)		3:15	(TRURO – from A3078									
			via King Harry ferry)	x	x	x		x	x	x	x	
			FALMOUTH	x	x	x	x	x	x	x	x	

TIMES ARE BASED ON AVERAGE WALKER LIGHTLY LADEN.

NB.
1. STAGE: is the distance between that point and the preceding point.
2. CUMUL.: is the cumulative distance from the beginning of the chapter.
3. TIME: is the time for the stage (between that point and the preceding one) calculated at 4 kilometres per hour – the rate for a lightly loaded person walking without halt.
4. Brackets enclose places not on the Path but easily reached from it, together with distances and times from the Path.
5. CUMULATIVE DISTANCE: is the total distance from South Haven Point.

leaves the road here and goes straight on to regain the coast a couple of hundred metres farther on at Portgiskey. Continue along the cliff path around Penare Point, past Polstreath, to the harbour at **Mevagissey**.

Walk around the harbour and out to Stuckumb Point. Then

go past Polkirt Beach and Portmellon Cove into **Portmellon** on the road. On the far side of Portmellon, take off left on to the coast again, past Rowards Quay, across Chapel Point – where you will cross the road leading to the Point itself. Dip inland to cross a stream, pass behind the walled pond and back on to the coast around Turbot Point, keeping seaward of the fence. You now climb up over the National Trust property of **Bodrugan's Leap** and continue along the cliffs past Pabyer Point, across another stream, and along through gorse and bracken behind Perhaver Beach. Then descend on a metalled road into **Goran Haven**.

Walk through the village and out along the cliffs to Pen-a-Maen (or Maen-ease) Point. Go down past the coast guard look-out, around Cadythew Point and then inland up a track for abut 500 metres before striking off left along the coast again, across National Trust land above Bow (or Vault) Beach.

The path now climbs across fields and through gorse and bracken up to Dodman Point. The path up is not always easy to follow here but if you keep generally to the line of the cliffs you should have no problem. On the Point itself you will find a triangulation point, a disused coast guard look-out, and a large cross, erected in 1896 as an aid to shipping. In good conditions views from the point are magnificent. You now begin the descent along the cliffs to Hemmick Beach, going around above Lizard Pool, crossing High Point and Gell Point, before going down through gorse to meet the Penare-Boswinger road just behind the beach.

Follow the road for 250 metres and, just after crossing a stream, take off left along the cliff edge past Black Rock, Attimidday Rock, and Greeb Point and down through trees to cross a stream behind Lambsowden Cove. Climb up again to the headland above another Black Rock and down across fields to the road which separates **Caerhay's Castle** from the delightful Porthluny Cove.

Keep to the road as it climbs through trees away from the Castle and, after about 350 metres, a coast path sign directs you left into a field. Go straight out along the coast and turn right to pass seaward of a disused coast guard look-out and continue along down to **Portholland Cove**. Go through East and West Portholland on the road and then climb up around Perbagus Point, down through bracken to cross a stream above Cellar Rock, and up again to follow the cliffs. Take care not to be led off along the track inland to Tregenna but turn left along the coast itself, around past May's Rock, Carn Pednathon and down to Caragloose Point with its Shag Rock. When you have crossed a stream climb up past Hartriza Point, past a coast guard look-out and down steeply, by steps, to **Portloe**.

Walk around the cove on the road, and then on a path back to the cliffs to cut across Jacka Point and climb up around Menare Point. The path cuts back to go around the bay and you pass in front of an isolated house which dominates it. This is National Trust land and in spring the woods here are yellow with daffodils. After passing in front of the house, ignore the first path going off seawards, take the next one, down to the low cliffs on a long flight of steps. Turn right at the bottom, cross the stream on a foot-bridge and follow the cliffs around past Parc Cargloose Rock, the Blouth Point and down around Kiberick Cove, looking out over Coggan Rock and Horse Rock in the sea below. You now climb up to Nare Head, from which there are good views, and then descend to cross a stream before climbing up over Penarin Point. After another stream, the path climbs around behind Pendower Beach. At the western end of the beach it crosses over a bridge and follows the road for about 500 metres before dipping sharply seaward, opposite Pibyah Rock, and then taking to the cliffs again.

Just before Creek Stephen Point a footpath leads inland to **Dingerein Castle**. The coast path goes out to the Point and down a flight of steps leading on to Porthbean beach. After a few metres the path climbs up to the cliffs once more, past the coastguard look-out on Pednvadan Point and back around Porthcurnick beach into **Porthscatho**. (Here you should ask whether the Place–St Mawes ferry is operating. If it is not you may prefer to cut across to St Mawes from here.)

Follow the street nearest the bay through Porthscatho and regain the coast on the other side, after deciding how you intend crossing to Falmouth (see Place). Continue along the low cliffs around Greeb Point and down around Towan, Killigerran Head and Porthmellin Head, then past Elwinick Cove and along behind Porthbeor Beach.

The path now climbs gradually, around Zone Point, to pass inland of the lighthouse on St Anthony's Head, and then on round the coast until, crossing a field at the neck of Amsterdam Point, it takes you into **Place**. If the seasonal and infrequent ferry is not running you must make your way to **St Mawes** in order to cross to **Falmouth**. If the Place ferry is not running the only sure way to reach St Mawes is on foot or by car around the Percuil estuary, via Gerrans and the A3078.

Gazetteer

MENABILLY

The house was the seat of the Rashleigh family for 400 years, although Pevsner dates it at around 1600. Wherever he lived, John Rashleigh was already making a name – and a fortune – for himself in the 16th century by accompanying Drake and Raleigh on their voyages with his ship Frances of Foyle, which he also used against the Spanish Armada in 1588. There were other distinguished Rashleighs: Charles founded Charlestown a little farther down the coast in the 18th century, and Philip made a detailed study of Cornish mineral deposits. His extensive collection of mineral specimens, formerly displayed in the house and in a grotto on the estate, is now in the Truro museum. More recently, Daphne du Maurier has lived in Menabilly and she made the house the setting for her novel *Rebecca*, as well as featuring it in other books.

POLKERRIS

The ruins of a 300-year-old fish cellar used for salting and storing pilchards in the days of plenty points to the past of this tiny, unspoilt fishing village. There was a dramatic rescue here in 1865, when the village still had its lifeboat station. Two ships, one a barque – the Dryden – and the other the brig Wearmouth, got into difficulties during a gale. The lifeboat was launched but lost its oars. Somehow, in spite of the heavy seas, it reached Par under sail, collected new oars, went out again and rescued 21 men and a cat from the two ships.

The Rashleigh Arms inn is like a small museum. It has a collection of strange and exotic ornaments from many corners of the world, and many less exotic liquids for the weary walker to quench his thirst. The village also has a post office and shop.

PAR, CHARLESTOWN, AND CHINA CLAY

The histories of these two, and of Pentewan further West, are intimately connected with the extensive mining carried on in the hinterland. The countryside around and to the north of St

Austell has been an important source of china clay for nearly 250 years. Tin and copper were originally mined in the area, and workings at Caralaze, 3 kilometres inland, go back to the Phoenicians. That mining was the main source of revenue until about 1750, when William Cookworthy, a chemist, discovered clay deposits near Helston which he considered suitable for pottery manufacture. Much larger deposits were found on Henbarrow Downs to the north of St Austell and this area soon became the centre of the Cornish china clay industry.

One of the main problems the infant industry had to solve was that of transport from the mines to manufacturing areas such as the potteries of the midlands. The various small workings started to come together under families like the Rashleighs, the Hawkins and the Treffreys, who were all large landowners. There were no natural harbours along the south coast close to the pits, so Charles Rashleigh decided to construct his own. He engaged the famous engineer John Smeaton to design the harbour at West Polmear and construction began in 1791. He also built roads from the workings and from the copper mines at Crinnis, to the port. He built a small settlement there, a row of cottages and an inn, and the name was changed to Charlestown; it rapidly became the most important port in England for the export of china clay. Today, 200 years later, the cottages still stand, but with the growth of Fowey and Par, the importance of Charlestown has declined. The harbour is still very much as Smeaton designed it, but only the occasional ship uses it.

About 30 years after Charlestown was opened, Sir Charles Hawkins decided to go one better than Rashleigh and built his own harbour at Pentewan. Instead of using roads to bring the clay to the port, he constructed a railway in the valley from St Austell which came into operation in 1826. The wagons were originally horse-drawn, but steam gradually replaced the horses. Although it continued as a port longer than Charlestown, business was eventually lost to Par and Fowey, and today, with its sandy beaches, Pentewan is a popular resort. The church and a row of cottages built by Hawkins are still there.

The last of this group of three, Joseph Treffrey, was a gifted landowner, industrialist, shipowner and banker. In 1837 he was almost sole owner of Fowey Consols copper mine just north of Par. He constructed his own harbour at Par in 1842 to export copper mined by Fowey Consols, and although this mine is now closed, 150 years ago it was a thriving centre with engine house, crushing and stamping machines, pump houses, shafts, tramways and thirteen water wheels to supply power. Treffrey built a canal along the St Blazey valley to connect his tramways with his port and erected smelting works on land next to the harbour to produce lead and silver. With admirable foresight he recognized that Fowey Consols would decline and built a railway along the Luxulyan valley, from Par to Bugle, in the middle of the china clay district. It crossed the valley by the famous Treffrey Viaduct, 30 metres high, 210 metres long and built of granite. Although disused today, it is an impressive memorial to the man who, when he died in 1850, could claim to have been the greatest employer of miners and other labourers in the West of England.

Par has all services including accommodation, refreshments, post office, shops, and buses.

Hotel: Trecarrel Hotel; Tel. Par (072681) 4101
B&B: Grigg, 88 Par Green; Tel: Par (072681) 3203
Bus: To Fowey and St Austell

CARLYON BAY

Refreshments, telephone and accommodation are available at the Cornish Riviera complex.

Hotel: Carlyon Bay Hotel; Tel. Par (072681) 2304
B&B: Trevean, Chatsworth Way, Carlyon Bay; Tel. Par (072681) 3305
Bus: To St Austell and Par

CHARLESTOWN

See above for description.

Hotel: Pier House Hotel, Charlestown; Tel. St Austell (0726) 5272

PENTEWAN

In addition to Sir John Hawkins' harbour, Pentewan has quarries whose stone has been used for building throughout Cornwall. There is an Inn, post office and store.

MEVAGISSEY

St Mevan and St Issey combined to give this picturesque village its name. Renowned for its fishing, it was the fourth largest pilchard centre in Cornwall in the 18th century, exporting 35 million pilchards per year to Italy alone. There was a harbour pier here as early as the 16th century and it was rebuilt when pilchard fishing revived after the Napoleonic wars. By the middle of the 19th century Mevagissey yards were building trading schooners to carry the fish away and bring back timber for barrel staves from places as far apart as Russia and North America. In 1886 a second, outer pier was built. This enlarged the harbour area from 1½ to 4 hectares, making it a low- as well as a high-tide harbour. Although the pilchards, like the ship building activity, have long since departed, fishing for whiting, turbot, plaice, skate, lobsters, crab and other fish remains the locals' main occupation. The village is unspoilt and the cottages clinging to the hillside around the harbour are quite charming.

Hotel:	Trevalsa Court Hotel; Tel. Mevagissey (0726) 842468
B&B:	Ship Inn; Tel. Mevagissey (0726) 843324
Buses:	To Gorran Haven and St Austell

PORT MELLON

A small village which is really an extension of Mevagissey, with a public house and a telephone box.

BODRUGAN'S LEAP

The Bodrugans (also called Trenowth or Treworth) were a flamboyant family, which had already grown fat and extremely wealthy by 1250. Sir Henry, who built Bodrugan Castle in 1475 as a fortified manor house, owned a fleet of trading ships and supplemented their income by a heavy and profitable involvement in piracy. A supporter of Richard III at the Battle of Bosworth Field in 1485, he fled when the battle was lost and was pursued by Sir Richard Edgcumbe, who was fighting for the victorious Henry VII. Bodrugan leapt over the cliff on his horse into the sea and then escaped by boat to France, leaving the startled Edgcumbe behind him on the cliffs. His property was confiscated and given by Henry VII to the Edgcumbe family.

GORRAN HAVEN

This, with its twin village of Gorran Churchtown, just inland, once formed part of the manor of Bodrugan. The small port was of some importance in the Middle Ages and a Bodrugan built its pier in 1585. The church of St Just, which was largely rebuilt in 1885, used to be a chapel of ease for Gorran Churchtown. The church of St Gorran, in Gorran Churchtown, is surprisingly big for the size of the community. It dates from the end of the 15th century and has a tower which is more than 27 metres high.

Many ships have come to grief on the Gwineas, or Gwinges rocks, 1½ kilometres off Gorran Haven. One of the more recent ones was the 5200 ton Ardangorm in 1940, which went down without a single loss of life. The village has refreshments, accommodation, a store, and a bus service.

Hotel: Smugglers Hotel, Gorran Haven; Tel.
            Mevagissey (072684) 3228
B&B: Lawnrock Hotel, Gorran Haven; Tel.
            Mevagissey (072684) 3461
Bus: To Mevagissey and St Austell

THE DODMAN OR DODMAN POINT

The National Trust owns nearly 200 hectares stretching from Gorran Haven to Hemmick Beach, including Dodman Point (114 metres high) and its well-preserved Iron Age fort. The views from the top towards Black Head on the Lizard in the west, or to Bolt Tail in south Devon in the east, are magnificent. A massive granite cross was erected by the Rector of St Michael Caerhayes as a daymark for shipping in 1896, and ten years earlier Sir Arthur Quiller Couch set his famous novel *Dead Man's Rock* on the Dodman.

PORTHLUNY COVE

Caerhayes Castle stands just behind this pretty cove surrounded by low, wooded hills. The house was built by John Nash in 1808 for J.B. Trevanion, one of whose ancestors, Sir Hugh Trevanion fought at the Battle of Bosworth field in 1485. It is built on the site of a much older manor house, none of which remains today. The gardens, which are quite splendid, are open to the public at certain times of the year.

The 15th-century church (with some Norman features) contains monuments to the Trevanion family; it lies in the village 1½ kilometres inland behind the house.

PORTHOLLAND COVE

A small cove with a port office and village stores which sells refreshments in summer.

PORTLOE

An unspoilt fishing village which offers refreshments, accommodation, post office stores and a public telephone.

Hotel: Lugger, Portloe; Tel. Veryan (087250) 322
B&B: Ship Inn, Portloe; Tel. Veryan (087250) 356

VERYAN

This is a very old, relatively unspoilt village 3 kilometres inland due west of Portloe. It was recorded as Elerkie in the Domesday Book in 1086, when it belonged to the Earl of Montaigne. St Symphorian's church is partly Norman but mainly medieval, and the village has five white-washed cottages, thatched and completely circular, with gothic windows, known unsurprisingly as the Round Houses. They were built in the early 19th century by Hugh Rowe, a builder from Lostwithiel. Cornish superstition had them built round, so that no corner existed for the devil to hide in – and each roof bears a cross as added protection. Parc Behan is an attractive house you should look out for if you visit the village.

Veryan (or Carne) Beacon, 114 metres high and 114 metres around its base, is just outside the village. It is traditionally regarded as the burial place of Gerennius, 6th-century King of Cornwall. The mound was opened in 1855 and found to contain a kistvaen, or Bronze Age tomb, with charred bones in it.

DINGEREIN CASTLE

This large earthwork lies just off the path, to the west of the village of Curgurrel and due north of Porthbean beach. Dinas Gerin means Geraint's Castle, and Geraint appears in the Anglo Saxon Chronicle as an 8th-century King of the Britons.

He may, however, be the same person as the King Gerennius of Carne Beacon, although there seems to be some confusion about the dates. In any event, he was also nown as St Gerrans or St Gerant among other names, and founded the church named after him at Gerrans near Portscatho.

PORTSCATHO

This is yet another of this coast's many attractive fishing villages. St Gerrans church, just outside the village, has one of the rare octagonal Cornish spires to survive Victorian rebuilding. The village has a fine view over Gerrans Bay, and all services associated with a resort town: refreshments, accommodation, post office, shops and a bus service.

Hotel:	Rosevine Hotel, Porthcurnick Beach; Tel. Portscatho (087258) 230
B&B:	Clifton House; Tel. Portscatho (087258) 414
Bus:	To Truro, St Austell, St Mawes
Early closing:	Wednesday

ST ANTHONY

The peninsular is known as St Anthony in Roseland and most of it belongs to the National Trust. 'Roseland' has nothing to do with roses, it is a corruption of the Cornish word 'rhos' which means heathland, little of which is left on the largely agricultural peninsular. St Anthony has a 12th-century church, founded in 1124 by William Warlewast, Bishop of Exeter, and dedicated to the 3rd-century Egyptian monk St Anthony. One of the pews has the crests of Henry VIII and Anne Boleyn, and this has given rise to the legend that they spent their honeymoon at Place Manor, a house built next to the church after the dissolution to incorporate a priory.

The ferry to St Mawes is highly erratic. It operates only in high summer and can not be relied upon. The only sure way to reach St Mawes is on foot or by car.

ST JUST IN ROSELAND

Walking to St Mawes, St Just is on your right shortly after crossing the head of the Percuil estuary. The church of St Just was consecrated in 1261 and the windows of the north transept date from this time, while the windows in the tower are clearly 14th-century. There are ruins of a much earlier chapel at Roscassa to the north and traces of an old circular fort at Bartini Hill nearby.

TRURO

Up river at the head of the Truro river estuary and far from the path, Truro is the county town of Cornwall, and has played a key role in the county's development. Truro was to Cornish mining what St Austell was to her china clay industry. The derivation of the name is uncertain: it could be 'tru-ru' (three streets) or 'tre-ru' (the castle on the water). The latter seems more likely as there was a castle here once though only Castle Hill survives. The town received its charter in the 12th century during the reign of Henry I (1100 to 1135), and during the reign of Edward I it sent two members to Parliament.

By the middle of the 12th century tin was being shipped from Truro to the Isle of Oléron, off the coast of Brittany, which was then the tin market of Europe. By the end of the 13th century Edward I had 'nationalized' the tin industry for the purpose of financing his military adventures. In the 16th century an assay office was established at Truro, and a third of all the tin produced in the county was assayed there and duty paid to the Duchy of Cornwall.

As ships grew larger and their draught increased the importance of Truro as a port declined although the town remained prosperous and important as a commercial centre, as the many fine buildings show. Truro cathedral is modern, but it does incorporate one aisle of the 16th-century parish church of St Mary. The Almshouses of 1631 still exist and parts of Boscawen House are of the same period, but most of the town is Georgian, and Lemon Street is one of the best examples of Georgian town architecture in England. The facade of the Assembly Rooms in Cross Street dates from 1722 and the imposing Infirmary in Calenick Street from 1799. The Mansion House and Prince's House were both built in the mid 18th century and deserve a visit, as does the Quaker meeting house (1830) at the end of Moresk Road. A visit to the County Museum is essential for those interested in the history of Cornwall.

Richard Lander was born in Truro in 1804 and in his short life became well known as an African traveller. He took part in three expeditions between 1826 and 1834 to explore the river Niger and open Central Africa to trade. On the last of these expeditions he was shot and killed in an ambush and is buried on the island of Fernando Po. He was the first person to be awarded the Gold Medal of the Royal Geographical Society. His monument stands in Lemon Street.

The National Trust property of Trelissick is south of Truro, on the shores of Fal estuary. The neo-Greek mansion, built in 1825 with a portico copied from the Erechtheion in Athens, is of no particular interest but the gardens are magnificent and give superb views over the estuary and Falmouth Harbour.

ST MAWES

The name comes either from St Machatus, an Irish saint, or from a Welsh Prince turned monk called St Mawe or St Mauditus. He was driven from Wales by the Saxons and built himself an oratory here. At one time it belonged to Plympton Priory but, following the dissolution of the monasteries, it passed through various families to become the property of the Duke of Buckingham. The Castle, designed like a clover leaf, was built between 1540 and 1543. It was one of the many forts built by Henry VIII as protection against possible invasion by the French. During the Civil War it was attacked by Fairfax, and Hannibal Bonython, the Governor, surrendered without firing a shot. The Roundheads then took possession of the fort together with its 13 cannons and 160 muskets.

There was a pier at St Mawes as early as 1536 but the present harbour was not constructed until 1854. Today St Mawes is a yachting and tourist resort and has most facilities for the traveller – refreshments, accommodation, shops and post office.

Hotel:	Idle Rocks Hotel, Tredenham Road; Tel. St Mawes (0326) 270771
B&B:	Braganza, Grove Hill; Tel. St Mawes (0326) 270281
Ferry:	All year, frequent. Information Tel. Falmouth (0326) 318534
Early closing:	Thursday
Buses:	To Truro, St Austell

FALMOUTH

In 1600 Falmouth consisted of only two houses, an alehouse and a smithy. Today it is the most important place on the Fal estuary and a port known throughout the world. The site was occupied in Roman times, when it was called Voluba. Sir Walter Raleigh was so impressed when he visited the area in 1613 – he stayed with the Killegrews at Arwenack House – that he recommended that the site should be developed as a port.

As a result of this recommendation Sir John Killegrew was granted permission to build, and a small village started to grow. Originally called Smithwick or Smithike, the name was changed to Pen-y-come-quick ('the head of the narrow-vale'). A Royal proclamation changed it to Falmouth in 1660, and the town was granted a charter of incorporation the following year.

Falmouth grew in importance, mainly because of the large safe anchorage of the Carrick Roads. It became the first port of call in Britain for trading ships from all over the world. Masters were invariably instructed 'to Falmouth for orders'. There they would receive orders telling them where to discharge or load a cargo. From the late 17th century it was the home base of the Post Office packet ships. By the mid 19th century it was not uncommon to see 350 ocean-going sailing ships at anchor in the Roads at any one time, and in 1862 it was named a Head Port (one which administered a number of other ports) by Act of Parliament.

Another Act of Parliament, of 1859, granted permission to build docks, and two large dry docks were constructed. The Admiralty took over the docks in the 1914 War and in the Second World War Falmouth was one of the ports from which the Allied Forces sailed to invade Normandy in 1944. It was also the headquarters of the exiled Royal Netherlands Navy. Extensions have continued over the last thirty years and the new Queen Elizabeth dock can accommodate ships of up to 90,000 tons.

Compared with many places along the coast. Falmouth is modern, the oldest building being the Elizabethan manor of the Killegrews, Arwenack House. This was largely destroyed during the Civil War but the ruins were incorpoated in the house which replaced it, built in 1786 and standing today. The church of King Charles the Martyr was built between 1662 and 1664 and the tower was added in 1684. Various other additions were made up to 1813 when a new east end was built. Some of the original 17th- and 18th-century cottages can still be seen, off the main streets, beside Market Street, down Fish Strand Hill and on Quay Hill.

Pendennis Castle, on Pendennis Point below the town, is another in the girdle of protection woven by Henry VIII as a defence against the French. It was built between 1539 and 1546. The outer fortification is Elizabethan and the castle was first attacked during the Civil War. It held out for the Crown, under the 80-year-old Colonel John Arundel of Trerice, from March 1646 until August of that year, when he surrendered with 24 officers and some 900 men to Fairfax. The defenders were accorded the full honours of war and were allowed to march out with their weapons and their banners.

The town has all the facilities of a port and market town which is also accustomed to receive many tourists.

Hotel:	Greenbank Hotel, Harbourside; Tel. Falmouth (0326) 312440
B&B:	Harbour Guest House; Tel. Falmouth (0326) 311344
Early closing:	Wednesday
Tourist Information:	Tel. Falmouth (0326) 312300
Buses:	Cambourne, Helford Passage, Helston, Penzance, St Ives, Truro

9

Falmouth to Porthleven

*Daw's Hugo and the Lion's Den may be fairly taken as
characteristic types of the whole coast scenery about the Lizard
Head, in its general aspects. Great caves and greater landslips
are to be seen both eastward and westward. In calm weather
you may behold the long prospects of riven rock, in their finest
combination, from a boat . . .*

*On stormy days your course is different. Then, you wander
along the summits of the cliffs; and looking down, through the
hedges of tamarisk and myrtle that skirt the ends of the fields,
see the rocks suddenly broken away beneath you into an
immense shelving amphitheatre, on the floor of which the sea
boils in fury, rushing through natural archways and narrow
rifts. Beyond them, at intervals as the waves fall, you catch
glimpses of the brilliant blue main ocean, and the outer reefs
stretching into it. Often, such wild views as these are relieved
from monotony by the prospect of smooth cornfields and
pasturelands, or by pretty little fishing villages perched among
the rocks — each with its small group of boats drawn up on a
slip of sandy beach, and its modest, tiny gardens rising one
above another, wherever the slope is gentle, and the cliff
beyond rises high to shelter them from the winter winds.*

*But the place at which the coast scenery of the Lizard district
arrives at its climax of grandeur is Kynance Cove. Here, such
gigantic specimens are to be seen of the most beautiful of all
varieties of rock — the 'serpentine' — as are unrivalled in
Cornwall; perhaps, unrivalled anywhere. A walk of two miles
along the westward cliffs from Lizard Town, brought us to the
top of a precipice of three hundred feet. Looking forward from
this, we saw the white sand of Kynance Cove stretching out in a
half circle into the sea.*

COLLINS, William Wilkie (1824–89). Novelist. Extract from *Rambles Beyond Railways* (1851).

Introduction

A seasonal ferry across the Helford River, and a ford across Gillan Creek are the practical problems you will have to face on this stretch. If the ferry is not running, the detour to the nearest crossing point will take time. After Gillan Creek the country is unsatisfactory until you pass Coverack. From there on, you regain the high cliffs and have a marvellous walk as far as Gunwalloe, where a low cliff walk brings you past Loe bar into Porthleven. There are one or two steep gradients but none is beyond the scope of a fairly fit walker.

The geological structure of this region is varied, which gives rise to a rich mix of scenery, plant life and wild life. There is a succession of low and high cliffs, bays, coves, headlands and quarries, and the first signs of mining activity. From Falmouth to Gillan Harbour you have the slates and shales of the Middle Devonian. From Gillan to Porthallow is another slate complex, followed by schists to Porthoustock, gabbro from Porthoustock (where it is quarried) to Coverack, and serpentine round Pedn Boar to Carrick Luz. A short patch of gabbro and then serpentine take you to Mullion with the exception of the tip of the Lizard Peninsula and Predannack Head, which are schist. After Mullion it is Middle Devonian to Gunwalloe and Lower Devonian to Porthleven, where the first of the granite outcrops occur.

Loe Bar is a natural phenomenon thrown up by a freak tidal wave in the 18th century. Behind it lies the lagoon-like freshwater lake of Loe Pool. The Helford River is a good example of a drowned river valley, or ria. Both have a large, varied bird population.

Worth looking at are the Chapel at Church Cove, the Marconi Memorial at Poldhu, marking the first trans-Atlantic wireless transmission, and Manaccan where Titanium ore was first discovered, but the main excitement from Helford to Porthleven is the natural beauty and spirit of the region.

DISTANCE STAGE	DISTANCE CUMUL.	TIME	FALMOUTH TO PORTHLEVEN	TELEPHONE	TRAIN	BUS	FERRY	SHOPS	CAMPING	ACCOMMODATION	REFRESHMENT	CUMUL. DIST. KMS
			FALMOUTH	x	x	x	x	x	x	x	x	433
14	14	3:30	HELFORD PASSAGE/HELFORD		x	x	x			x	x	447
3	17	:45	ST ANTHONY				x					450
(2½)		(:40)	(MANACCAN)	x				x		x	x	
2	19	:30	CARNE									452
3	22	:45	GILLAN	x						x		455
4	26	1:	PORTHALLOW	x		x		x		x	x	459
(2)		(:30)	(ST KEVERNE)	x		x		x		x	x	
5	29	1:15	COVERACK	x		x		x	x	x	x	466
10	39	2:30	CADGWITH	x				x		x	x	476
(1)		(:15)	(LIZARD)	x		x		x	x	x	x	
14	53	3:30	PORTH MELLIN							x	x	490
2	55	:30	POLDHU POINT			x				x	x	492
1	56	:15	CHURCH COVE	x				x				493
2	58	:30	GUNWALLOE			x					x	495
4	62	1:	PORTHLEVEN	x		x		x	x	x	x	499
(4)		(1:)	(HELSTON)	x		x		x		x	x	

TIMES ARE BASED ON AVERAGE WALKER LIGHTLY LADEN.

NB.
1. STAGE: is the distance between that point and the preceding point.
2. CUMUL.: is the cumulative distance from the beginning of the chapter.
3. TIME: is the time for the stage (between that point and the preceding one) calculated at 4 kilometres per hour – the rate for a lightly loaded person walking without halt.
4. Brackets enclose places not on the Path but easily reached from it, together with distances and times from the Path.
5. CUMULATIVE DISTANCE: is the total distance from South Haven Point.

Guide

From the pier turn left and walk through the town, past the lifeboat station, behind the main dock area and out to Pendennis Point, with its coastguard station, Tudor Castle and coastguard look-out on the Point itself. Swinging around the Point, the path goes first north west and then west around Gyllyngvase Beach to Swanpool Point, then on past the Swan Pool itself, around Swan Pool Beach to Pennance Point. The path now continues on the cliffs past Newporth Head down to **Maen Porth**, with its beach and headland.

Climb up over the headland and continue along the cliffs to the National Trust Property of Rosemullion Head. Go round the Head and up and down along the cliffs past **Mawnan**. Walk inland and go along behind Parson's Beach to round Mawnan Shear and Toll Point before descending towards the hamlet of **Durgan**. Just over 1 kilometre further on you enter **Helford Passage** with its seasonal ferry to Helford (subject to weather conditions).

From the ferry point in **Helford** the path goes through the village on the road and where the road turns sharp right, continues along the estuary. It crosses streams behind Bosahan Cove and Ponsence Cove, crosses over the Gew and, cutting across the neck of **Dennis Head**, enters **St Anthony**. Here there is no ferry and the Gillan Creek must be waded, which is possible for one hour each side of low tide. Otherwise you must make the detour around the head of the Creek and back or take the alternative path from Helford via **Manaccan** and Carne to Flushing.

From Flushing the path follows the shore of the creek past **Gillan**, Men-aver Point and around Parbean Cove to Nare Point. Pass inland of the coastguard look-out and climb up around Polnare Cove to Nare Head, where there are pleasant views. From the Head the path crosses the next Head and keeps close to the cliff edge, descending steeply and finally by steps to the beach at **Porthallow**.

From Porthallow the path goes inland to avoid the disused quarries around Pencra Head and Porthkerris Point. With one short passage of 800 metres across fields north of Tregaminion it follows the road to Porthoustock and on to Rosenithon, opposite Godrevy Cove. About 1500 metres east of the cove lie the treacherous Manacles Rocks. The path follows the stream towards the cove for a few metres and then turns right, taking you through Dean Quarries (if the Red Flags are flying you must wait) and round Polcries to Lowland Point.

Rounding the point the path turns west again, just above sea level on the low, flat 'Raised Beach'. This continues for about 2 kilometres until you reach a track, by the sewage works, which leads you on to the road and into **Coverack**. Go round the beach and harbour, through the village, out to

Dolor Point and through the car park. Then come back along the cliffs around Perprean Cove, where you are diverted inland a little and then cross fields towards Trewillis Farm, which you pass well to seaward, rejoining the cliffs just before the final climb up on to Black Head. Go around the head, past the coastguard look-out and continue on along the cliffs around Dinas Cove over Treleaver Cliff to Pedn Boar. From here to Beagles Point is National Trust property. Go down, cross the stream and climb up over Beagles Point, steeply down to Downas Cove, across another stream and up on to the cliffs again behind Zawn Vinoc, taking care to keep to seaward all the while. Now keep inland behind Lankidden Cove, on the edge of farmland, to cross a stream and cut across the neck of the **Carrick Luz** peninsula in front of Borgwitha Farm.

From the farm road, a good path takes you along the cliff tops around Spernic Cove, over Eastern Cliff and down quite steeply to Kennack Sands. Pass behind the sands along the road for about 300 metres, taking care not to go too far inland, and up over Thorny Cliff past Polbream Point to the steep rocky head of Carlyon Cove. Cross over the bridge over the stream and turn back on to the cliffs, past Black Rock and on to Enys Head. Go around the head and then on the cliffs around Kildown Cove and Kildown Point before descending into **Cadgwith**.

Climb up out of Cadgwith on to the cliffs again, around the Devils Frying Pan – formed by the collapse of a cave roof – across the National Trust property of Caron Barrow, and on along the well trodden cliff path. Pass Dollar Ogo, Chough's Ogo, Porbarrow, Whale Rock and dip down across a stream and up again past a landmark for shipping above Parn Voose Cove. You will then pass through a disused serpentine quarry to the National Trust property of Church Cove. A path leads inland here to **Landewednack**. Up again on to the cliffs to pass Kilcobben Cove (where the Lizard Cadgwith lifeboat is stationed), Prilla Cove and Hot Point and out seaward of the coastguard station at **Bass Point**.

The path continues on along the coast passing a signal station used by Marconi, and the Housel Bay Hotel on the path at Housel Bay. Climb back up on to the cliffs and on around the Bay, passing landward of the Lion's Den (another impressive shaft formed by the collapse of a cave roof), and Bumble Rock where you turn west again to pass the Lizard Lighthouse, above Polbream Cove. A path leads inland and 300 metres further on there is a road to **Lizard**.

Climb down along the coast to cross the stream behind Polpeor Cove and then up again on to Lizard Point itself, the southernmost point in Britain, with its coastguard look-out and the Mulvin and Quadrant Rocks offshore. The path now turns due north, keeping close to the cliff's edge, goes round Holseel Cove, down to cross a stream above Caerthillian Cove and up again above Pentreath Beach.

From the cliff top Lion Rock can be seen and beyond it along the coast Gull Rock and Asparagus Island. Go past the car park and cafe, across the headland and down into **Kynance Cove**. Cross the footbridge over the stream and climb up onto Kynance Cliff – with Gull Rock and Asparagus Island to seaward. Keeping to the cliffs, go round above Rill Cove, Rill Ledges and Rill Point, around the Pound Cove past the Horse Rocks and the dramatic cliffs of Pigeon Ogo. Inland a little you will cross over a stream and pass some old quarry workings (soapstone or steatite used in china making) at Gew Graze. As you descend, look out for the path up on the other side. It runs straight up the cliffs slightly further inland than you might expect.

Climb up towards Pengersick and Vellan Head. You can follow the cliffs around the Head but the path runs across the (often boggy) moorland neck of the head to rejoin the cliffs above George's Cove. It then follows the edge of the sheer cliffs around Pol Curnick before dropping down to cross a stream above Ogo-Dour Cove. Up again through National Trust land, over Predannack Head, past Men-Te-Heul and the Chair (with a good view of Mullion Island in the Bay before you). Then down to cross a stream, before climbing up again over Mullion Cliff. Both Mullion Cliff (a nature reserve) and Mullion Island are National Trust properties, as is **Mullion Cove** which you now descend to.

Climbing up out of Mullion Cove, past the Mullion Cove Hotel, and over Henscath past a coastguard look-out you will find yourself on the road for a couple of hundred metres before taking to the cliffs again, and descending to Polurrian Cove. Cross a bridge over a stream behind the beach and climb up on to the National Trust property of Meres Cliff, where you will follow a well-worn cliff-top path around past the Marconi Monument at **Poldhu** to the Poldhu Hotel.

Passing seaward around the hotel to join its drive, you will reach the road behind Poldhu Cove. Turn left on the road over the stream and left again, still on the road, up over Carrag-a-Pilez Cliff. Here the road becomes a track which leads down, through a car park and past a golf course, steeply into **Church Cove**. Walk around the limit of the beach past a hut, to cross the stream by a footbridge on to the road. Avoiding the subsidence, climb back on to the cliffs again beyond the church and follow a good path around Pedngwinian Point over Halzephron Cliff, until you reach Baulk Head and descend to **Gunwalloe Fishing Cove**.

If the tide is out you can walk along the beach to Looe Bar; if not take the track just above the beach, which is fenced to landward at first, and passes some ruined buildings and the rusty remains of machinery. It continues as a low cliff path to the National Trust property of **Looe Bar**. Just before reaching the bar, it passes seaward of a white cross, Memorial to H.M.S. Anson.

Cross the bar, between the romantic Looe Poole, with its sloping wooded banks, and the sea, and climb up on to a good path which takes you, above Porthleven Sands, down into the town of **Porthleven**.

Gazetteer

MAWNAN

This village is just off the path, not far from the beautiful National Trust property of Rosemullion Head, and has a 14th- and 15th-century church. Dedicated to the two Saints, Macmanus and Stephen, it is built in the centre of an oval Celtic entrenchment in woodland some way from the village.

HELFORD PASSAGE

Helford River made an important, secret contribution to the Allied success during the Second World War. At Durgan a slipway was constructed for the embarkment of American tanks for the Normandy invasion in 1944. More important was the work of the Inshore Patrol Flotilla who had their head-quarters here. This very special unit, equipped with Breton fishing boats, used to deliver and recover Agents from Brittany. Many escaped RAF and United States airmen were brought back by these boats. On Christmas Eve 1943 they pulled off a most important mission: they brought back a French professor from the Sorbonne with the plans for the V2 rocket experimental establishment at Peenemunde in Germany. There is a bus service to Falmouth.

FERRY

The ferry operates only in season (normally Easter to October). Call Mawnan Smith (0326) 250278 for information. When it is not in operation a long detour must be made around the Helford Estuary.

HELFORD

Formerly a small port from which granite was shipped, this place was once notorious for its pirates. There is a private seal sanctuary at Gweek, farther up the Estuary, run as a hospital for injured seals and birds. Both children and adults love to visit it. Helford has facilities for refreshment and shopping and a public telephone.

ST ANTHONY

This tiny settlement at the neck of Dennis (or Dinas) Head, has a church, St Dunstan's, founded in the 13th century. The window in the chancel is all that is left of the original 13th-century church, the rest being 15th-century. The ancient British camps of Great and Little Dinas on the Head itself were fortified and used as military posts during the Civil War and were among the last to surrender to the Parliamentary forces.

There is no ferry but normally, for one hour either side of low tide, you can wade Gillan Creek from just beyond St Anthony to just West of Flushing. The alternative is to make the short detour around the estuary past Manaccan.

MANACCAN

Coins found at the double-trenched camp at Rasmorden nearby suggest that a settlement existed at Manaccan from Roman times. The church of St Manaccan is Norman, with additions in the 13th and 15th centuries, and was restored and enlarged in 1824. Look for the fig tree growing with Biblical symbolism out of its south-west wall.

The most important event in Manaccan's history was the discovery of the metal titanium (also called gregorite or manaccanite) in 1791. The gentle Reverend W.M. Gregor can hardly have suspected that the harmless ore he took from the stream of Tregonwell Mill would one day be a vital ingredient in the world's space and arms industries.

CARNE

The two stone and cob cottages you pass here are typically Cornish and were given to the National Trust with 2½ hectares of land in 1945.

GILLAN

The Tregildry Hotel (032 623) 378, is open from March to October.

PORTHALLOW

This pleasant village has a shop, a telephone, a pub and bed and breakfast. It was not so pleasant on the night of the Great Blizzard in March 1891. The Bay of Panama was wrecked that night off Porthallow, all 2,282 tons of her. She was one of the finest sailing ships afloat – four-masted, square-rigged, built of steel and bound for Dundee with a cargo of jute from Calcutta when the blizzard caught her and blew her on to the rocks just North of Porthallow. The captain, his wife and part of the crew were swept overboard. The rest were ordered into the rigging to avoid the huge waves crashing over the decks. When the cold light of day swept in from the East they were seen hanging inert like winter washing on the halyards, frozen to death. Seventeen survived and eventually, most of the cargo and the metal superstructure was salvaged. The ship's bell hangs in Helford chapel and a skeleton like hull can still be seen, lying in sand in 4.5 metres of water.

B&B: Valley View; Tel. St Kevern (0326) 280596.

ST KEVERN

Almost due South of Porthallow and 2 kilometres south west of Porthoustock, this largish village has shops and refreshments. Although frequently prospected, minerals have never been found in the area. This is because St Kevern, having been treated with disrespect, put a ban on his parish, saying 'no

metal will run within the sound of St Kevern's bells.' So no
metal, but there is a church. The church of St Akeveranus is
not the purest of styles. It was built in the 15th century out of
bits and pieces left over from a 13th- or 14th-century one
which stood on the site. The spire was added in the 18th
century after the old one was destroyed by lightning. The
Domesday Book tells us that there was a collegiate church
here at the time of the Norman Conquest which became the
property of the Cistercian Abbey at Beaulieu in the 13th
century and was taken from them at the Dissolution in the
16th century. Leland, writing later that century, reports
'within the land of Menke (Menage) is a parish church of St
Keveryn and there is a sanctuary with ten or twelve dwelling
houses and thereby was a cell of monks. The ruins of the
monastery yet remaineth.'

THE MANACLES

These fearsome rocks lie just 1½ kilometres offshore, due
east of St Kevern and it is a deadly tally of lives and ships that
have been lost on their jagged teeth. Over 400 sailors have
been consigned to eternity beneath the sods of St Kevern's
yard alone. On a January night in 1809 H.M.S. Dispatch,
homeward bound with troops from Corunna, and H.M.S.
Primrose both came to grief there. Out of over 200 only 8
survived, and another 191 were lost when the emigrant ship
John was lost on an outward voyage in May 1855. One
hundred and six went down with the liner Mohegan in 1898.

LOWLAND POINT

This is a good example of a raised beach in the last great Ice
Age. It overlooks The Manacles and is a treacherous rival to
those violent rocks. In 1899 Lowland Point claimed the
biggest ship yet to come to a sad end on the English coast. This
was the United States Lines' Paris, 10,499 tons. Miraculously
the crew of 370 and the 386 passengers were all saved. Even
the tons were eventually salvaged. 13 tugs towed the ship off
the rocks to Falmouth for preliminary repairs, and after a
complete refit in Belfast she was renamed 'Philadelphia' and
sailed again. A happy escape for a ship which, ten years
earlier, had won the Blue Riband for the fastest crossing of the
Atlantic – 5 days, 23 hours and 7 minutes.

COVERACK

The inn at Coverack is named after the determined liner Paris (mentioned above). Pretty fishermen's cottages and a generous little harbour, souvenirs of its importance in pilchard days. But fishing was always rivalled by smuggling as the principal activity of this community whose geography lent itself so well to both.

The Gunvor sank in Beagles Hole, just South of Coverack, beyond the aptly sinister Black Head. The three-masted Norwegian barque foundered in fog in April 1912, and, although her crew were saved, a cargo of nitrate from Chile went down with her. Nearby, the multi-coloured panels you see on the clifftop are there for colour testing. The village has all facilities:

Hotel:	Headland Hotel, Coverack; Tel. St Kevern (0326) 280243
B&B:	Beach House, Coverack; Tel. St Kevern (0326) 280261
YHA:	Parc Behan, School Hill, Coverack; Tel. St Kevern (0326) 280687
Bus:	To Helston and Porthallow
Early closing:	Tuesday

CHYNALLS POINT, CARRICK LUZ, KENNACK SANDS, GOONHILLY DOWNS

An Iron Age fort, or cliff castle, crowns Chynalls Point. The men who built it no doubt knew that the serpentine country started here in earnest. What they could not have foreseen is the range of gaudy bric-a-brac the tourist souvenir industry would make of this red, black and green rock. Its very soft relation, called soapstone, when ground into powder is known as French talc, and is indispensable to tailors and beauty specialists alike. The hinterland, monotonously flat and bare of trees because of the serpentine, is known as Goonhilly Downs. Infertile, impossible to drain or to cultivate, its value lies in its prehistoric remains. Goonhilly is the ancient Cornish name for a donkey, or ass, and British Telecom have their communications and satellite tracking station here.

There is another Iron Age fort on Carrick Luz, and the Post Office cable to Spain and Portugal comes ashore on Kennack

Sands. At Carleon, a little further South, the ruins of the Carleon Serpentine Factory are National Trust property. Many of the Oxford and Bond Street shop fronts were made there. An abandoned flour mill stands nearby, one of its walls decorated with a primitive (probably Celtic) crucifixion figure carved in the stone.

CADGWITH, RUAN MINOR

At Ruan Minor, next door to Carleon, the church of St Ruan has a Norman font, some 13th-century elements and a 15th-century tower built out of massive serpentine blocks.

Cadgwith was another pilchard port which enjoyed prosperity a century ago when the Huer's House lodged the Huer and he had work to do shouting out the news of the pilchard shoals' approach. Pilchard cellars remain too, where the fish were salted. The village has facilities for refreshment, accommodation and shopping.

Just south of the village is the Devil's Frying Pan – a vertical hole in the cliff formed when the roof of a cave collapsed in 1868. Its size is impressive: 0.8 hectares in area and 73 metres deep. And out to sea, the Tregwin Rocks have claimed a ship or two. The steamer Clan Malcolm was a total wreck when she ran foul of them in September fog in 1935. The Bass Point rocks are almost as treacherous; they sank the full-rigged ship Cromdale on its return from Chile in May 1913.

Hotel: Cadgwith Hotel, The Lizard; Tel. St Kevern
            (0326) 290513
B&B: High Massets, Cadgwith, The Lizard; Tel. St
            Kevern (0326) 290571)

LANDEWEDNACK

The Manor here belonged to the Earl of Mortaigne at the time of the Norman Conquest. It has a Norman door, although the building itself probably dates from the 13th or 14th century, and the font has an inscription by the vicar who was there from 1405 to 1415. An unusual feature is the squint, or hagioscope, a hole cut in the wall of the South transept to allow a view of the chancel and altar. The West tower is built of serpentine, and it looks ethereal when the light catches its shiny shades of blue, green and black. The graves of 1645 are poignant reminders of the plague. St Winwallow claims to be the most southerly church in England, and the last church to have a sermon preached in Cornish, a boast made also by St Feoca at Feock near Truro.

MARCONI

Before arriving at the most southerly point in England, you pass the Marconi Signal Station, above Housel Bay, the building he used in his early experiments. Guglielmo Marconi was born in Bologna in 1874. Obviously this Bolognese achieved so much because his mother was Irish. Marconi arrived in England in 1896 and formed the Marconi Company and an association with the Post Office. From then on things moved fast. In 1897 he sent a signal across the Bristol Channel, in 1898 from Poole to the Isle of Wight and in 1899 across the English Channel. Then, in 1901, he united the Old and the New World through wireless technology. He received messages at St John's Newfoundland, with the aid of an aerial suspended from a kite, transmitted from Poldhu 2000 miles away in Cornwall.

THE LIZARD

This is the most southerly point in England. The town is grey in any light and full of shops selling serpentine artwork. It does have most of the facilities a walker might need, however.

No one knows how the Lizard got its name. Was it from its shape, or its serpentine colouring, or from the Cornish word for Headland, 'Liazherd'. We do know however that Ptolemy called it Ocrinum and Promontorium Damnonium. His last name for it seems rather apt. The Point has always been a hazard for shipping: 700 unmarked graves of shipwreck victims dot the cliff top. One hundred and sixty one bullocks had an unusual experience when the schooner-rigged steamer Suffolk, which was carrying them from Baltimore to London, hit the Lizard at full speed in dense fog in September 1886. The crew and passengers were saved, and 50 of the beasts were hauled alive on to the cliffs, but the rest went to a watery grave with cargo and ship.

In 1913 the Lighthouse itself seems to have caused an accident. The captain of the four-master Queen Margaret lost ship and cargo when, in perfectly calm seas, he stood too close to this tricky shore to speak with the Lighthouse keeper – and lost his ship.

Sir John Killigrew of Falmouth built the first lighthouse on the Point, in the 17th century, although his reputation as a pirate suggests that his intentions weren't simply philanthropic. This Lighthouse was replaced by the present one in 1753 and has been modified since. Originally it consisted of two towers 57 metres above sea level and 70 metres apart and these were altered to today's single tower in 1903. The original coal-fired lamp was replaced by oil in 1813, and today the light is equivalent to that of four million candles. You can visit the lighthouse in the afternoon.

Although flat and dull, the Lizard heathland is world famous as an area of interest to both geologist and botanist. The colourful serpentine makes up the bulk of the peninsula, but it is relieved by intrusions of granites and schists. Together these Pre-Cambrian rocks are among the oldest in the British Isles, more than 570 million years old. Apart from producing pretty serpentine pebble beaches they influence the flora and fauna. The soil has both acid- and base-rich habitats, which support a variety of plants. The rarest of these is Erica Vagans or Cornish Heath, which grows purple in spring and summer. But the fact that the peninsula has been chosen as the site for an experiment into tree growth under extremely exposed conditions (the 40 hectare Croft Pascoe plantation) points to another peculiarity. The area is windswept and there are very few high-growing plants. This has led to an absence of bird life. The Point itself is a privileged view-point for migratory birds, but the indigenous population is not what you might expect. Red deer are sometimes to be seen but otherwise you must look to the odd small herd of cattle for the only signs of animal life.

Hotel:	Housel Bay Hotel, The Lizard; Tel. St Kevern (0326) 290417
B&B:	2 Parc Grous, Cross Common, The Lizard; Tel. St Kevern (0326) 290430
Bus:	To Helston
Early closing:	Saturday

KYNANCE COVE

The Worcester Pottery (Royal Worcester, today) used to get their steatite here, a rocky substance which was ground up to make china body. Developments in china manufacture, however, have made this raw material redundant. Half a kilometre inland of the cove, on the west bank of the stream, is the site of a settlement dating from 1300 BC.

ASPARAGUS ISLAND

Don't expect to find delicate provisions for your evening meal here. The asparagus is a plant called *Asparagus Officianalis*, which doesn't have quite the same flavour as its near namesake. The Devil's Throat and the Devil's Bellows are two chasms on the Island. The latter at least deserves its menacing name, it 'projects a volume of water, with loud rumbling noise, at certain states of the tide' according to a 19th-century account.

PREDANNACK HEAD

This has been a Nature Reserve since 1969 and belongs to the Cornwall Naturalists' Trust.

PORTH MELLIN

This is a small fishing port on Mullion Cove which was prosperous during the high point of the pilchard fishing industry. The church of St Melina is 16th century and contains some of the finest carved bench ends to be seen in Cornwall.

Hotel: Mullion Cove Hotel; Tel. Mullion (0326) 240486
B&B: Journey's End, Polurrian Cliff; Tel. Mullion (0326) 240103

POLDHU POINT

The monument to Marconi's first trans-Atlantic wireless transmission of 1901 makes interesting reading. Just beyond the monument is the rather grand-looking Poldhu Hotel (Tel. Mullion (0326) 240339).

CHURCH COVE

There seems to be no reason for the siting of this small chapel here in the lee of the cliff on this sheltered cove. It may have belonged to Winnianton Manor, on the hill above it, which was entered in the Domesday Book as the property of the King, Earl of Cornwall. The present church was built in the 14th century, close to the tower of an earlier one. St Winawalloe, from whom it takes its name, was a 6th-century Breton Abbot, who is reputed to have visited Cornwall and several early churches are named after him. The skilled and lucky may find gold in Church Cove's sands. Two treasure ships were wrecked there in the 16th and 18th centuries. Much of their precious cargoes was recovered, but some gold coins have been found quite recently. The cove also saw its share of smuggling (was the wreck of the two treasure ships really fortuitous?) and the Halzephron Inn nearby has a hidden smuggler's tunnel burrowing down through the cliff.

GUNWALLOE

Gunwalloe Fishing Cove is no longer a fishing cove. Today there are only a couple of cottages and the twisted, rusting remains of some tackle connected with the quarry nearby.

LOE POOL

This pretty freshwater lake with its peaceful, wooded shores was formed when Loe bar, the shingle bar across its mouth reminiscent of Chesil Bank, grew up. The bar is 550 metres long and encloses the largest area of fresh water in Cornwall. The pool is a preferred haunt of bird watchers, particularly in winter, when there is a colourful population of wintering water birds. It is part of the Penrose Estate which was given to the National Trust in 1975 by Colonel Rodgers, whose family had owned it for more than 200 years.

The Bar has seen some pretty spectacular ship wrecks. One ship was thrown clear over it in a storm. In 1807 the frigate H.M.S. Anson was wrecked on it with the loss of a hundred lives. Henry Trengrouse of Helston witnessed the disaster and was so moved by it that he devoted the rest of his life and fortune to the development of a line which could be fired by rocket from ship to shore or vice versa, a safety device still in use today. In recognition Henry received £50 from the government, 30 guineas from the Royal Society, a silver medal and a diamond ring from the Czar of Russia, which he had to pawn to continue his research. The discreet monument to the right of the path as you reach the bar, also commemorates the tragedy which led to his dedicated work. His original apparatus can be seen in the Helston Museum.

HELSTON

A little way up the Cobber, north-east of Loe Pool is this ancient town, known as Henliston in the Domesday Book. Each year, on the 8 May, the Furry is held there, a pre-Christian tradition to celebrate the passing of winter and the approach of summer. It has picked up one or two Christian associations along the way, as well as the hopeful name, the 'Floral Dance'. There's even a Furry song with the optimistic chorus:

'With Hal-an-Tow, Rumble O! for we were up as soon as any day O!
And for to fetch the summer home, the summer and the may O!
For summer is a-come O! and winter is a-gone O!'

Edward I made it a stannary town, where the Courts exercised a jurisdiction peculiar to the tin mines. The sovereign decreed that tin miners should be exempt from any other jurisdiction, although stannaries had existed from the time of Athelstan who reigned from 924 to 940. In addition, Edward named it as a place where tin was to be taken for 'coinage'. A corner of the metal was cut off and a seal stamped on it as a guarantee of quality. The stannary courts were not abolished until 1896.

The main street of Helston is called Coinagehall, or Coinagel, Street, and you can still see the old stannary building. The park at the bottom of the main street was the site of a castle already in ruins in Edward IV's time (1461–1483). The Earl of Godolphin built St Michael's church in the middle of the 18th century, modelled on designs by Thomas Edwards of Greenwich. A monument inside to T. Bougins, dated 1602, suggests that he rebuilt an existing one. Helston remained an important mining town until the middle of the 19th century, and the Wheal Vor mine nearby was the richest mine in the world at one time.

Several attractive buildings make the town worth a visit. The Helston Aeropark and the Poldark Mine Museum are both open daily from April to October.

PORTHLEVEN

As you approach the town from the east you pass the remains of the Wheal Prosper lead mines, first worked in Roman times. These have been disused for many years and the fishing village is surprisingly unspoilt. The harbour faces south-west and is exposed to the prevailing weather. Several attempts were made to protect and develop it, beginning in 1811 when the Porthleven Harbour Company was formed by Act of Parliament. The harbour was completed by 1818 but was completely destroyed in the great gales of 1824. It was rebuilt in 1825 but because it was dangerous and difficult to enter it stayed a sleepy fishing port with only 46 boats registered there by 1850. In 1855 Harvey & Co of Hayle bought it and fitted lock gates to the inner harbour. Shipyards and a canning factory were established, but both these industries have died. Only tourism survives the stormy weather.

To the west of the village, as you climb towards Tregear Point is a cross erected by the parson who first gave Christian burial to ship-wreck victims. Until then the Church decreed that they must be buried in unconsecrated ground, or simply thrown back into the sea, although it is not clear which of religion's incongruities was responsible for that barbaric rule. His humanity was endorsed by an Act of Parliament in 1803, the effect of which was to allow those drowned to be buried in the nearest parish churchyard at the expense of the county rate. Porthleven has all facilities and is very crowded in season. It also has some charming inhabitants who may offer you madeira cake and sage advice on walking and the more abstruse aspects of pack carrying.

Hotel:	Torre Vean Manor House, Porthleven; Tel. Helston (03265) 62412
B&B:	Beacon Crag Hotel, Porthleven; Tel. Helston (03265) 62209
Bus:	To Falmouth and Penzance
Early closing:	Wednesday

10

Porthleven to Sennen

The Land's End terminates in a point of great rocks which runs a good way into the sea. I clambered over them as far as safety permitted me. There are abundance of rocks, and shoals of stones stand up in the sea a mile off, some here and there, some quite to the shore, which they name by several names of Knights and Ladies rolled up in mantles from some old tradition or fiction.

The poets advance description of the amours of some great persons; but these many rocks and stones, which look like the Needles in the Isle of Wight, make it hazardous for ships to double the point, especially in stormy weather. Here at the Land's End they are but a little way off France; two days' sail at farthest convey them to Hauve de Grace in France, but the peace being but newly entered into with the French, I was not willing to venture, at least by myself, into a foreign kingdom, and being then at the end of the land, my horse's legs could not carry me through the deep, and so returned again to Pensands ten miles more, and so came in view of both the seas and saw the Lizard Point and Pensands and the Mount in Cornwall, which looked very fine in the broad day, the sun shining on the rock in the sea.

FIENNES, Celia (1662–1741). *Through England on a Side Saddle* (1695).

Introduction

With the exception of the three granite outcrops of St Michael's Mount, Trewavas Head and Rinsey Head, greenstone and killas (the local name for the slates and shales of the

Devonian) continue to Lamorna, just beyond Penzance. From Lamorna it is granite, at its most dramatic and glorious, all the way to Land's End and on to Sennen. This stretch offers some of the most outstanding scenery of the whole coastal path, and indeed the coast from Gwennap Head to Land's End is some of the finest in the British Isles.

There is great natural variety here as conditions swing from sheltered cove to blasted headland, from the typical Devonian structure to the starkly beautiful granite. The luxuriant vegetation about the wood at St Loy is almost tropical, and tropical shrubs and trees can be seen in the gardens of Penzance. Granite has the intrinsic beauty of its own crystalline structure, that of its mineral veins where it meets foreign geological formations and the subtle tones of the lichens and mosses which espouse its healthy surface.

In addition to the birds which have cheered our route since we left Poole Harbour, the great freshwater lake, Loe Pool, welcomes mallard, teal, gadwill, shoveler, tufted duck, pochard and dabchick in winter as well as mute swan, heron, moorhen and various warblers in summer. Land's End and its approaches afford a veritable feast for the ornithologist with herring gull, great black-backed gull, lesser black-backed gull, kittiwake and fulmar. The swallow, swift, sandmartin, warblers, dotterel and flycatchers come in spring to leave again in autumn. Kestrel, wheatear, buzzard, stonechat, cuckoo and meadow pipit breed there and in autumn guillemots, razorbill, shearwaters, kittiwakes, skuas, terns, puffins and sea ducks use it as their final staging post in England before they migrate.

The South Cornwall path is much more taken up with agricultural land than the northern sector and there are not such extensive heathland areas. However sessile oak, turkey oak, common oak, Cornish elm and Montery pine will be encountered, as well as gorse, bell heather, tamarisk and a great variety of lichen (on the rocks) and ferns, such as hay-scented buckler fern, hart's tongue and lady fern.

This is a varied section of about 50 kilometres with an abundance of magnificent scenery. For the most part the path is clearly marked and in reasonable condition, although the woods to the west of Mousehole demand a certain amount of attention as in places the path is indistinct. Similarly, the stretch between Boscawen Point and St Loy is not well marked. The built-up areas of Penzance and Newlyn are best dealt with by some form of transport from boundary to boundary – and the same is true even from the eastern approaches to Penzance right through to Mousehole, as the path is road-bound for most of the way. Otherwise, there is a variety of walking experiences: some brisk steep ascents and descents about the coves, picturesque villages and ports, beaches, high cliff walking and the magnificence of the approach to Land's End.

Guide

Continue along the road, skirting the harbour and climb up out of the village to Tregear Point, leaving the road just before the cross. Take care after the point, the path has been diverted away from the crumbling cliff edges. But the line of the path is clearly traced and continues to be so, following the coast past Wheal Trewavas Copper Mine, to seaward, round **Trewavas Head**, past Wheal Prosper Copper Mine, to landward, then by an unmetalled road to Rinsey Head. The path then drops down through bracken to Praa Sands. Here you can either take the metalled road above the beach behind the sand hills or walk along the long, safe sandy beach itself to **Praa Sands**.

Climb up the Hoe Point and then up and down through bracken along the cliff above Keneggy Sand past Bessies Cove and Piskies Cove to **Prussia Cove**. Follow the coast path round, cutting across Cudden Point, scene of many ship-wrecks, and down slightly round Stackhouse and Trevean Coves to Perran Sands. The path goes inland here 400 metres to **Perranuthnoe**. But if you do not wish to visit the village, continue along the beach and rejoin the path at the western end. Climb slightly to Maen-Du (Black Rock) Point and then, skirting some fields, down to the rocky beach of Trenow Cove, then up on to the low cliffs and down into **Marazion** on the main A394 road. (It is possible to catch a No. 502 or 503 bus into Penzance from here, from Henfor Terrace).

In the centre of Marazion, turn left towards the **St Michael's Mount** causeway. If the tide permits you may wish to visit the mount on foot, otherwise you will have to take the ferry. If you decide not to visit it turn right onto the beach, which you follow for about two miles until reaching a railway crossing, opposite the Heliport. Cross here and follow the main A30 into Penzance, either walking along roads through **Penzance** and **Newlyn** or taking a bus or some other form of transport.

DISTANCE STAGE	DISTANCE CUMUL.	TIME	PORTHLEVEN TO SENNEN	TELEPHONE	TRAIN	BUS	FERRY	SHOPS	CAMPING	ACCOMMODATION	REFRESHMENT	CUMUL. DIST. KMS
			PORTHLEVEN	x		x		x	x	x	x	499
(3)		(:45)	(BREAGE)									
6	6	1:30	PRAA SANDS	x		x		x		x	x	505
3	9	:45	PRUSSIA COVE						x			508
(½)		(:10)	(PERRANUTHNOE)	x							x	
6	15	1:30	MARAZION	x		x		x	x	x	x	514
(2)		(:30)	(LUDGVAN)			x						
5	20	1:15	PENZANCE	x	x	x		x	x	x	x	519
2	22	:30	NEWLYN	x		x		x	x	x	x	521
(2)		(:30)	(PAUL)							x	x	
3	25	:45	MOUSEHOLE			x			x	x	x	524
(3½)		(:55)	(ST BURYAN)			x		x	x			
9	34	2:15	LAMORNA	x				x	x	x	x	533
3	27	:45	PORTHCURNO					x				536
2	39	:30	PORTHGWARRA	x							x	538
6	45	1:30	LAND'S END	x		x				x	x	544
2	47	:30	SENNEN COVE	x		x		x	x	x	x	546

TIMES ARE BASED ON AVERAGE WALKER LIGHTLY LADEN.

NB.

1. STAGE: is the distance between that point and the preceding point.
2. CUMUL.: is the cumulative distance from the beginning of the chapter.
3. TIME: is the time for the stage (between that point and the preceding one) calculated at 4 kilometres per hour – the rate for a lightly loaded person walking without halt.
4. Brackets enclose places not on the Path but easily reached from it, together with distances and times from the Path.
5. CUMULATIVE DISTANCE: is the total distance from South Haven Point.

From Newlyn the official path is mainly along the road to **Mousehole** (pronounced 'Mowzel'). There is, however, an alternative route which takes off to the right, just before Newlyn Harbour, up a steep lane, past a chapel, then past the huge Penlee stone quarry (on your left) to the villages of St Paul and Trevithal and down into Mousehole, where you turn left at Treen Villas and emerge at the harbour by the Lobster Pot pub. The path leads you up out of Mousehole on the road and then by a metalled right of way to the coastguard look-out at Penzer Point. The path now turns inland a little, through bracken and then into a wood. Continue around the headland of Carn-Du and down into the village of **Lamorna**.

When you climb up out of Lamorna you walk around Carn Barges and past Tater Du automatic lighthouse. On this stretch, between Tater Du and Paynter's Cove, you cross the properties of two well-known writers, Derek Tangye (a notice reads 'Don't feed the donkey, don't pick the daffodils' – you are unlikely to see either) and John Le Carré. After Boscawen Point the path runs inland a little through high scrub and bracken and then drops right down to the rocky beach at St Loy's Cove, follows the beach for about 50 metres before climbing up quite steeply through a wood and coming out onto the cliffs again just above Merthen Point. There is then a steep drop down to Porthguarnon and a brisk climb up and then down again to **Penberth Cove**, a fisherman's village.

Up out of Penberth, pass the **Logan Rock** and **Treryn Dinas** before dropping down into **Porthcurno**. Climb up out of Porthcurno, past the Minaek Open Air Theatre, past the memorial to the first transatlantic cable at Pedn-Mên-An-Mere (Great Rock Headland). Opposite **St Levan** (inland) you will see the remains of a radio mast. The path skirts **Porthchapel** and dips down to **Porthgwarra** then up again past two red and black land-marks for shipping, a large hole which was formed by the collapse of a cave, and the coastguard look-out, just beyond Gwennap Head.

The path continues to follow the line of the cliffs past the finger of the Black Carn. From here to Land's End you have what is arguably the finest part of the finest stretch of the path. Go around Pendower Cove and **Mill Bay**, leaving an old mine shaft to landward, just after which the boilers of the City of Cardiff, wrecked in 1912, may be seen at low tide rusting away at the foot of the cliffs. Keep to the good cliff-top path close to the sea, and after several intermediate points and bays you come to **Land's End**. Turn right here and follow the well defined coastal path round into **Sennen Cove**.

Gazetteer

BREAGE

If you have time, visit Breage, 3 kilometres North West of
Porthleven. The 15th-century church is dedicated to the Irish
St Breaca, who founded the original settlement. It houses a
rare collection of 15th-century wall-paintings, depicting the
saints, and a touching naked Christ squeezing blood from his
heart onto the tools of different professions. This is known
ominously as 'Warning to the Sabbath Breakers' or, more
benignly, as 'Christ of the Trades'. Two other things to look
for are a Roman milestone inside the church with an inscription referring to Marcus Cassianus Posthumous (258–268)
and, in the churchyard, a sandstone cross. This is the only
example of a four-holed wheel-cross with Hiberno-Saxon
decoration that exists in Cornwall.

TREWAVAS HEAD, GRANITE AND MINING

Trewavas Head is the most easterly of the coastal granite
out-crops. Granite is the magnificent hard rock that has
fashioned much of the dramatic scenery in Cornwall and
Devon. In the great shakedown of the Earth's substance
granite retained its heat longer than the surrounding rocks. As
it cooled it gave off gases and liquids which set against its rocky
neighbours and within the granite itself, forming the seams of
minerals which were to make young Cornwall rich. Tin,
copper, silver were the first to be identified and mined,
drawing traders from Phoenicia (the coastal region of Syria),
Rome and ancient Greece. Wolfram, lead and zinc followed.
The richest mineral deposits occur where granite meets other
rocks, and for this reason Trewavas Head marks the Eastern
coastal limit of Cornwall's mines. The mines were worked
from as early as the Bronze Age, until the 19th and 20th
centuries when the discovery of richer deposits in the Far
East, Africa and South America where labour costs were
lower made operations of the English mines uneconomic.

Climbing up to Trewavas Head you pass Wheal Trewavas
copper mine. Its shafts went far out under the sea and it was
forced to stop production in the middle of the 19th century
when the sea broke through its bed and flooded the submarine
mine. Just beyond the head is another copper mine, Wheal

Prosper, which operated until 1860. It now belongs to the National Trust. Three kilometres inland, due North of Trewavas Head, at Tregonnig Hill, Cookworthy discovered the first English deposits of china clay in 1746. This is another valuable mineral produced in rocks surrounding the cooling granite, and is basically decomposed granite.

PRAA SANDS

A typical holiday development with little charm, it does have facilities for shopping, refreshment and transport.

Just north of Praa Sands is Pengersick, which used to be called Pen-giveras-ike, 'The Head Fort Of The Cove'. Sure enough there is a fortress – a Tudor castle built by Milliton in Henry VIII's reign. Only two towers still stand, but there are interesting allegorical paintings and carvings. Local legend tells how it came to be destroyed – tales of frustrated love, witches, dusky maidens from the East, the young Lord Pengersick and a sun-burnt Bey's revenge.

B&B: Gwynoon, Praa sands; Tel. Germoe (073 676) 2475

Buses: To Helston and Penzance

BESSY'S COVE and PRUSSIA COVE

This is the start of real smuggler's country, a scalloped, craggy coast with countless tricky coves and a wild and desolate hinterland. Here Bessy Burrow kept an inn or, in Cornish, a kiddleywink (an inn licenced only to sell beer but where a wink would get you stronger stuff from underneath the counter). She used the inn for storing smuggled brandy landed in her cove, and next door, in Prussia Cove, the Carter family were raised into a similar profession.

Prussia Cove, formerly called Portleah, was renamed after the King of Prussia Inn, the house John Carter built for himself and his three delinquent sons, John, Charles, and Henry, early in the 18th century. The name was popular for inns at that time and John, who looked like Frederick of Prussia, enjoyed the soubriquet himself. The family formed one of the most successful smuggling bands along the coast. Born seamen, they knew every inch of it and could handle any boat in any seas. Their business made them rich, and John's reputation for fair trading, albeit with goods of doubtful provenance, earned him the grudging respect of the enemy Revenue. Tales of their dashing exploits abound. Acton Castle, a mid-18th century castellated mansion just behind the cove, belonged to the Stackhouse family, local gentry who often gave shelter to the Carters.

A concrete pillar on the point marks the demise of the battleship Warspite, wrecked in the cove in 1947 en route to the breakers yard.

PERRANUTHNOE

The name is derived from St Perranus and is normally shortened to Perran. Although 1.2 kilometres inland, the church of St Piran and St Nicholas is worth a moment's detour. It was substantially rebuilt in the 19th century but the 15th-century tower remains intact. The Perran Inn provides liquid sustenance. A little further inland, at Goldsithney, in noisy contrast to sea and God is the 'World of Entertainment', a unique collection of amusement machines. Occult palm reading machines, test-your-strength devices, magic lanterns, and vast brash Wurlitzer organs, mostly rare and carefully restored intrigue, fascinate, and simply bring back memories. Open Easter to September.

MARAZION

Longevity is Marazion's only feature. It was a market town before Penzance and received its charter early in the Middle Ages. Its name is a source of speculation: was it two towns, Market Zion and Market Jew, or are those names (and today's amalgamation of the two) semitic relics of early visitors from the Eastern Mediterranean? Supporters of the later possibility cite other similar names like Morvah and the fact that miners houses were once called Jews' houses. But that could just as easily be derived from the Cornish words for small 'jew' and big 'zion', although the philological source of these is unclear. I fear that, rather like the sex of angels, the question will remain open for quite some time. Marazion gave way to Penzance in commercial importance but it continued as the base for pilgrims to St Michael's Mount facing it in Mount's Bay.

ST MICHAEL'S MOUNT

The causeway connecting it to Marazion can be used for about an hour either side of high tide. At other times a ferry service operates throughout the season. St Michael's Mount (not the Lizard) may have been the Ocrinum referred to by Ptolemy in the 1st century. It is certainly the Ictus described by Didorus Siculus: the place where the ancient Greek merchants came to trade for tin in the 1st century B.C. Tin was shipped from here to Normandy, then overland to Marseilles, then shipped again to the great Mediterranean destinations of Phoenicia, Greece or ancient Rome.

A Celtic monastery existed there from the 8th century until Edward the Confessor founded a Benedictine Priory on the Mount in 1044, a cell of the Abbey of St Michel in Brittany. Both are named in honour of the saint who appeared to a fisherman of the isle in 495 A.D. After the Norman conquest it passed to the Earl of Mortaigne, who annexed it to the abbey of St Maria de Pericula in Normandy. Henry V (1422–1461) took it when he seized all foreign monasteries on English soil, and Edward VI (1461–1483) transferred it to Sion Abbey. The Arundells were given it in the 16th century at the time of the Dissolution, and the St Aubyn family acquired it in 1659. It has been their seat ever since. The present Lord St Aubyn gave it to the National Trust in 1954 but continues to live in the castle.

The Mount's military history goes back to Richard I (1189–1199), who captured it from Henry de la Pomeroy, in the service of Prince John, on his return from the Crusades. It was seized by the Earl of Oxford in the 15th century, and twice by Cornish rebels in the reign of Edward VI (1547–1553). During the Civil War it held out strongly for the Crown, but eventually fell, and after the Restoration rested peacefully in St Aubyn hands.

Architecturally the buildings belong to no one style or period. The original buildings date from the 12th century but have been much added to and altered. The refectory was part of the original monastery, but the chapel was not built until the 15th century, and when the St Aubyns acquired the island in 1659 they converted the main buildings into a mansion which they continued to 'improve' from then on. Additions were made as recently as 1927.

The rock near the mainland end of the causeway is called Chapel Rock, but a chapel where pilgrims sheltered whilst waiting for the tide to clear the causeway is no longer there. When the giant Cormoran was building St Michael's Mount his wife, Cormelian, was helping him by bringing stone. When the woman arrived with an apron full of serpentine, the short-tempered giant, incensed by her stupidity, (islands are built of granite) struck her dead. She fell, buried beneath the offending load. Marazion has all facilities.

Hotel:	Cutty Sark Inn, The Square; Tel. Marazion (0736) 710334
B&B:	Tolvadden Cottage; Tel. Marazion (0736) 710375
Bus:	To Penzance and Helston
Early closing:	Wednesday

LUDGVAN

Not on the path, but only 3 kilometres north of Marazion, this medieval tin-smelting centre was recorded in the Domesday Book as yet another possession of the Earl of Mortaigne. The church, of Norman foundation, was re-dedicated to St Ludgvan and St Paul in 1336, and the chancel dates from this period. The rest is 15th-century, but the unusual Norman font probably belongs to the original church. In the church are memorials to Christopher Borlase, the Cornish historian (1696–1772), who was rector here for 50 years, and to the inventor of the miner's safety lamp, Sir Humphry Davy, and his family. A few kilometres north east of the village is the Iron Age fort, Castle An Dinas with its three impressive lines of ramparts 230 metres in diameter, and a little further still Chysauster an ancient settlement whose site and houses are carefully preserved.

PENZANCE

An ancient chapel to St Anthony once stood on the point by the pier but nothing of it remains today. Indeed, nothing is very old in Penzance. Sacked by the Spaniards in 1595, none of its buildings is earlier than 17th century. A market town, with an annual fair, in the 14th century, in the 15th century it was exporting wool to Gascony. The only artefact that remains from before 1595 is a crude and ancient cross which stands in Penlee Park.

The town was granted a charter by King John in 1614 and in 1663 was made a Stannary town for the West of England, which it remained until the abolition of the tin tax in 1838. Tin was the fuel of the town's prosperity from the 17th to the mid 19th century, when the Cornish mining industry started to decline and pilchards replaced tin as traffic for the Port. When the pilchard fishing industry also went into decline, tourism took over as the principal livelihood of the town. Penzance is still a small port providing both ferry and helicopter services for the Isles of Scilly.

There are some Georgian and Regency houses to be seen but the bulk of the town, like the Market House at its centre, is Victorian or later. Castle Horneck, now a Youth Hostel on the border of the town, was built for the Borlase family in 1720. Rosecadgehill House was built in the 17th century, Nancealverne House in the 18th, and Lescudjack Castle is not a castle but a very old hill fort overlooking the town from the North East.

The raw newness of Penzance is aesthetically discouraging but there is quite a lot to see. There are several museums and the beautiful Morrab Gardens. Penzance has a sub-tropical tolerance for plants and vegetation, and a fascinating variety of plants grow in both public and private gardens. Trengwainton gardens 1½ kilometres north west of the town have an outstanding display of shrubs which you can visit. The mother-church of Penzance is a little beyond Trengwainton at Madron. St Madern dates from the 14th century but as usual has been considerably added to and altered. There are many pre-historic remains around Madron and St Madron's well was once visited for its curative properties. If you have time you should visit the Scilly Isles, only 2½ hours by boat, or minutes in a helicopter from Penzance.

NEWLYN

This is really a part of Penzance now. It too suffered the indignity of being sacked in 1595 and only the 1435 pier survived that humiliation. Newlyn is still Cornwall's largest fishing town, and its superior harbour facilities have given it the edge on its more distinguished neighbour. If you walk along the quays, you will find the general stores very much as they were in the 19th century, a jumble of clothing, tackle and other sailorly things and full of evocative smells of rope and tar and the sea. But there is nothing 'olde worlde' about the docks themselves, with their ultra modern trucks, refrigeration facilities, hi-tech trawlers and busy, bustling fishermen and dockers. Just down the road is the Penlee quarry, one of the most important sources of greenstone in Europe, used in building roads and as the ballast between the rails on railway lines.

Newlyn preceded St Ives as a centre for artists in Cornwall. The Newlyn School was founded here in 1884 by Walter Langley, Edward Harris and the others in imitation of their impressionist friends across the Channel who painted at the seaside of Normandy and Brittany. A large art gallery, built there by Passmore Edwards in 1895, is open to visitors.

Both Penzance and Newlyn have all the facilities associated with a modern country town, and both cater for tourists. Penzance also has the train.

Hotel:	The Abbey Hotel; Tel. Penzance (0736) 66906
B&B:	The Yacht Inn; Tel. Penzance (0736) 2787
YHA:	Castle Horneck, Alverton; Tel. Penzance (0736) 2666
Early closing:	Wednesday (Newlyn and Penzance)
Tourist Information:	Tel. Penzance (0736) 2343
Buses:	All major destinations
Trains:	Plymouth and London

PAUL

You pass through this village if you take the alternative route avoiding the main road. The village is named after St Pol de Leon, a Cornishman who became a Breton Saint and was victim of the Spaniards in 1595, so little of the original village exists. The 15th-century church of St Paul was rebuilt in the 17th century. Dolly Pentreath, the last person to speak Cornish as her mother tongue, is buried in the churchyard, and part of the inscription on her grave is in Cornish. The Hutchens Almshouses beside the churchyard were built in 1709.

MOUSEHOLE

The locals pronounce it 'mowzel', and if you're asking for directions you'd be well advised to do the same. In 1337 the

Duchy of Cornwall designated the port the most important fishery harbour in West Cornwall. Pilgrims sailed from here to the Holy Land and to Santiago. Salt for the pilchard industry was imported through the port and the oil extracted from the fish exported from it. Maritime courts were held there, and an artificial harbour was built and can be seen today, although there are very few working boats among the pleasure craft, but the port is still closed against bad weather with the huge wooden door.

Mousehole was called Port Enys – port of the island – and this could be a reference to St Clement's Isle opposite, once inhabited by a hermit. It has all facilities, shops, post office, accommodation, refreshment and transport.

Hotel:	Lobster Pot; Tel. Mousehole (073 673) 251
B&B:	Revovelle, Mousehole (no number available write to Mrs Bartlett)
Bus:	To Penzance.

PENZER POINT

The 4068 ton steamer Ansgir ended her short life on these rocks. Completed in a German yard just at the end of the Great War, she was immediately handed over to Britain in 1918 as part of the reparations. In 1920 she set sail under the British flag to North America with a cargo and then to France with another. In France the captain was told that the ship had been transferred to Japan as part of that country's war reparations. This time he got no further than Penzer Point, which he struck in a howling gale. The crew were saved and the ship hung on to the rocks for nearly a year before finally sinking.

LAMORNA COVE

This is one of the most beautiful coves on the Cornish coast. The Lamorna river flows sweetly down the pretty wooded valley to join waters with the sea just here. The village of Lamorna, with its quaint cottages and its colony of artists, is strung slightly inland along the valley. Up there, too, is the Lamorna Inn, another Cornish 'kiddleywink', where a wink to the innkeeper would get you stronger stuff than the beer, which was all he was authorized to sell. In fact this inn was known as 'The Wink', and its sign shows a patron tipping the wink. The village used to be a fishing village, but like many others had to learn to live on her charms. Luckily she has many and is famous as a beauty spot. In addition to the inn there is a post office stores and the smart Lamorna Cove Hotel (Tel. 073 673 411).

Tragedy struck the peaceful spot in December 1981, when the Mousehole Lifeboat went to the aid of the coaster Union Star. The ship, on her maiden voyage, was driven on to the rocks between Lamorna Cove and Mousehole. The lifeboat capsized and was washed up in Lamorna Cove, after taking 4 people off the ship. All the members of the lifeboat crew and all on board the coaster drowned, including the captain's wife and his two teenage daughters. The public responded by contributing £3 million to a fund set up for the dependents of the lifeboat's eight crew members.

MERRY MAIDENS, PIPERS AND PRE HISTORY

North-west of Lamorna, on either side of the B3315, are two curious sites. South of the road is the stone circle known as the Merry Maidens. The 19 stones are Bronze Age, about 3500 years old. In stony morality, these stones are really 19 young girls who were foolish enough to dance on a Sunday. They were punished by being turned to stone. It wasn't outright misogyny; their accomplices, the pipers who played for them, are just across the road, on the northern side, condemned to stony stoicism in the very same way. A short way off, and unrelated to that salutary tale, is Tregiffian Entrance Grave, another Bronze Age artefact. It already had an occupant when it was found, so it wasn't meant to harbour sinners. Until the charred remains of the burial were found, some thought that it might be an Iron Age meat safe similar to those found on Skomer Island and in the Hebrides – trenches lined with stone and covered with salt slats, in which dried meat was preserved for winter consumption. The grave was used by Royalists during the Civil War to hide from Fairfax.

TREWOOFE AND ST BURYAN

There is a 17th-century farmhouse at Trewoofe with a 16th-century doorway. Nearby is an 18th-century clapper corn mill.

St Buryan is a little to the west of Trewoofe, still well off the path. Pevsner described the church of St Berian as 'one of the proudest churches of West Cornwall'. It was built after the previous church was demolished in 1473, in the Perpendicular style. Only the tower of its 13th-century predecessor was kept and incorporated in the new building. The collegiate church of St Berian had been founded by King Athelstan (925–940) and re-founded by Bishop Brewer of Exeter in 1238, which explains its grandeur. A 13th-century memorial inside the church commemorates Clarice de Bolleit in Norman French.

SHIPWRECKS

This part of the coast down to Land's End has been particularly cruel to ships and their sailors. A treacherous rocky shore, jagged rocks peppered at random in the sea, unpredictable, often violent weather, and the hand of man, who sometimes assisted nature in her devilish schemes, has caused catastrophe to countless ships. Lamorna Cove has claimed more than the Penlee lifeboat and from there to Porthcurno the toll has been heavy. Public agitation brought about the installation of the 30,000 candlepower automatic lighthouse at Tater Du in 1965. Just before you come to the lighthouse you cross the property of the writer Derek Tangye. This stretch of coast has always been England's market garden for early flowers, and Tangye and his wife fled the rat-race of post-war London to come here to create these early spring treasures and to write in tranquillity, beauty and peace.

PENBERTH

The National Trust owns this little group of granite fisherman's cottages. They have done their best to preserve it as the typical fishing community. They rent the cottages only to working fishermen and reserve the slipway for them. You can sometimes rent a room in one of the cottages. Try Mrs George of Fernleigh (Tel. 073 672 281).

TRERYN DINAS AND THE LOGAN ROCK

Treryn Dinas means 'fortress settlement'. This one is just beyond Penberth Cove and, like the cove, it was given to the National Trust in 1933 by Sir Courtenay Vyvyan of Trelowarren, whose family had owned it for 800 years. An Iron Age promontory fort, it is composed of three inner ramparts protected by a high outer one, all of different periods. It commands good views up and down the coast as well as inland.

In the rocky mess below it you can distinguish one huge rock balancing precariously on another. That is the Logan Rock. 'Log' is the Cornish for 'move', and the Logan rock could be rocked with one finger, but could not be toppled. At least that's what they said. But *they* had not counted on Lieutenant Goldsmith, commander of H.M.S. Nimble and nephew of Oliver Goldsmith the poet. In 1824 he took a party of his sailors and dislodged the stone. Public outcry was so great that the Admiralty mounted an enquiry and ordered Goldsmith to replace the stone at his own cost. It took several months and cost him a small fortune (the accounts for the operation can be seen in the Morrab Library in Penzance). On the 1 November 1824, after several months and an expenditure of £130.8.6, the rock was back in place, and Goldsmith never rose above the rank of Lieutenant.

PORTHCURNO

Almost midway between the Logan Rock and Porthcurno a white pyramid marks the place where the first transatlantic cable came ashore in 1880, linking England with the American continent via the Compagnie Francaise du Telegraphe's cable from Brest. In 1919 the cable was moved to the Eastern Telegraph Company's hut further down the cliff near Porthcurno where it remained operational until 1962.

Porthcurno was known to cable-men everywhere as 'P.K.', and at one time 14 lines came ashore here. Today it is the site of the Cable and Wireless Company's engineering college. On the headland of Pedn-Mên-An-Mere, just beyond the village, are the remains of a radio mast by which Cable and Wireless attempted to monitor the experiments of Marconi, which culminated in the transmission of the first wireless message from Poldhu to Newfoundland in 1901. Not the first case of industrial espionage by any means, but a nice early electronic one.

On the headland to the west of the village is the Minack Open Air Theater – a brilliant jewel in a perfect setting. It would be reminiscent of the classical sites of Greece or Rome, if the weather were a shade warmer. The experience of sitting in Minack's privileged site looking out to sea, the last light of a perfect summer's night fading softly in the west, players giving their enthusiastic all to entertain you with *The Tempest* or *The Pirates Of Penzance* on the stage below, is unforgettable.

ST LEVAN

The Norman church was named after the 5th-century Breton Saint, St Selvan, whose baptistry lies in ruins at St Levan's Well nearby. The church was added to in the 13th and 15th centuries. There is a fine Celtic cross in the church yard, as well as a monument to Captain Henry Rothery and the crew of the Khyber, who went down in a gale off Tol-Pedn-Penwith in March 1905. Only three of the crew of 20 were saved and at that time it was the worst disaster recorded at Land's End.

Tol-Pedn-Penwith is the Cornish name for Gwennap Head (which sounds pretty Cornish itself). It means 'holed headland of Penwith', and Penwith is one of the nine administrative districts, or hundreds, into which Cornwall was divided. No one knows how the hundreds came into existence, but the list goes back to the 11th century and the hundreds themselves still further. The hole in Tol-An-Pedn was caused by another cave collapse, similar to that of the Devil's Frying Pan further east. This one is 30 metres deep and 2.5 metres across, and the sea rushing into it makes a most fearful noise.

THE RUNNEL STONE

This independent rock, far out off Gwennap Head, gave headaches to more than one ship's captain until the City of Westminster took the top off it in 1923. The 6,000 ton ship was a total loss but all on board were saved. The Runnel Stone's granite tip is now 6 metres below the surface, and no ship has struck it since. Between 1880 and 1923 alone more than 30 steamers and heaven knows how many sailing ships had come off second best in brushes with it.

MILL BAY

This is also called Nanjizal. There are the ruins of a mill once used for crushing both corn and ore. Close by is a disused mine shaft. At the western end of the bay the rusting metal you can see on the rocks is what remains of the boilers of the steam ship City of Cardiff – a 3,089 ton collier which struck Carn Boel in 1912. Everyone on board was saved, but the sea made short work of the ship, breaking her up completely in under 24 hours.

LAND'S END

Land's End is not the most westerly point of England. Dr Syntax' Head, a few metres further on is. The Cornish name for Land's End is 'Pedn an Laaz', the 'End of the Earth', which takes the misconception one stage further. Ptolemy called it 'Belerion' and wrote of it as such in his geographical works; the Romans knew it as 'Bolerium', so as not to plagiarize the Greek. Dr Syntax' Head probably got its name from William Combe's (1742–1843) satirical traveller Dr Syntax, about whom he wrote three 'tours'. Rowlandson created an amusing series of cartoons around him, copies of which can still be found as coloured engravings.

Land's End, depressingly down at heel and vulgar, is a tourist trap which deserves to be hurried past, eyes cast firmly down or turned fixedly out to sea. But all that is going to change. Charles Neave-Hill, whose family had owned the land since the 17th century, sold Land's End to a Welsh millionaire, David Goldstone in 1981. (The reason he sold had nothing to do with the £2 million or so he received for it. He simply felt no longer able to safeguard the future of the site and of the community of Sennen Village.) The new owner intends to spend a further £3.5 million recovering the site and creating a . . . 'tasteful tourist complex'.

Two kilometres off Land's End are the Longships Rocks, a name which goes back to Viking times. Since 1795 a lighthouse has warned sailors, not always successfully, of the rocks. In 1898 the 2,205 ton steamer Bluejacket went on to the rocks where it perched for 14 months under the lighthouse, swaying like an unhappy seesaw.

MAEN CASTLE

The Castle is another finely preserved promontory fort handed down to us from the Iron Age. It is well sited: the two ramparts and the ditch cover the promontory and have only one entrance. Pieces of Iron Age pottery have been found there.

Close by is the granite pinnacle known as the Irish Lady, after a protestant noble-woman who fled James II's persecution in Ireland and whose ship was wrecked. She showed the tenacity of her class and race by clinging to the rock until dawn. Alas she finally disappeared beneath the waves.

SENNEN COVE

This has developed as the tourist centre for Land's End, with shops, hotels pubs and night life as well as all the normal daytime seaside distractions. A few fishermen can still be seen, inhabitants left over from a more suitable age when the village was the fishing port for Sennen. It was a fishing village as far back as 1086 when the Domesday book records that it had a salt works. Evidence has also been found of Roman occupation. St Sennen's church in Sennen Churchtown is 13th-century with 14th-century additions. Fragments of a sculpture of the Virgin and Child are 13th-century, and the font has an inscription dated 1441. It was on a rock a little to the north of the church that King Arthur and his knights celebrated the defeat of the last Viking invasion, feasting on the big flat table rock called Table-men.

Sennen Cove has all the facilities associated with a holiday resort.

Hotel:	Old Success Inn; Tel. Sennen (073 687) 232
B&B:	Myrtle Cottage; Tel. Sennen (073 687) 466
Bus:	To Penzance
Early closing:	Thursday

11

Sennen to Portreath

*Behind the house rose the great sweep of towans, many times
larger than those between Church Cove and Cury Churchtown,
and stretching for most of the length of St Ives Bay, being
bounded on the west by St Ives itself and on the east by Godrevy
lighthouse below the cliffs of Dead Man's Cove. To my
pleasure I saw that the towans at the back of Riviere were
covered with cowslips.*

*Mostly these towans presented to the beach a low line of
serrated cliffs some thirty feet high; from time to time they
would break away to gullies full of fine, drifted sand, whose
small cavities hoarded snail-shells wind-dried to an ethereal
lightness and rabbit-bones bleached and honey-combed by
weather. The beach itself was at low water a very wide and flat
and completely desolate expanse, shining near the sea's edge
with whatever gold or silver was in the air, shot with crimson
bars at sunset, crinkled by the wind to a vast replica of one of its
own shells, ribbed and ploughed by tempests.*

MACKENZIE, Sir Compton (1883–1972). Novelist. Extract
from *My Life and Times* published by Chatto & Windus,   .

Introduction

This is a stretch of fine, rugged walking, less dramatic than the
previous section but with attractive coastal scenery once you
have left mines and holiday resorts behind. After following
the beach of Whitesand Bay the path takes to the cliffs again.
From Porth Nanven it follows roads – from time to time
through mine workings – and there are one or two steep climbs
and descents. After Pendeen the path is generally wild,

desolate and magnificent, running along the cliff top and crossing bleak moorland. There is no refreshment or refuge on the path for over 30 kilometres until St Ives; so be prepared. From St Ives to the other side of Hayle, and indeed to the northern end of Gwithian Towans, the path is of little interest and, if the St Ives – Hayle ferry is not running, could involve quite a lot of road walking. The walk around Godrevy Point and on to Portreath is high, open cliff walking with some steep climbs and superb scenery.

Minerals occur where changes in rock structure from killas to granite have allowed minerals to spurt up from the earth's molten core, and this is mining country. The Land's End Peninsula is virtually solid granite meeting Lower Devonian slates and so on at its neck. A thin strip of this Lower Devonian lines the north coast of the peninsula from Porth Narven to St Ives, and some outcrops of miscellaneous igneous rocks occur as well. It is the meeting of this strip with the main granite mass that has given rise to the intensive mining activity along the coast.

The Hayle Estuary has one positive quality: it is a satisfying area for bird-watchers. Navax Point is another, particularly for watching birds migrating in summer and autumn. There are sometimes seals along this coast and they often bask near the Carracks rocks off Mussel Point. Apart from the mass and variety of sea birds, other wildlife is rare.

The mines themselves, proof of an industrial activity going back over thousands of years, are almost museums of mining technique and of industrial architecture. Some, like Geevor and Levant, are still in operation, whereas parts of others have been preserved as part of England's industrial heritage. Going further back in time, the area abounds in antiquities; stone circles, chamber tombs, promontory forts and so on are everywhere, and more modern settlements, like St Ives, Zennor and Gwithian, also have their contributions to make to the architectural and social portrait of the area.

Guide

Go out of Sennen along the sea front road which ends at Whitesand Bay. The path continues on behind the beach for about 1½ kilometres and at the northern end climbs up to go around Aire Point. You will pass Carn Aire and then go

STAGE	CUMUL.	TIME	SENNEN TO PORTREATH	TELEPHONE	TRAIN	BUS	FERRY	SHOPS	CAMPING	ACCOMMODATION	REFRESHMENT	CUMUL. DIST. KMS
			SENNEN	x		x		x	x	x	x	546
(2)		(:30)	(ST JUST)	x		x		x	x	x	x	
(1)		(:15)	(BOTALLACK)	x		x		x	x	x	x	
12	12	4:	PENDEEN	x				x	x	x	x	558
6	18	1:30	PORTHMEOR									564
(1)		(:15)	(ZENNOR)	x		x				x	x	
13	31	4:15	ST IVES	x	x	x		x	x	x	x	577
5	36	1:15	LELANT	x	x	x		x			x	582
3	39	:45	HAYLE	x	x				x	x	x	585
(6)		(1:30)	(CAMBORNE)	x	x	x			x	x	x	
(6)		(1:30)	(REDRUTH)	x	x	x			x	x	x	
18	57	4:30	PORTREATH	x		x			x	x	x	602

TIMES ARE BASED ON AVERAGE WALKER LIGHTLY LADEN.

NB.
1. *STAGE: is the distance between that point and the preceding point.*
2. *CUMUL.: is the cumulative distance from the beginning of the chapter.*
3. *TIME: is the time for the stage (between that point and the preceding one) calculated at 4 kilometres per hour – the rate for a lightly loaded person walking without halt.*
4. *Brackets enclose places not on the Path but easily reached from it, together with distances and times from the Path.*
5. *CUMULATIVE DISTANCE: is the total distance from South Haven Point.*

seaward of a mine; dip down to cross a stream by the Maen Dower Rocks, and on over the cliffs around Polpry Cove, before going down – taking care to stay above the land-fall – across Gribba Point. Carry on down, finally by way of steps, to Porth Nanven. Here the path goes inland along the road (which leads to St Just) for about 300 metres, before climbing back across the hillside, past an unfenced mine shaft, up to **Carn Gloose**. Then, following an unmade road, the path goes down past Priest's Cove and on to the car park and the mine chimney at Cape Cornwall. (From here a road leads inland to St Just.)

The path goes around the car park, inland along the road, past the chapel and then down behind Porth Ledden to cross the stream. The official route goes inland close to the ruins of Kenidjack Mines to make the crossing. It then climbs back along the sides of Zawn Buzz and Gen, partly on tracks, towards North Zawn Headland, with its **Kenidjack** cliff castle. It is possible, after leaving the track past the chapel on **Cape Cornwall**, to head straight down, cross the stream on large boulders near its mouth, and climb straight up the other side again towards the castle. The path climbs up over the cliffs above Wheal Edward Zawn, on an old mining road for a couple of hundred metres, to pass seaward of **Botallack**. It then continues on old unmade roads, through country marked by generations of copper and tin miners, passing in succession Botallack mine, the Crowns Mine, **Levant Mine** (from which a road leads inland to Pendeen), and the **Geevor Mine**. This last is still in operation and also works some of the Levant property.

Passing through Geevor, head for the three tall chimneys above Trewellard Zawn. Shortly after passing them, you leave the mine road and continue along the cliffs past the Avarack Point and down to cross a stream. Here it is possible to turn left along the north side of the valley and climb around the cliffs to **Pendeen Watch**. The path, however, crosses the stream and climbs inland slightly to join the road from Pendeen, which serves the lighthouse. Turn left along the road, pass inland of the Pendeen Watch Lighthouse, seaward of disused mine workings and on along the cliff tops.

Go past the Kenidjack rocks, down around Portheras Cove, up around its northern limit and then inland a little, through open pastures, following the general line of the cliffs past Blinker's Bed and Greeb Point. The path now turns inland to go around the head of Morvah Cliff. (From here a sunken path leads inland for 400 metres to the hamlet of **Morvah**.) The path bends back on to the cliff top, across National Trust land, past the Manankas Rocks, landward of an exposed disused mine shaft, down to cross a stream and up around Whirlpool and past Brandys Rocks. It now descends steeply to cross the stream above Porthmoina Cove before climbing up to the Headland of **Bosigran Castle**.

Since the cliffs here are popular with climbers, there are many well-worn tracks which could lead the unwary astray. Your path cuts across the neck of the headland and continues along as a good, grassy, cliff-top path around Halldrine Cove, past Great Zawn and steeply down to **Porthmeor Cove**.

Climb up out of the cove, along the cliff, past Porthmeor

Point, heading north-east towards the long finger of **Gurnards Head**, with its coastguard look-out and the Iron Age cliff castle of Trereen Dinas. The path cuts across the neck of the Head, crossing a footpath inland to **Treen**, and follows the cliffs round and down into Treen Cove. It then climbs up over Lean Point, across another stream and up over the headland and down, again crossing two further streams, around Porthglaze Cove. It goes on seaward past more disused mine workings and up on to the cliffs around Veor Cove. Down then to Pendour Cove, to a bridge which takes you over the stream to a road leading inland to **Zennor**.

The path now climbs up along the cliffs to Zennor Head, 95 metres, National Trust property. Go around the Head and down, behind Porth-Zennor Cove, on down along the cliffs to cross two streams in a narrow coomb. Climb up slightly and on down past Gala Rocks, to cross another stream by **Wicca Pool**, where the path climbs again around the cliffs at Mussel Point. Continue up past the Carracks, two imposing rocks off-shore, and down to cross the stream by River Cove. The path now climbs up to Ting Point on Trevega Cliff, above Carn Naun Point, from which there are fine views. It then continues along the cliff top past Brae Cove, the abrupt Polgassick Cove, and across the neck of the National Trust property of Hor Point. Go on down, past a number of nameless coves, to Clodgy Point, where you turn right, past Carrick Du Point, to pass behind Porthmeor Beach. Go around the western end of the putting green, along Fore Street and into St Ives.

Continue along the main road around the harbour, past the railway station, keeping between the railway and the sea behind Porthminster Beach, until you cross over the line just before Porthminster Point. Continue close to the landward side of the track until you cross to seaward again just before Carbis Bay. Then go on between railway and beach, around Carrack Gladden, along Porthkidney Sands, by the golf course. Cross over again at the mouth of the Hayle Estuary and walk close to the landward side of the track, past **Lelant** and on the A3074 main road to the head of the estuary. Cross the track again, go around the estuary and, on the A30, into **Hayle**. Having done this, however, you may wonder why you did not take a bus from St Ives.

Cross over the canal on the bridge and go out of Hayle, keeping close to the estuary shore, past the harbour and the power station, around past the mouth of the estuary itself to Black Cliff. You now have a 4 kilometre walk along the sands of St Ives Bay. You will find it easier along the beach than through the dunes. At Strap Rocks the path goes inland to the village of **Gwithian** and then north along the road to cross the Red River, before turning seawards again along its northern bank towards Magow Rocks. At low tide it is possible to walk straight across the Towans to avoid this detour.

The path continues on along the road to Godrevy and on around **Godrevy Point**. Then it follows the coast to the Trig Point at Navax Point, 76 metres, National Trust property, and around above Fishing Cove to the National Trust property of Hell's Mouth, whose sheer dark cliffs and seething seas look just like their name. The path remains a good open cliff path with fine coastal scenery, passing above Deadman Cove, Greenbank Cove, Basset's Cove, across Reskajeage Downs before dropping down steeply to cross one and then another stream on Carvannel Downs by Porth-Cadiack Cove. Climb up from the cove onto the downs once more, past Ralph's Cupboard and The Horse, around Tregea Hill, with Gull Rock off-shore, and down around the beach into **Portreath**.

Gazetteer

WHITESAND BAY

Abbot Sinnius came from Brittany with his friends, Germochus and Breaca, and settled here to live. He gave his name to Sennen. King Athelstan landed here in 980, triumphant after his conquest of the Scillies, and King John returned here after exercising his malignant folly on Ireland at the end of the 12th century. Today a host of happy holiday makers surf and swim along the 1½ kilometres of fine white sand.

Mining debris and disused mines appear about the path fairly soon after crossing Whitesand Bay, as does a wealth of pre-historic remains.

ST JUST

A path leads inland from Aire Point to Land's End (St Just) airport – a private airport with flights to the Scilly Isles and elsewhere. From Porth Nanven, there is a road which takes you to the Land's End Youth Hostel (Letcha Vean, St Just, Penzance; Tel: Penzance (0736) 788437) and into St Just.

St Just was another Breton, a monk and brother of St Selvan. It is just possible that St Selvan is buried in the church but no one is sure. The town is ancient and was probably already important in Saxon times, but it was as a centre for tin and copper mining in the west of Cornwall that St Just grew to its present size.

The church of St Just is 15th-century, although it has a couple of details pointing to earlier times. A Romano-Christian grave-stone with Selus Ic Jacet inscribed on one side, and a cross on the reverse was found walled into the chancel. Adventurous thinkers have stretched Selus to Selvan to introduce their theory of St Selvan's burial here. The shaft of a Hiberno-Saxon style cross was found in the north wall of the North Aisle, and two medieval wall paintings recall those at Breage and Porthleven. One is of St George and the other shows Christ surrounded once more by tools. The open air theatre in the centre of the town is one of only five to survive in Cornwall. They were used to boost the moral spirit of the community by the showing of miracle plays until well into the 17th century. The town has all facilities.

CAPE CORNWALL AND CARN GLOOSE

Just after Porth Nanven, the coast path passes seaward of Carn Gloose, the site of a memorial to a people we have not seen, a culture we may never know. Indeed, the age of these stones has not been accurately assessed. This cavernous chamber, 4.5 metres under its dome, with a pit beneath it cut 2.5 metres down into the living rock, remains an enigma. Seven burial cysts, an amulet, lambs' bones and some pottery shards were found when the site was excavated a century ago. Although the shards are Bronze Age, the tomb itself could well be neolithic. There are stone circles at Botallack and Tregeseal, inland and a little further north, which are surely Iron Age.

Cape Cornwall is the only cape on the map of England and is really rather more impressive and very much less spoilt than its precocious neighbour, Land's End, which sticks out a few hundred metres more further west. The chimney on its summit was a ventilation shaft for Cape Cornwall Mine, which closed in 1870. The chimney bored down to the workings below, a fire kept going at its base forced great draughts of air up the shaft and so improved the circulation of fresh air. Down the hill is the site of St Helen's Chapel; its actual date is not known but it was certainly there in Roman times. Only the outline of the building, however, remains today.

KENIDJACK

This is another Iron Age cliff castle dominating the coast north of Cape Cornwall and providing both home and protection for the early settlers. Inland, up the valley, Wheal Owles (or Kenidjack) mine produced copper until 1893, when flooding killed 23 miners and prompted the closure of the mine.

On either side of Kenidjack Castle the inlets are called 'Zawn'. This is a word you will meet frequently along this mining coast. A zawn was a copper or tin-bearing lode which, since it was softer than the surrounding rock, wore away into a gully, giving access to the shore. Mining has turned them into steep and ragged corridors which are always precarious and often impassable.

BOTALLACK MINE

You will probably recognize this engine house at once, perched on the side of the cliff ten metres above the Atlantic. It is one of the most photographed mines in the West. Queen Victoria visited it in 1846, although she had to wait on the top while Prince Albert went down below. The mine went down 130 metres, ran 165 metres out under the sea and twice as far as that in its inland tunnels. A flourish of patriotic pride in 1873 made the Imperial Gazetteer declare that it was altogether as wonderful a work as the Great Pyramid of Egypt. You can judge for yourself.

The Manor House in Botallack village, 1 kilometre inland, is an unusual 'L' shape. It was built in 1665. The village has a public telephone, facilities for accommodation and refreshment during licensing hours and a small shop (with odd opening hours) on the camp site.

B&B: Manor Farm, Botallack; Tel. Penzance (0736) 788525

LEVANT MINE

This was one of the largest mines in the area, over 600 metres deep and going more than 1½ kilometres out under the sea. It had a complicated platform lift for the miners to get from level to level. The lift consisted of two reciprocating series of platforms worked by an engine; one set descended as the other rose. It saved the miners a lot of leg-work on ladders between the different levels but in 1919, the engine failed and 31 men died, bringing about the closure of the mine. However, parts of it have been re-opened and are being worked by the Geevor mine next door.

GEEVOR MINE

This is the biggest mine still producing tin in the West Country and it also exploits part of the Levant and Boscaswell Mines. You get quite an eerie feeling as you walk through the workings from Levant past Geevor, the sea permanently discoloured with the effluent and the ground looking rather like archaeological excavations in Arabia. In a way it is an historical site: the impact of mining on Cornwall was at least as important as the effect of the pyramid building in Egypt, although much smaller and with rather less colourful artefacts. Geevor has one of the big steam beam engines, built in 1840, and now preserved, with four others, by the National Trust. It can be visited by arrangement with the Trust's office in Bodmin or by calling the manager of the Geevor Mine; Tel. Penzance (0736) 78862.

PENDEEN

Only the church is of interest in the village and that only because it was designed by the parson and built by the villagers themselves in 1851.

Pendeen Watch is another rocky headland sticking proudly out to sea. Inevitably, it too has been the site of many wrecks, particularly of colliers south-bound from Wales. Many of these have ended their working lives striking the rocks in fog whilst seeking the open seas around Land's End. A lighthouse was built here in 1900 but in spite of that the toll remains quite high.

Pendeen House lies inland of the Watch, its entrance left off the made-up road. The house is a good example of a 16th-century Cornish farmhouse and was the home of the first great Cornish archaeologist, William Borlase. He was born there in 1695 and died there in 1772.

It was probably the presence of the Iron Age fogu in his yard that determined the course young William's life was to take.

The fogu is a Celtic food-store more than 2,000 years old. It is easy to imagine the youngster's enthusiasm being fired as he stepped down into that stone-faced, stone-roofed, sloping passage. It runs 7 metres north-east into a 7 metre chamber, cut into the clay, then turns north-west as another passage for 10 more metres before opening into a field. The exit is now blocked but if you ask at the farm you can visit it.

MORVAH

Inland due south of Greeb Point, the name's semitic ring has caused much speculation, none of which has been resolved. The hamlet has a 14th-century church – St Bridget or St Morwetha, depending on your taste. For Pevsner's taste, who makes no choice in the matter of the name, the 19th-century nave and chancel are more interesting than the church's 14th-century tower – even though it is a mite unbuttressed for its years. It defies the Church Commissioners' ruling on style at that time, having been built without an aisle and of rough granite, in a clear attempt to masquerade as medieval.

Castle Chun is a Danish hill fort just south of Morvah. It is the only stone-built fort in Cornwall. Its two concentric stone-built ramparts, 3 metres high, have only one entrance each, and excavations have revealed huts within the ramparts which show that they were raised to protect a settlement of early tin smelters.

The area is rich in pre-historic sites. On the same hill, Chun Quoit a Megalithic burial chamber capped by a massive stone 2½ metres square, lies at the centre of a round barrow, 10.7 metres in diameter.

Lanyon Quoit, 3 kilometres south-east of Morvah, is another Megalithic chamber. This one lies at the end of a barrow 27 metres long and 12 metres wide and is capped by a 9 metre square stone, even bigger than Chun Quoit.

Mên-an-Tol, the Holed Stone or the Crick Stone, another Megalithic tomb, lies just 1 kilometre north of Lanyon Quoit. Crawl through it nine times against the sun and your illness will be cured. (John Hillaby tried it on his journey through Britain but I am not sure that he gave himself the full dose of nine.) Due north of this, heading for the coast, Bosigran Castle, another Iron Age fort, stands on Bosigran Head looking out to sea.

PORTHMEOR

A Romano-British courtyard settlement has been excavated here and twenty similar sites have been found in the 30 square kilometres around Morvah and Zennor. These were farmers' houses, although some evidence of tin smelting on the premises has been found. Each courtyard house was surrounded by circular huts, whose purpose is not clear, but they may have been farm buildings or work-shops. Porthmeor has two courtyard houses, and coins dating from 160 to 180 A.D. have been found in the area of the settlement. Ask at Porthmeor Farm if you wish to visit the site.

GURNARD'S HEAD

Trereen Dinas, another promontory fort, had two groups of Iron Age huts within its inner rampart. The rampart still stands, 2 metres high, and you can trace the stones of the huts it sheltered. If all this pre-historic delving has made you thirsty, the Gurnard Head Hotel is only a few hundred metres inland.

ZENNOR

A road leads 1 kilometre inland from Pendour Cove to Zennor village, where the Tinner's Arms will give you refreshment, and tell you something of the village's past. St Sennen Church belonged to Tywardreath Priory in the 12th century, then one of the chief monastic houses in Cornwall. In 1270 it was given to Glasney College by its founder, Bishop Bronescombe. Now it is just the Parish church; partly Norman but added to up until the 15th century.

Zennor Folk Museum is housed in an old mill just south of the Tinner's Arms. A private collection of old mining and domestic tools, furniture and equipment, farm implements and models of a tin mine, illustrate Cornish life back to pre-historic times.

Zennor Quoit, 1 kilometre east of Zennor, is a massive Megalithic Chamber tomb. Although it looks much as it was when Borlase discovered it in the 18th century, it was pretty roughly handled in modern times.

One local farmer took away the upright pillars to make a cart shed, then another blew it up with dynamite. Although a little clumsy, he might have done pre-history a service. His explosion revealed a perforated whetstone similar to others found in early Bronze Age graves, and probably 3,500 years old. The tomb itself could be a thousand years older still. Most of it has been put back together, although one end of the capstone is resting on the ground, and the round barrow, which used to cover it, has almost totally disappeared. The Sperris Quoit is a similar chamber 350 metres to the east.

At Pennance, north of Zennor, the Giant's House is another similar pre-historic tomb. Its chamber is 4 metres long and covered by a barrow. Eight hundred metres south and west, four other round barrows mark the place of tombs. Two of them still have large stone chambers inside.

The Nine Maidens south-west of Zennor are no relation to those close to Lamorna. Indeed here there are 11 stone pillars in the circle and a Bronze Age barrow cuts the circle on its southern side. However, the story is the same: wicked girls found dancing on a Sunday and turned to stone for shame.

D.H. Lawrence lived in Zennor from the end of December 1916 to October 1917. After his arrival he thought about establishing his long-dreamed of Utopia on the Black Rocks of the Peninsula and persuaded Katherine Mansfield and John Murry to come to Zennor from their house in Bandol. They soon saw that northern Cornwall in a war-time British April bore little resemblance to the south of France. They left and the Lawrences were eventually expelled. The locals, zenophobic and suspicious at the best of times, thought Lawrence's German wife a spy. Lawrence and she used to sing German folk songs in the evenings. Finally a careless blackout and, coincidentally, a German submarine seen cruising off Zennor Head, caused them to be banished from the county.

B&B: Boswednack Manor Farm, Zennor; Tel.
            Penzance (0736) 794183
Bus: To St Ives

WICCA POOL

Lifeboatmen have to be admired; like firemen they can be called upon at any moment to put their lives at risk for the safety of others. We tend to think of this only when a tragedy occurs. The Penlee disaster is a recent example. In January 1939 Wicca Pool saw another; the steamer, Wilston, ran into difficulties in a 150 kilometre per hour gale. St Ives Lifeboat went to her aid, capsized three times and was smashed to pieces on Godrevy Rocks with the loss of all eight lives but one. Meanwhile, the 3218 tons of the Wilston were being subjected to the same cruel treatment. By morning, only her cylinder head and boilers were distinguishable among the mass of twisted metal. All 34 crew were drowned.

The Bessemer City met a similar, if slower fate there in October 1936. That time there was no loss of life but the hardy locals, proud descendants of stout smuggling stock, made short work of her cargo. Larders from Zennor Head to Newquay were stocked for months with tinned fruit and salmon, dried raisins, currants and sultanas.

ST IVES

St Ia, the missionary daughter of an Irish King, landed in the Hayle estuary and persuaded a local lord to build a church. The church was given her name and the town which grew around it became St Ives. The first town was on the promontory to the east, Porthminster Point. But that was overcome by drifting sand, and the ruined walls lie silent now beneath the railway, whilst the modern town has grown up further to the north and west, closer to the sea.

It is from the sea that St Ives first earned its living. By 1377 it had taken over from Lelant as the most important port of West Cornwall. In 1487 the town became a borough with the right to hold a market and two fairs, and in the same year, Sir Willoughby de Broke built the first pier. A second pier was built in 1770 by Smeaton, fresh from his construction of the Eddystone Light, and a third pier was built in 1894. In the 19th century, St Ives vied with Newlyn for the title of premier pilchard port, but mining too was of importance. Sadly, both industries were destined to decline and die before the century was out.

The closing years of the 19th century brought a hint of the new trade which was to save the town. Artists found St Ives and established there the most important colony of outdoor artists in the country. Their names are household words: Sickert and Whistler, Ben Nicholson, Barbara Hepworth and the potter, Bernard Leach. These were the first tourists to patronize St Ives, portray it, and make it popular. Those that followed were plentiful but not always quite as talented. The St Ives' Society of Arts was founded in 1927, followed closely by that of Penwith. Barbara Hepworth's home has become her museum and is open daily. One of her bronzes is in the cemetery at Carbis Bay, another sculpture in the Library, and a Madonna and Child can be found in St Ia's Church. Bernard Leach's pottery is still manufactured in the town.

St Ia's church was completed in 1434. The granite tower is over 24 metres high, one for each year it took to build. There is a memorial brass to Trenwith dated 1463, and in 1500 the family gave the aisle which is now the Lady Chapel. In the churchyard stands a solid medieval lantern cross, a rare survivor of an old tradition. Near Smeaton's Pier there is a chapel where a friar used to bless fishermen before they set sail, and the patron saint of seamen, St Nicholas, had his chapel on St Ives' Head. The Head was once separated from the mainland and is still called 'The Island' today. Only a ruin remains of the chapel but in its time it must have served as lighthouse as well as a House of God, for Leland in the 15th century referred to it as 'a Pharos for light for shippes sailing by night'.

In 1782 John Knill, then mayor, built himself a granite pyramid to the south of the town. It was meant to be his mausoleum and, as an added treat in death, his will provided for a five-year plan: every five years, ten little girls must dance around the tomb to the music of fiddles, although what perversion caused him to add that they should be accompanied by the vicar and the mayor and sing a psalm can only be guessed at. The provision is respected and the occasion has become a jolly event, like the Helston Furry; not at all sinister and solemn as the will suggests. The next dates for this will be 1986 and 1991.

St Ives is a busy tourist resort today, a pretty one at that, although at the height of the season it can get uncomfortably crowded. It has all facilities.

Hotel:	Tregenna Castle Hotel; Tel. St Ives (0736) 795254
B&B:	The Grey Mullet, 2 Bunkers Hill; Tel. St Ives (0736) 796635
Bus:	To Hayle, Penzance and Camborne
Early closing:	Thursday
Train:	Penzance, Redruth, London

LELANT

The silting up of the estuary meant that this port, so powerful in the Middle Ages, gradually lost ground to St Ives, its neighbour. King Theodorick, ancient king of Cornwall, had a castle here which also sank beneath the sands. St Ia's brother, Uny, also a saint, gave his name to the Norman church, and in St Uny's churchyard there are two ancient Cornish crosses, much older than the church itself. The town has shops and trains, refreshment and accommodation.

West and slightly south of Lelant is Trencrom Hill, crowned by an Iron Age fort. The hill was given to the National Trust in 1946 as a memorial to the men and women of Cornwall who had died in the two world wars.

HAYLE

'Eyl' is Cornish for estuary, which is just where Hayle is. The town grew up on mining and was the principal port for the mining areas of Camborne and Redruth. In the 18th century a sizeable smelting business grew up too, and even today the northern end of Hayle is called Copperhouse.

Ore was brought from Redruth on trains drawn by horses to the foot of Steamer Hill. Then the train was hauled up the hill by a stationary steam engine. This was the first steam railway to be built in Cornwall, in 1834, and you can still see the engine house in a field at the top of Steamer Hill.

Economics killed the smelting trade. It took three tons of coal to produce one ton of copper, and it was eventually decided to ship the ore to the coal in South Wales. As Copperhouse declined, the firm of Harvey's grew. It was founded to manufacture machinery for the mines, and Harvey's engines were exported throughout the world. From foundry work they went into ore crushing, winding and pumping machinery and finally into ship-building. By 1860 the ship yard alone employed 1,000 men and made ships of up to 4,000 tons. It was one of the largest yards in Cornwall. The machines too were sometimes monsters. In 1844 Harvey's made the largest pump in the world to drain Haarlem Lake in Holland. The cylinder had a bore of 365 centimetres, huge by any standard. However, the mining industry was falling off and, in ship-building, competition from Belfast and the Tyne proved too strong and Harvey's went into decline.

Hayle lost its importance as a direct result of this. The little port is still active, however, and a certain amount of fishing still goes on.

The parish church of Hayle is at Phillack, and it could be

one of the oldest churches in England. The porch is 6th century and a stone in the churchyard is 7th or 8th century, as is the ancient wheel cross you see there. The tower is 15th century, however, and the rest of the church was re-built in 1856.

YHA: Riviere House, 20 Parc-An-Dix Lane, Phillack; Tel. Hayle (0736) 752381

THE TOWANS

This large area of dunes used to be mining country, but the sand has covered the abandoned mines and probably much else. Now nature has re-asserted her control.

GWITHIAN

There was once an oratory here which *might* have been the oldest Christian building in England, but this again is speculation. Pevsner tells us that it was excavated in the 19th century and was a rectangular building dating back to Celtic Christianity. The remains of the chapel were still visible in Leland's time; he saw it in the 16th century. There is also an important Bronze Age settlement on three levels on the site but today you see nothing but sand. If you visit St Golianus' church at Gwithian, you will find a booklet by Charles Thomas on the history of the settlement. The church itself was built in 1866 but it incorporates a 15th-century tower and a 13th-century chancel arch.

GODREVY

It took a public outcry to have a lighthouse installed on Godrevy Island, a pile of rocks just off Godrevy Point, in 1859. The day Charles I was executed, 31 January 1649, his son, the Prince of Wales, lost all his wardrobe on the rocks. The good ship Garland went aground there and only one man, one boy and one dog were saved out of the complement of 60. But it was the wreck of the *Nile* that made the greater impact. She went down in November 1854 with another 60 hands and an unknown quantity of passengers. There were many more wrecked ships but this one tipped the scales and the lighthouse was installed. Manned at first it is now automatic.

CAMBORNE

The town is well inland of the path and of little interest architecturally, but it cannot be ignored since it was the mining capital of Cornwall. The 15th-century church of St Martin and St Meriadocus is worth a visit. The altar slab is 10th century and came from St Ia's chapel near St Ives, and the church itself is relatively unspoilt.

Richard Trevithick, who invented the high-pressure steam engine for draining mines and adapted it for vehicles, was born in Lower Penponds in 1771. His memorial is in Station Road. In spite of being in some ways the father of motorized rail and road travel, he died penniless whilst building the Dartford Tunnel in Kent in 1833. Another inventor, William Bickford, lived here too. He invented the safety fuse and there is a monument to him at Tucking Mill.

The Royal School of Mines is in Camborne and so is the Holman Mining Museum with its mining and rock-drilling machinery. Even if you do not think you are interested in mining, you are sure to be fascinated by the exhibits and the history. Two more engine houses are open to the public, magnificently refurbished and maintained by the National Trust, at East Pool and Agar, and South Crofty Mines on the Redruth Road.

The most westerly Roman villa in England was found due north at Magor, between Camborne and the Nordic-sounding Reskajeage Downs; excavations have shown it to be 2nd century. To the east stands Carnbrea, 225 metres high, capped by Lord de Dunstanville's tall monument (of interest as a landmark but little else) and an ancient camp, once the chief seat of Druid power in the west of England.

REDRUTH

Although the A30(T) now by-passes built-up areas, the old main road runs from Camborne to Redruth through houses all the way. This is another mining town and interesting for that fact alone. The Scotsman, William Murdoch, settled here and lived in a fine old house in Cross Street which was originally a chapel and then a prison before he took it as his private house. He invented gas lighting and put the first installation into this house.

When the mine workings caved in at Gwennap Pit, 3 kilometres south-east of the town, they formed a natural amphitheatre. John Wesley preached there in 1762 and the acoustics were so good that he came back 15 times, his congregation numbering tens of thousands, and the place became a Methodist Mecca. A service has been held there every Whit Monday since Wesley's death in 1791. North of the town is Togus Tin, a unique tin streaming mill which still produces tin using methods 200 years old.

PORTREATH

This was another important mining port, shipping ore and metal from the mines and smelting works around Camborne and Redruth. By 1840, 100,000 tons of ore a year were going through the port. Today a little fishing still takes place but it is really just a small resort which appeals to surfers and bathers.

Hotel:	Glenfeadon House Hotel; Tel. Portreath (0209) 842650
B&B:	Rockaway, Lighthouse Hill, Tel. Portreath (0209) 842293
Bus:	To Redruth
Early closing:	Wednesday

12

Portreath to Newquay

Mr Penwarne said that Opie was born at St Agnes, a village in Cornwall, about 4 or 5 miles from Truro. That his father was not in so low a situation as has been reported. That he was a Carpenter & Joiner in a decent situation of life. Opie's education must have been very limited, as good schools were not established in that part, but he was taught to read & write. The first time that he showed an inclination to drawing has been thus related by his sister. He was acquainted with a young man of the name of Mark Oates who is now a Captn. of Artillery. — Opie happened to call upon him and saw a drawing of a Butterfly made by him, was seized with a desire to attempt to make one like it. In this (he) succeeded so well as to become quite eager to make further attempts in drawing. His father kept a horse on which Opie rode to Truro & purchased some pencils & colours.

Penwarne told me that Opie's sister had informed him that Opie was at ten years of age a very good arithmetician, & at that early age he set up a sort of school, & taught writing and acounts to many much older than himself. Before he was twelve years of age he had for some time been under the tuition of Dr Wolcot so far as to receive advice & instruction in painting, the Doctor having much love for the art & a few pictures in his possession. He began to paint portraits at a very early period, and when not more than thirteen years of age went to Padstow a town at some distance where he remained three months, and at the end of that period returned to his fathers dressed in a new suit of clothes & having twenty or thirty guineas in his pocket.

FARINGTON, Joseph (1747–1821). Extract from *The Farington Diary* quoted in A.L. Rowse's *A Cornish*

Anthology (1968) by permission of the Hutchinson Publishing Group.

Farington was better known as a landscape painter. The diary was edited by James Greig and others and published in 8 volumes in 1922–8.

Introduction

The cliff walking is good all the way to Perranporth, although the first couple of miles are somewhat marred by the proximity of the unkempt perimeter fence of Nancekuke, Ministry of Defence property. After Perranporth the path runs along the sands of Perran Bay for about 5 kilometres before rounding Penhale Camp. Walking is then good again to Crantock, where a seasonal ferry should take you across the Gannel. Out of season you can wade (but state of tide and weather are critical), walk round, or take a bus into Newquay. Apart from the crossing of the Gannel and possible confusion where the path has been disrupted by quarry workings at Cligga Head, this stretch is quite straightforward.

With the exception of granite outcrops on St Agnes Head and Cligga Head the rocks are Devonian Slates: Middle Devonian from Portreath to Penhale Sands and Lower Devonian on to Newquay. There are traces of mining activity at both St Agnes Head and Cligga Head. At Perran Bay the great expanse of Perran Sands, stretches from Perranporth to Penhale along the coast and runs well inland in flat windswept areas and dunes.

Portreath, with its natural harbour, used to be a busy port for the mining industry, and in the 19th century St Agnes was a thriving miners' settlement; both deserve a visit and St Piran's Oratory, an 8th-century Chapel on Penhale Sands, is worth the kilometre detour inland.

St Agnes Head, in addition to being a monument to mining and an excellent coastal viewpoint, is a marvellous place for birdwatchers, there they can observe nesting kittiwakes, herring gull, fulmar and guillemot. In autumn skuas, petrels, shearwaters and diving gannets pass on their migration south. In the Gannel Estuary numerous different waders potter about among the varied salt-marsh plants, while on the stretch from Portreath to St Agnes stonechat and wheatear vie for your attention with buzzard, kestrel and raven.

DISTANCE				T E L E P H O N E	T R A I N	B U S	F E R R Y	S H O P S	C A M P I N G	A C C O M M O D A T I O N	R E F R E S H M E N T	
STAGE	CUMUL.	TIME	PORTREATH TO NEWQUAY									CUMUL. DIST. KMS
			PORTREATH	x		x			x	x	x	602
5	5	1:15	PORTHTOWAN	x				x	x	x	x	607
(1½)		(:25)	(ST AGNES)	x		x		x	x	x	x	
11	16	2:45	PERRANPORTH	x		x			x	x	x	618
12	28	3:	CRANTOCK	x		x	x				x	630
5	33	1:15	NEWQUAY	x	x	x		x	x	x	x	635

TIMES ARE BASED ON AVERAGE WALKER LIGHTLY LADEN.

NB.
1. *STAGE: is the distance between that point and the preceding point.*
2. *CUMUL.: is the cumulative distance from the beginning of the chapter.*
3. *TIME: is the time for the stage (between that point and the preceding one) calculated at 4 kilometres per hour – the rate for a lightly loaded person walking without halt.*
4. *Brackets enclose places not on the Path but easily reached from it, together with distances and times from the Path.*
5. *CUMULATIVE DISTANCE: is the total distance from South Haven Point.*

Guide

Follow the road inland around the harbour in Portreath and then back towards the cliffs with their shipping marker above Horse Rock. The path now continues along the cliff tops, cutting across Gooden Heane Point, where it passes seaward of the high fencing of the Nancekuke Defence Area, which will remain with you for the next 3 kilometres or so. Descend to cross a stream and climb up over a small headland by the Diamond Rock. Go on up along the cliffs past Sheep Rock and, further on, Gullyn Rock; down to cross two more streams and up above Tobban Horse past an old mine shaft with its chimney. Carry on along the cliffs for half a kilometre and then go down into **Porthtowan**.

Pass around behind the Sandy Beach, inland a little to cross the stream bridge and climb up on to the cliffs again. Continue past the spoil heaps and disused mine shafts of Wheal Charlotte before turning inland and down to cross the stream behind the National Trust property of Chapel Porth. Climb up on to the cliffs again past the Wheal Coates mine with the restored engine house of the Towanroath shaft, and, passing the disused mine shafts and spoil heaps near Tubby's Head, climb on up to **St Agnes Head**. Pass seaward of the coastguard look-out and continue along the cliff top to New Downs Head and through more disused mine workings before descending steeply to Trevaunce Cove, just below **St Agnes**.

The path climbs up out of the cove on to the cliffs again, past more abandoned mine workings, before descending sharply to cross a stream behind Trevellas Porth. A steep climb up from Trevallas Porth brings you on to the cliffs again, past some Second World War fortifications, with Green island out to sea and Trevellas Airfield inland. The path continues on high above the sea, past evidence of former mining activity, around Hanover Cove up on to Cligga Head. Here there has been much upheaval among the remains of Mr Nobel's (of Peace Prize fame) dynamite works, and the path between the spoil heaps is not clear. You should keep as close to the coast as possible, continuing below the top of the cliffs down past Droskyn Castle Hotel and into **Perranporth**. Walk around the little bay and set off for just over 3 kilometres across Perran Sands. Inland there is first a golf course, then the large holiday camp at Gear Sands, just after which there is a footpath leading inland 800 metres to **St Piran's Oratory**. The path leads across the sands climbing right out to Ligger Point. Go around the point and between the double fencing around Hoblyn's Cove. Then follow the white posts which mark the way through the Penhale Military Camp Area. If the Red Flag is flying – indicating that firing is taking place – the Range Sentry will show you which path to use. At the far side you cross the fence, out of the Military Area by a stile and steps. Continue along the outside of the fence for a few metres, before turning left to cross the stream at **Holywell**.

Walk along behind the beach at Holywell Bay, across National Trust land, around the north end of the Beach and up to **Kelsey Head** with its Cliff Castle. Go around the head and follow the coast down to cross the stream by Porth Joke. Continue along the coast, up around Pentire Point, west and then down around the low cliffs above Crantock Beach. Go on past West Pentire to the seasonal **Crantock** Ferry for the crossing of the Gannel. If the ferry is not operating, you can wade across at very low tide in good conditions. Otherwise you must make the detour by road.

Having crossed the Gannel to Pentire continue out around Pentire Point East, back around Fistral Bay, passing either just behind or along the beach itself, around Towan Head and back along Gazzle Bay into **Newquay**, where the main road through the town serves the path.

Gazetteer

PORTHTOWAN

The Nancekuke Defence Area dominates the path between Portreath and Porthtowan and mining debris is common around the path beyond the village. Porthtowan is a small resort of no great interest but has facilities for refreshment, revictualling and accommodation.

Hotel: Westcliffe Hotel; Tel. Porthtowan (0209) 890
                228
Bus: St Agnes, Camborne, Truro

ST AGNES HEAD

If you have energy to spare, climb St Agnes Beacon, which is 192 metres high. There are magnificent views on to Trevose Head, back to St Ives and south to St Michael's Mount as well as a bird's eye view of the mines and mining area.

In St Agnes there are three typical Cornish wayside cottages which belong, like the beacon, to the National Trust. The church was virtually rebuilt in the 19th century, but the octagonal font is 15th-century. The town was never of much importance but its port – down in Trevavnance Cove – acted as a port for Truro, enabling cargoes destined for Bristol and South Wales to avoid the perilous journey around Land's End. The Tonkin family proved indefatigable builders and rebuilders of ports in the harbour between 1632 and 1710, but as fast as they built them the sea swept them away and by 1736 nothing was left. A more resistant one was built in 1793, which lasted into the early part of this century, but it too was washed away.

St Agnes has a bus service to Truro, facilities for shopping, refreshment and accommodation.

Hotel: Trevaunance Point Hotel, Trevaunance Cove;

Tel. St Agnes (087 255) 3225

B&B: Sea Spray, Quay Road, Trevavnance Cove; Tel. St Agnes (087 255) 2991

Early
closing: Wednesday

PERRANPORTH

This little resort is larger than it seems to be. Much of it has grown up in this century – including the huge car park, which is practically on the beach. John Opie the painter was born at Trevellas, just outside the town, in 1771. At Rose, 2 kilometres east, there is another outdoor theatre, an amphitheatre called St Piran's Round, where miracle plays were performed in Cornish in the Middle Ages.

Perranporth has fine sandy beaches, dunes and all facilities: good shops, refreshment, buses and accommodation.

Hotel: Lamorna Hotel, Twarnhayle Road; Tel. Perranporth (087 257) 3398

B&B: St Pirran's Rose; Tel. Perranporth (087 257) 3338

YHA: Youth Hostel, Droskyn Point; Tel. Perranporth (087 257) 821

Buses: To Newquay, Truro and Redruth

Early
closing: Wednesday

ST PIRAN'S ORATORY

St Piran was the Patron Saint of Cornish Miners. St Patrick sent him to Cornwall in the 6th century and he built his oratory at 'Perranzabuloe', Perran in the Sands, now Penhale Sands. It yielded to the encroaching sands and had to be abandoned in the 11th century. It was excavated in the 19th century: a single hall 9 metres long 5 metres wide and 6 metres high made of granite, porphyry, slate and rubble. It had a pitched roof with gables east and west, a stone seat around the inside and a canopied altar. The Victorians vandalized it and now the site is protected by a concrete cover marked with a large white cross.

A new church was built in the 11th century, but that too became engulfed in sand and a third St Piran's was built in 1804 at Lambourne by Perranzabuloe, south east of Perranporth.

The church was not the only institution to come off second best to Perran's Sands. Followers of the Devil did rather badly too. Longarrow – a lost city in every sense, a sort of Cornish Sodom – is also reputed to lie beneath the sands.

HOLYWELL BAY

There is a cave with a fresh water spring, the Holy Well. It was credited with magic powers, and its waters were sought by those in need. Holywell has a Pub and shops.

KELSEY HEAD

This is another well-sited Iron Age cliff castle, which covers a whole hectare of land. Four kilometres south east inland – it's not really worth the detour – is St Cuthbert's 13th-century Church. Unusually, for Cornwall, it has a spire.

CRANTOCK

Only the church is of interest in this little village behind Pentire Head. It is made of 'Blown Sandstone', an amalgam of sand, shells and pebbles welded together by the action of the sea. The building is Norman and was made a collegiate church by Bishop Brewer of Exeter in 1236 and was given a dispro-portionately long chancel to accommodate the dean and canons that its promotion required. The present chancel is 14th-century and a little smaller than its predecessor.

NEWQUAY

This is the Bondi Beach of England. You have to be careful not to get crushed on the roads by the vans and mini-buses stacked with surf boards, or to get run through on the beach by a board as its weather-beaten owner dashes off 'to catch a wave'. Newquay's life has not always been as frivolous. A port was built there in 1440 and was improved in 1586. The town was then known as Towan Blistra, but by the time Carew passed through in 1602 it was called Newquay.

The inhabitants lived by pilchard fishing in the 19th century. On Towan Head, beside the path the Huer's house still stands. From there the Huer watched the shoals of pilchards approach and called out to warn the fishermen, who jumped into their boats and hauled the fish ashore by the ton. When the railway came a new trade grew up in the export of china clay. But by 1920 both trades had died away and Newquay set course to become the resort it is today.

It is the surfing centre of the south, with miles of golden sand and great white rollers swishing in from out at sea. But other tastes are catered to as well. There is a Zoo, a Marine Aquarium, Old Newquay Gallery, and the Trenance Cottages Museum. Outside the town there is the Lappa Valley Miniature Steam Railway at Newlyn East and a working dairy and country life museum called Dairyland. By far the most precious visit you could make, however, is to the magnificent house Trerice, 5 kilometres south east of Newquay. This National Trust property is quite superb: an Elizabethan manor house rebuilt by Sir John Arundell in 1571, complete with all contemporary detail, plasterwork, fireplaces etc. It also has fine furniture and objects, attractive gardens and delicious home-made teas. Newquay has all facilities including trains and buses.

Hotel:	Bristol, Narrowcliffe; Tel. Newquay (063 73) 5181
B&B:	Mr Row, 7 St Pirian's Road; Tel. Newquay (063 73) 4944
YHA:	Alexandra Court, Narrowcliffe; Tel. Newquay (063 73) 6381
Early closing:	Wednesday
Tourist Information:	Tel. Newquay (063 73) 2119
Train:	Penzance, Plymouth, London
Bus:	Bude, Camborne, Padstow, Plymouth, Tintagel

13

Newquay to Port Isaac

You, who in these days of vehement bustle, business, and competition, can still find time to travel for pleasure alone — you, who have yet to become emancipated from the thraldom of railways, carriages, and saddle-horses — patronize, I exhort you, that first and oldest-established of all conveyances, your own legs! Think on your tender partings nipped in the bud by the railway bell; think of crabbed cross-roads, and broken carriage-springs; think of luggage confided to extortionate porters, of horses casting shoes and catching colds, of cramped legs and numbed feet, of vain longings to get down for a moment here, and to delay for a pleasant half-hour there — think of all these manifold hardships of riding at your ease; and the next time you leave home, strap your luggage to your shoulders, take your stick in your hand, set forth delivered from a perfect paraphernalia of encumbrances, to go where you will, how you will — the free citizen of the whole travelling world! Thus independent, what may you not accomplish? — what pleasure is there that you cannot enjoy? Are you an artist? — you can stop to sketch every point of view that strikes your eye. Are you a philanthropist? — you can go into every cottage and talk to every human being you pass. Are you a botanist, or geologist? — you may pick up leaves and chip rocks wherever you please, the live-long day. Are you a valetudinarian? — you may physic yourself by Nature's own simple prescription, walking in fresh air. Are you dilatory and irresolute? — you may dawdle to your heart's content; you may change all your plans a dozen times in a dozen hours; you may tell 'Boots' at the inn to call you at six o'clock, may fall sleep again (ecstatic sensation!) five minutes after he has knocked at the door, and may get up two hours later, to pursue your journey, with perfect impunity and satisfaction. For, to you, what is a timetable but waste paper? — and a 'booked place' but a relic of the dark ages? You dread, perhaps, blisters on your feet — sponge your feet with cold vinegar and water, change your socks every ten miles, and show me blisters after that, if you can!

COLLINS, Wilkie (1824–89). Novelist. Extract from *Ramble beyond Railways* (1851) quoted in S.H. Burton's *A West Country Anthology* published by Robert Hale, 1975.

Introduction

This is a relatively gentle section of the coast. Trevose head (74 metres) is the highest point you climb and there are few steep gradients to be negotiated. The path sticks close to the coast with one important diversion inland from Portquin to just before Port Isaac. The coastline varies from good high grassy cliffs, which drop sheer to the sea with their neat stone walls, pastures and arable land, to stretches of long, flat, sandy beaches which have attracted bathers and surfers for many years. The views from Trevose Head and, to a lesser extent, Pentire Head can be spectacular in good conditions. There are several prehistoric forts and settlements on or near the path, including probably the most important of the Cornish cliff castles, at Trevelgue Head.

The land is composed of the slates and shales of the Upper and Middle Devonian, giving an indented coastline of which the softer shales have been worn into coves by the action of the sea. Headlands are mainly of the harder greenstone, while the cliffs at Pentire Head are volcanic, formed from pillow lavas. Bedruthan Steps, the giant's stepping stones on Bedruthan Beach, are similarly volcanic in origin.

The cliffs above Porthcothan were the last known breeding grounds in its native county of the Cornish Chough, the emblem of Cornwall. It has now adopted Wales as its habitat. The Camel Estuary, the most important drowned river valley of the North Cornwall Coast is particularly rich in birdlife. Both the Hawke's Wood Nature Reserve (South of Wadebridge) and the Chapel Amble Regional Wildfowl Reservoir are on the Estuary. In winter many water birds and and waders make it their home and in summer you can often see osprey among the more familiar sea birds and the red throated diver with its magnificent head which resembles the nose of a deadly submarine.

DISTANCE				TELEPHONE	TRAIN	FERRY	BUS	SHOPS	CAMPING	ACCOMMODATION	REFRESHMENT	CUMUL. DIST. KMS
STAGE	CUMUL.	TIME	NEWQUAY TO PORT ISAAC									
			NEWQUAY	x	x	x		x	x	x	x	635
(10)		(2:30)	(ST COLUMB MAJOR)									
9	9	2:15	MAWGAN PORTH	x	x				x	x	x	644
7	16	1:45	PORTHCOTHAN	x				x		x	x	651
10	26	2:30	HARLYN	x	x						x	661
10	36	2:30	PADSTOW	x	x	x	x	x	x	x	x	671
4	40	1:	POLZEATH	x	x			x	x	x	x	675
11	51	2:45	PORT ISAAC	x	x			x		x	x	686

TIMES ARE BASED ON AVERAGE WALKER LIGHTLY LADEN.

NB.
1. *STAGE: is the distance between that point and the preceding point.*
2. *CUMUL.: is the cumulative distance from the beginning of the chapter.*
3. *TIME: is the time for the stage (between that point and the preceding one) calculated at 4 kilometres per hour – the rate for a lightly loaded person walking without halt.*
4. *Brackets enclose places not on the Path but easily reached from it, together with distances and times from the Path.*
5. *CUMULATIVE DISTANCE: is the total distance from South Haven Point.*

Guide

Go out of Newquay on the main road following the sea front and branch off left along a path just after the junction with the A3075. This leads along the coast around Lusty Glaze to St Columb Porth where it joins the road, passing under the B3276 road bridge, up some steps on the left by the Porth House Hotel and around the head of the beach, going along the road for about 400 metres. Where the road turns sharp right, the path carries straight on, following the coast out to **Trevelgue Head**, with its impressive cliff castle.

Come back down the peninsula towards the road and turn left along the cliff top above Watergate (or Tregurrian) Beach, which is over 6 kilometres long. As you turn left along the cliffs you can see the tiny Flory Island to seaward and, 800 metres further on, Zacry's Islands, before dipping down to cross the stream by a road bridge at Watergate. Just before the hotel, climb steeply up again to go over Strase Cliff, around Stem Point, and then steeply down to cross two streams at the neck of **Griffin's Point**, where there is another cliff castle. The path climbs up again around Beacon Cove and Berryl's Point before descending sharply into **Mawgan Porth**.

Cross the river on the road bridge and then walk across the edge of the beach back on to the cliffs. Climb up quite steeply to Trenance Point, from which there are good views back to Newquay. Walk on through gorse along the cliff tops, past Trerathick Point and Carnewas Island. Dip down to cross a stream and climb up again opposite Pendarves Island, past steps leading down to the beach and the huge rocks of Bedruthan Steps, (200 metres further on you pass seaward of Iron Age Redcliffe Castle) carry on, past Diggory's Island to Park Head, National Trust land with fine views of the English countryside in a wide sweep inland from Trevose Head. Walk round Park Head, around High Cove and on for about 1 kilometre before descending steeply to cross a stream above Porth Mear. Climb up again, past Trescore Islands and, dipping to cross another stream, on down into **Porthcothan**.

Go down past the holiday villas to the road, turn left to pass behind the beach, over the stream, and then left off the road and up on to the cliffs again. Pass Minnows Islands, Fox Cove, Warren Cove and Trethias Island and go down into Treyarnon Bay. Cross the beach and, passing the youth hostel, go around Treyarnon Point and along the beach at Constantine Bay, then climb up, past Booby Bay onto **Trevose Head,** 74 metres, with its coastguard station, lighthouse, and its superb views in both directions along the coast.

Go past the Round Hole, down through the cliffs, cross the neck of Dinas Head – to the west of which you can see the Bull and Quies Islands – past Stinking Cove, inland of the light-house and Cat's Cove, before going down past Merope Rocks and the Padstow Lifeboat Station to Polventon (or Mother Ivey's) Bay. Here you pass inland of Mother Ivey's Cottage, past a caravan site and go up around Cataclews Point. The path continues on around **Harlyn bay**, St Cadoc's Point and Newtrain Bay and into **Trevone**. Come out of Trevone around the bay past another round hole, which bores down through the cliffs, past the Porthmissen Headlands – with its arch – and Longcarrow Cove to Gunver Head. Go inland slightly here to cross a stream and then climb up past Butter Hole and Pepper

Hole and Seal Hole, all invisible from the path (you can see them from the sea), on to Stepper Point.

Go past the tower around the coastguard look-out and down, along the shores of the Camel Estuary, around Hawker's Cove, Harbour Cove and Gun Point in front of the Padstow War Memorial, through the Deer Park of Prideaux Place and into **Padstow**.

Take the ferry from Padstow (from the harbour or the War Memorial, depending on tide) to Rock. Walk up the beach in front of the sailing club, seaward across the car park and through the dunes along the path which lies closest to the estuary. Go seaward around Brae Hill (although a path inland, with white marker stones, takes you across the edge of the golf course to **St Enodoc's Church** and back on to the path) to Daymer Bay.

If the tide permits, cross the sands of Daymer Beach – from either route – otherwise walk around just behind the beach and climb the low cliffs on a well trodden path around into **Polzeath**. Here again you can either cut across the beach of Hayle Bay or walk around behind it. In either case you turn left down a small path behind the last house, 'Medla', on the low cliffs of **New Polzeath**. Dip into a small cutting, cross a stream and climb up over a headland into another gully before the long climb up to Pentire Point.

A high cliff path, with magnificent views along the coast in both directions, leads on past **Rump's Point** with its ancient castle and the Mouls Rock seaward off it. It then takes you down steeply past Pengirt Cove and on, up and down, on a coastal path easy to follow alongside farmland, through gorse and bracken, dipping into gullys, crossing streams, and up again around Portquin Bay.

After rounding Carnweather Point, go down steeply and, keeping to the path nearest to the sea, pass the deep and impressive Lundy Hole, which pierces right through the cliff to the sea below. Go around Lundy Bay, up over the headland, and down into Epphaven Cove. Cross a stream and go on up over Trevan Point. Descend again, past two fenced mine shafts, to the National Trust property of **Doyden**. Head for the House, leaving the tiny castle and Doyden Point to seaward, and pass to seaward in front of the house, around on its drive to the road, on which you turn left down into **Portquin**.

Cross over behind the Port and follow the road, past the National Trust cottages, out of the village. After about 300 metres the road bends sharply right and you head straight on across a stile beside some cottages, over fields which take you up a valley towards Roscarrock Farm.

As you pass the farm, cross a stile and turn sharp left. You have started to head back towards the coast. In a few hundred metres you reach the steep coomb of Pine Haven where you slant down inland to cross the stream, then turn seaward along the other side of the coomb to pick up the coast path which heads up over Lobber Point. A well worn path takes you down past houses into **Port Isaac**.

Gazetteer

ST COLUMB MINOR

This ancient village is practically a suburb of Newquay but its church, St Columba, is 14th-century. Just outside the town, Rialton was founded as a Priory by Thomas Vyvyan in the 1590s and is now a farmhouse. Only the main wing of the original house survives today and the study and bedroom of Prior Vyvyan of Bodmin can be seen on the first floor. There is a 5th-century Latin inscription on a stone in the wall of one of the farm buildings, but no indication as to where it came from; and there is a small holy well in the courtyard.

ST COLUMB MAJOR

The town is built on the hill site of a Danish Fort, 8 kilometres to the east and well inland of Newquay. The Church of St Columba dominates the town, and Pevsner calls it one of the major churches of Cornwall. But since he gives no reason why, it could be a rare flash of Pevsner humour, making a play on words.

Castle-an-Dinas, one of the more flamboyant Cornish earthworks, is 3½ kilometres south-east of St Columb Major, 225 metres above sea level with four concentric rings of earthworks and a single entrance, to the south-west. It was passed from hand to hand: first Britons, then Romans, then Danes inhabited it. Pevsner says that there were two levels of construction, corresponding to two entirely different periods. But the only artefacts discovered are shards of Iron Age pottery. The land to the north is just a mass of prehistoric debris: burial chambers, standing stones and so on. The Nine Maidens, north of Winnard's Perch, is an avenue of standing stones over 100 metres long.

TREVELGUE HEAD

Just north of Newquay is an outstanding promontory fort which probably housed a sizeable community. It has seven lines of ramparts and ditches to protect it as well as the superb defences nature gave it. Excavations made just before the outbreak of the Second World War revealed a Bronze Age battleaxe and retorts for smelting ore. Griffin's Point at the northern end of the bay, has another, smaller cliff castle not at all as impressive as its mighty neighbour.

MAWGAN PORTH

Is an imposing little resort with a long flat beach. Just behind it, in the Vale of Mawgan or Laherne, are the ruins of a settlement which started in the Dark Ages. All the huts were built around a courtyard.

Further up the valley at St Mawgan is St Mawgan's Church. A large 13th-century building added to in the 15th century, with a mass of memorials to the Arundell Family in it, (some of which reused early Flemish Brasses) and a Lantern Cross in the churchyard. There is also a peculiar headstone shaped like a longboat's Transom commemorating nine sailors and a cabin boy found frozen together in 1846 in the lifeboat of a ship called, ironically, Hope. There is accommodation, public telephones and refreshments.

Hotel: Seaview Hotel; Tel. Mawgan Porth (06374) 276
Buses: Newquay, St Columbmajor, Padstow, Camborne

LANHERNE

Inland and north of St Mawgan, this manor came into the possession of the Arundell Family in 1231. They gave it to Carmelite Nuns as a refuge in 1794 and it is still a convent. The façade is Tudor, though there are 17th- and 18th-century additions, and there is a rare and most elaborate Cornish Cross in the cemetery of the Chapel.

BEDRUTHAN STEPS

As with every inexplicable large natural phenomenon in Cornwall, a giant is blamed for these volcanic rocks which march across the sand from Pendarves Island to Diggory's Island. It was not a giant but the slow, systematic erosion of sea and sand that exposed and fashioned them, one of which is called the Samaritan, after a ship which was wrecked there in 1846. Nine lives were lost and the locals got the cargo of gaily printed cloths. They also composed this song:–

> 'The Good Samaritan came ashore,
> To feed the hungary and clothe the poor
> With Barrels of beef and Bales of Linen
> No Poor Soul shall want for a Shilling'.

From time to time the sands shift and expose the keel of the ship, close to the Samaritan Rock. Redcliffe Castle, a well-composed Iron Age fort, surveys this scene from the cliffs above.

PORTHCOTHAN

Once a tiny port, now a tiny resort – with a good sandy beach, shops and accommodation.

Hotel:	Bay House Hotel, Porthcothan Bay; Tel. Padstow (0841) 520472
B&B:	"Carncothan", Porthcothan Bay; Tel. Padstow (0841) 520282
YHA:	Tregonnan, Treyarnon; Tel. Padstow (0841) 520322
Buses:	Newquay, Padstow

CONSTANTINE BAY

The path to the bay is littered with pre-historic sites: there are six round barrows along the cliff edge above Park Head, more cliff castles above Pepper Cove and numerous tumuli scattered about. A kilometre inland from the bay, behind the Golf Course, lie the nave chancel, one aisle and the tower of St Constantine's Chapel. It was built in the 1390s, but is now in ruins.

TREVOSE HEAD

This head is notable for the simple statistic that twice as many ships were wrecked on her rocks from 1847 to 1900 as had been wrecked there in the first half of the century – the lighthouse was built in 1847. Not surprisingly, Padstow lifeboat is stationed on the eastern edge of the head.

HARLYN

Some poor fellow stumbled on 150 Iron Age grave cysts while digging foundations for his house in 1900. Subsequent excavations revealed evidence of a very large pre-historic settlement where Harlyn now stands. The Beaker Folk lived there 2000 years B.C., and a whole village dating from 300 B.C. was also found. Weaving, grinding and spinning instruments, Bronze and Pottery Ornaments and stocks of tin are now in Truro Museum. But the real gems were two Irish Gold crescent-shaped ornaments 3000 years old, which are also in Truro Museum. Inland from Harlyn, St Merryn's Church is 15th-century but has a Norman Arch into the nave and a board with the instructions for the bellringers in verse. There is a pub in Harlyn and occasional buses for Padstow.

THE DOOM BAR

This is a Sandbank which can only be seen at low tide close to the mouth of the estuary. The Cornish explanation is quite straightforward. A Saxon fisherman shot a seal but his arrow killed a mermaid. He'd hit a bad one, because as she died she cursed the Port and created the bar. Another explanation is that 'Doom' is a corruption of 'Dune' or 'Dun' – a sand bar – which sounds pretty harmless, but this one has taken 300 ships, 3 lifeboats and 150 lives in the past 150 years. The Padstow Harbour Association even went as far as to install a winch at Stepper Point in 1830, to heave ships out of the Harbour over the Bar when conditions were not right for them to cross normally. The wreckage of a number of ships can still be seen when the Bar is revealed at low tide.

PADSTOW

When St Pedroc landed in Lodenek in 560 A.D. the name was changed to Petrocstone in his honour. Then King Athelstan

(925–940) conquered Cornwall and the sycophantic locals changed the name to Atherstone. In the 16th century, for a reason which is not recorded, the name was changed again to Padstow. The town was a port when the Danes sacked it in 981 and it sent two ships to the siege of Calais in 1346. But the Doom Bar and general silting-up put paid to its portly pretensions. Elizabeth I granted the town its charter in 1583 and the port was cleared and opened up again. The sand was used as fertilizer, and continued dredging meant that by the 17th century Padstow was quite an important port again, exporting not only great quantities of ore to Bristol and other ports but, in the 18th century, quite a lot of agricultural produce as well. In the 19th century shipbuilding developed, one yard alone launching a ship every eight months for 20 years. Although some fishing still goes on and steamers leave on pleasure trips to Lundy and elsewhere, Padstow is now mainly a tourist resort.

St Pedroc's Church stands where the Saint built his Church, when he landed in the 6th century, although the present one was built in the 13th and 14th centuries. It has a fine octagonal font, sculpted in ornate detail by the Master of St Endellion in the 15th century. The pulpit is 16th-century and the churchyard gates are rare examples of 18th-century wrought ironwork. Inside the Church there are monuments to the Prideaux family and in the churchyard a Hiberno-Saxon decorated cross – look carefully at its Fleur de Lys motif, Pevsner found it odd.

Prideaux Place, opposite the Church, has been the Prideaux seat since 1530. The present House is late 16th-century but was added to in every century save ours. The Tropical Bird and Butterfly Gardens, though not connected, are quite close to the house and open daily.

Each May Day Padstow celebrates its Hobby Horse Festival. These are almost certainly pagan fertility rites and this festival is very similar to that of Minehead. A man dressed to look like a horse tours the town prodding women 'for luck' from 10 in the morning until late evening accompanied by dancers and singing crowds. A proclamation of 1830 declared that 'The Bones of every Padstow Boy are fired by the Hobby Horse . . .' which can leave little doubt about the purpose of it all. Weary walkers might be a little circumspect about arriving on the evening of the 1st of May.

Padstow is a pretty town, well-kept and with a character of its own. Just walking around it is a pleasure, provided that it's not too crowded. It has all facilities.

Hotel:	Old Custom House Inn; Tel. Padstow (0841) 532359
B&B:	The Cross House, Church Street; Tel. Padstow (0841) 532391
Buses:	Bodmin, Newquay, Bude, St Ives, Truro
Early closing:	Wednesday
Ferry:	All year to Rock, frequent sailings. Tel. Padstow (0841) 532239

ST ENODOC

Situated behind Brae Hill, on the Golf Course, this little church was buried in the sand until 1863. Any spire is unusual in Cornwall, but this one is 13th-century, which makes it rarer still. The rest of the church is Norman. Another rarity is the tomb to John Mably and his daughter, dated 1687. This is the latest known example of an incised slab with effigies in England.

POLZEATH AND NEW POLZEATH

These small resorts are of no great interest but they do have shops, refreshments and accommodation.

Hotel:	St Elmo Hotel; Tel. Polzeath (020 886) 3213
Bus:	Rock, Bodmin, Wadebridge

RUMP'S POINT

This complicated Iron Age castle on its well-formed promontory was occupied from 1 B.C. to 1 A.D. – dates confirmed by the Cornwall Archaeological Society during excavations in 1963–68.

DOYDEN POINT

The castle is a folly, built by the Landowner in 1830. He used it as a ballroom and a venue for his elaborate parties. The castle, the house and the land now belong to the National Trust.

PORT QUIN

This was once quite a busy little fishing village and is now almost deserted out of season. The long low building by the harbour used to be the Pilchard Palace, where they salted and barrelled the fish for export. The National Trust is the main landowner now.

ROSCARROCK

Parts of Roscarrock Manor Farm are 12th-century and the collection of stone buildings is a rare example of what these great farm settlements looked like in the Middle Ages. You need a little imagination, but the framework is there.

ST ENDELLION

Just south, behind Roscarrock, this tiny village has a Church with the enchanting name of St Endellienta. It is a very well-preserved 15th-century church, with a Norman Font and a delicately sculpted tomb chest, dated 1400, made by the Master of Endellion, who also sculpted the Stoup inside the south door and was one of the foremost sculptors of his generation.

PORT ISAAC

Once again there is great dispute about the name. Some say it means Corn Port, but it is more likely Lower Port. Issyke is Cornish for lower and locals pronoune the name Port 'Issik'. It is a delightful little village of narrow streets, twisted passages, and quaint old buildings. It used to be a thriving fishing port and the harbour was constructed in the 19th century when everyone believed that pilchards had become as indispensable as sliced bread. Well the pilchards have gone, the four great salting houses have found other uses, and the tourists who throng the town in summer ensure that the locals do not starve. The town has all facilities.

Hotel:	Headlands Hotel; Tel. Port Isaac (020 888) 260
B&B:	Gwel Avor, Tintagel Terrace; Tel. Port Isaac (020 888) 404
Early closing:	Wednesday
Buses:	Wadebridge, Camelford

14

Port Isaac to Bude

From Bossinny to Tintagel Castle on the Shore is a Mile. This Castelle hath bene a marvelus strong and notable forteres, and almost situ loci inexpugnabile, *especially for the Dungeon that is on a grat and high terrible cragge environid with the Se, but having a Draw Bridge from the Residew of the Castelle onto it. The Residew of the Buildingues of the Castel be sore wether beten and yn Ruine, but it hath bene a large thinge. The Castel had be likehod iii. Wardes, wherof ii. be woren away with gulfyng yn of the Sea, yn so much that yt hathe made ther almost an Isle, and no way ys to enter ynto hyt now but by long Elme Trees layde for a Bryge. So that now withowte the Isle renneth alonly a Gate Howse, a Welle, and a fals Braye dyged and walled. In the Isle remayne old Walles, and yn the Est Part of the same, the Ground beyng lower, remayneth a Walle embateled, and Men alyve saw theryn a Postern Dore of Yren. There is yn the Isle a prety Chapel of S. Ulette alias Uliane, with a Tumbe on the left side. There ys also yn the Isle a Welle, and ny by the same ys a Place hewen owt of the Stony Grownd to the Length and Brede of a Man. Also ther remayneth yn the Isle a Grownd quadrant walled as yt were a Garden Plot; and by this Walle appere the Ruines of a Vault. The Grownd of this Isle now nuryshyth Shepe and Conys.*

LELAND, John (1506?–1552). Librarian to Henry VIII and King's Antiquary. Extract from his *Itinerary* 1534–1543, first published in 1710.

Introduction

Parts of the coastline on this stretch are wild, beautiful and unspoilt. Be prepared, however, for a number of steep gradients and to use up nervous energy navigating in places where the path is not clear. But the price is small for the natural beauty you will enjoy.

Port Isaac to Port Gaverne is uninteresting. Port Gaverne to Trebarwith Strand is wild tough country with some fine high cliff walking mixed with problems of cliff fall and subsidence, bad signposting, sometimes indifferent maintenance and some of the steepest gradients of the whole coastal path. From Trebarwith to Tintagel the going is good and easy while beyond, to Boscastle, it is good – but hardish work. After Boscastle, right through to Crackington Haven, the scenery is wild and the walking good and strenuous. But the maintenance and waymarking between Pentargon and Ruset Cliff leave much to be desired. Crackington Haven to Bude has some good scenery, but much of the path has been disrupted by subsidence and there is an unnecessary diversion inland at Cleave Farm. Between Boscastle and Bude there are few refreshment facilities.

The rock is upper Devonian slates and sandstones with some igneous rock outcrops from Port Isaac to Boscastle. Upper and lower carboniferous rocks, sandstone and shale then take over all the way to Bude. These are all sedimentary rocks and yield a mixed coastline which varies – with the exposure and the subsequent erosion to which such rock is prey – from high wild cliff and rugged coves, to low cliffs and beaches where the structure has collapsed.

Apart from the birds and flowers you have already met (the rocks off Tintagel are a breeding ground for many seabirds including the puffin), there is a unique wood in a gully beyond Bynorth Cliff: it is the only sessile oak wood preserved in Cornwall. In spring its thick undergrowth is a mass of fresh pretty flowers and later wild strawberries and blackberries tempt observant walkers to linger here.

It is pleasant to wander around Port Isaac and Boscastle which are both attractive Cornish ports. Tintagel is of course the focus of the Arthurian Legend and no one should miss it. There are many pre-historic remains and the Bronze Age burial mounds beyond Start Point and Rocky Valley both deserve attention.

DISTANCE		TIME	PORT ISAAC TO BUDE	TELEPHONE	TRAIN	BUS	FERRY	SHOPS	CAMPING	ACCOMMODATION	REFRESHMENT	CUMUL. DIST. KMS
STAGE	CUMUL.											
			PORT ISAAC	x		x		x		x	x	686
1	1	:15	PORT GAVERNE	x		x		x		x	x	687
9	10	2:15	TREBARWITH STRAND	x		x				x	x	696
3	13	:45	TINTAGEL	x		x		x		x	x	699
7	20	1:45	BOSCASTLE	x		x		x	x	x	x	706
(2)		(:30)	(ST GENNYS)									
(7)		(1:45)	(WEEK ST MARY)									
(2½)		(:40)	(POUNDSTOCK)									
25	45	6:15	BUDE	x		x		x	x	x	x	731

TIMES ARE BASED ON AVERAGE WALKER LIGHTLY LADEN.

NB.
1. *STAGE: is the distance between that point and the preceding point.*
2. *CUMUL.: is the cumulative distance from the beginning of the chapter.*
3. *TIME: is the time for the stage (between that point and the preceding one) calculated at 4 kilometres per hour – the rate for a lightly loaded person walking without halt.*
4. *Brackets enclose places not on the Path but easily reached from it, together with distances and times from the Path.*
5. *CUMULATIVE DISTANCE: is the total distance from South Haven Point.*

Guide

Follow the road around, through Port Isaac, behind the harbour and up on to the cliffs on a path which leads off opposite Barclay's Bank. This takes you round the point, in front of the coastguard station, and on to the road leading to **Port Gaverne**.

Behind the harbour, turn inland towards the Port Gaverne Hotel, where a path leads straight up, metalled at first, to meet the road again above the Headlands Hotel. Turn right on to the road for a few metres and then left on to the cliffs along the path which passes in front of some cliff top cottages.

Continue along the cliffs, dip down to cross a stream and then climb up over Bounds Cliff, and after several dips, past a disused coastguard look-out, and up on to Tregardock Cliff.

197

You will then pass Tregardock Beach, go round the mountain and down to a stream by Tregonnick Tail.

From the stream climb up on to the cliffs once more and continue along the top, through gorse and bracken, past **Start Point** and the burial mounds, landward of the path just beyond the point. Drop steeply down to cross two streams above Backways Cove and climb up, on tracks which go landward round the hill above Dennis Point, before coming around the hill to the cliffs once more, and descending into **Trebarwith Strand**.

Cross the slipway and climb up on to the cliffs opposite. The path continues along the cliff tops past Hole Beach with its prominent pillar of rock, across Penhallic Point, past the youth hostel at Dunderhole Point, and past the 11th-century church. It then crosses over Tintagel Head, passing the remains of King Arthur's Castle and running seaward of the hotel, from which a path runs inland to **Tintagel**.

From Tintagel Head the path continues along the cliffs, across the neck of Willapark, with its Iron Age cliff castle. The two rocks known as the Sisters lie off Willapark to the north west and Lye Rock to the north east. A footpath leads inland here to **Bossinney**. The path then drops down very steeply, by steps at first, to cross a stream above Bossinney Haven, then it climbs up through gorse to run along the cliff top before going sharply down, and inland slightly, along the impressive rocky valley, where it crosses the torrent on a foot-bridge.

Now climb up the other side, past Long Island, Short Island, and the distinctive rock with a hole in it known as Ladies Window. (The house you see inland is Travelga Manor.) Continue along the cliff top, past Grower Rock and then steeply into the coomb before Willapark, with its white castellated coastguard look-out and the big Meachard Rock offshore. Cross the stream seaward of a ruined cottage and climb straight up the hill opposite. Go along the path which cuts across the neck of Willapark Headland (the second one), descend across the slope of the cliff, then go straight down to the natural harbour of **Boscastle**. Head for its protective wall and climb down on to the quay, following it inland to cross the water by the first stone bridge.

Leaving Boscastle, take the path which climbs seaward to the right of the Pixi Shop a few metres from the bridge. It passes in front of a row of cottages then goes out towards Penally Point, climbing up towards the flag pole with its fish-shaped weathervane on the summit of Penally Hill. It then continues on along the cliff, seaward of a fine stone wall, on the edge of the steep cliffs at Pentargon. At the head of the Rocky Cove the path drops sharply down to cross over a stream, which tumbles as a waterfall to the sea below, and then climbs up over crumbling cliff and around the headland. Continue on through gorse and bracken on a path which does not always look safe.

The path now crosses the sloping cliffs, midway between summit and sea, through gorse, heather and brambles, past Seal Hole and up over Fire Beacon Point. Beyond the point you can see two rocks with the sea foaming around them. These are the Beeny Sisters. Carry on along a badly kept, badly marked path through undergrowth and scrub. Dip down to cross a stream and climb up over Buckator, down sharply and briefly, then up again across the side of the cliff to pass in front of a seat dedicated to Charles Mervyn Scott.

Go down again gently at first, across rough ground, then steeply down to cross the stream above Rusey Beach. Climb up on to High Cliff, 223 metres, passing in front of a seat dedicated to John Weaver, from which you can see Lundy Island when visibility allows. The path now turns down, steeply at first, off High Cliff, and crosses a stream, with the Strangles Rocks seaward and landward, to arrive at the charming **Trevigue Farm**, a National Trust property well worth a detour for its farmhouse snacks, lunches, and teas.

Pass Samphire Rock, go down across a stream, up above Northern Door Arch and down towards the headland of Cambeak. Cut across the neck of the headland and back, following the coast, down into **Crackington Haven**, joining the road where it crosses the head of the beach.

Turn left on the road, along the head of the beach, and then follow the road out of the village for about 30 metres. A sign, just before a thatched cottage, directs you up left to the cliffs. The path climbs diagonally through low undergrowth up towards Pencarrow Point, crosses a stile into a field and doubles back along the upper fence, on the cliff edge above Great Barton Strand. Dip down to a stream and go steeply up on to the National Trust property of **Cleave**.

At the top, the path diverts inland to Cleave Farm and then back on to the cliff top, dropping down to cross the stream above Cleave Strand. Go up on to the cliff again, down very steeply and up, only slightly less steeply, on the other side. The path keeps to the cliff edge, past pastures and agricultural land, crosses a stream in a small copse above Chipman Sand,

and climbs up to the Trig Point above Dizzard Point. Passing a curious wire enclosure, it goes on, over Bynorth Cliff, to cross the steep combe, above Concleave Strand, which shelters a wood of dwarf oak trees and is filled with wild flowers in Spring.

The path is waymarked on both sides of the wood, but care should be taken to stick to it through the wood itself as the undergrowth is thick and the ground marshy.

Head back to the cliff top, down sharply on to the road for a couple of hundred metres through Millook, leaving it – just after the holiday flatlets – down a lane on the left (not the earlier private road). You climb up over Foxhole Point, down on to the road and sharply down on it for about 1 kilometre. Turn left off the road along the cliffs and down sharply to cross the stream at Wanson Mouth. Climb up just as steeply, and then down along the cliff edge to cross along Widemouth 'Widmoth' Sand. Go up past a house, to the road again where it crosses a stream, and continue along it behind the hotel before cutting back to seaward, passing landward of a cottage. The path now runs beside the road to Upton, where it takes to the cliffs again over Efford Down. You pass seaward of a coastguard look-out, landward of the tower into **Bude**, where you cross over the canal and, passing the Council Offices on your left, arrive in the town centre.

Gazetteer

PORT GAVERNE

A small fishing port almost part of Port Isaac, which, like its larger neighbour has become a small resort. Not far away Tregeare Rounds (3 kilometres east and inland of Port Gaverne) is an Iron Age earthwork, which was either sited by a very silly strategist or is not a fort at all. It is on the slope of a hill dominated by higher ground. It might have been a cattle enclosure, although it was obviously built by the same team who built the forts.

Hotel:	Port Gaverne Hotel; Tel. Port Gaverne (020888) 244
B&B:	Bodannon Farm; Tel. Port Gaverne (020888) 381

DELABOLE

If you are interested in extremes, visit the old Delabole Quarry, 3 kilometres inland from Tregardock Beach. It was the largest single open excavation in England, a pit 300 metres long and 75 metres deep, worked from the time of Elizabeth I, and once the most important slate quarry in the world. Its slates were shipped from Padstow, Port Isaac and Port Gaverne to cover roofs and to make hearths and blackboards throughout Europe and the British Isles. Today, like so many other pits and quarries, it is out of work. Look around for the rock-crystals, which were known as 'Cornish Diamonds'. They used to be plentiful here.

TREBARWITH STRAND

This tiny fishing village of Port William is now a resort with a pub, a public telephone and the Trebarwith Strand Hotel. The Mill House Inn, 800 metres inland, is on the site of a watermill with an ingenious slate-hung gantry. The massive water wheel operated this hoist, as well as grinding grain in the usual way.

TINTAGEL

> On either side the river lie
> Long fields of Barley and of Rye,
> That clothe the wold and meet the sky,
> And thro' the field the road runs by
>   to many towered Camelot

Of course Tennyson had already seen Tintagel when he wrote the Lady of Shallott, so if some of the facts fit the poem it is no cause for excitement, no supplementary proof that this was indeed King Arthur's capital. Geoffrey of Monmouth first associated Arthur with Tintagel in his 'History of the Britons' in about 1140, but whereas Arthur lived in the 6th and 7th century, the castle itself dates from about the time that Monmouth was writing. Do not let that distract you from your dreams as you walk about these majestic walls of stone.

Try to conjure up the towers that Tennyson talks of, the Gallant Knights, the beautiful richly clothed ladies, the whinny of a horse, the smell of leather, the jangle of a spur. No one can tell you that you're wrong, and there is no better place to give wings to phantasy than this mysterious headland, called 'The Island', where the misty myth of Arthur hangs like a light, late autumn cloud.

There was a celtic monastery on the site: the remains of small square huts you see were the cells of monks.

The 12th-century castle was probably built for Reginald Mortain, Earl of Cornwall, illegitimate son of Henry I. Beside it the Chapel of St Juliot or Julitta was built at about the same time. The Black Prince added to the Castle in Henry III's Reign (1216–1272), building a lower and an upper ward on the mainland and connecting them by a drawbridge to the inner ward and Great Hall on The Island. The Castle was used as a Prison in Elizabethan times, but was then abandoned, and by the beginning of the 17th century was in ruins. Like so many great houses, it fell victim to the cost of upkeep.

Tintagel village lives unashamedly on tourism and on the exploitation of the King Arthur Legend. The disneylike Hotel on the Cliffs gives some hint of the level to which Arthur has been pulled. There are some sights to see. The Old Post Office is probably a 15th Century Cornish Manor House. It was used by the G.P.O. for nearly 50 years, but the National Trust have owned it since 1903. Barras Nose, just beside the Castle is one of the earliest properties the Trust acquired – in 1897, two years after its foundation.

St Mertetriana's Church is early Norman and has a number of Saxon features, the hinges on the Saxon looking door are the original 12th century iron-work, and there is a Roman Milestone made in the Emperor Licinius' rein (308–324 A.D.). Among the monuments there is a well preserved 13th century slab and a brass of 1430, both are rare.

Willapark Headland, overlooking Bossiney Haven has an Iron Age Promonitory Fort which must have witnessed all the goings on on King Arthur's Island. But Forts cannot talk. Bossiney, behind it, was important enough to return two Members to Parliament from the 13th century right up to the 19th century. Sir Francis Drake was once its representative.

Tintagel has all facilities.

Hotel:	Bossiney House, Bossiney; Tel. Tintagel (08404) 240
B&B:	Pendrin Guest House, Atlantic Road; Tel. Tintagel (08404) 560
YHA:	Dunderhole Point; Tel. Tintagel (08404) 334
Early closing:	Thursday

Bus: To Camelford, Bodmin, Plymouth, Newquay,
                 St Ives

ST NECTAN'S KIEVE

A pretty rocky valley runs inland from Bossiney Haven, and at its head lies this 12 metre waterfall that the hermit St Nectan lived beside in the 6th century. A Kieve is the pool at the base of a waterfall. Nearby two sisters lived in complete seclusion, but only the ruins of their cottage now remain. No one knew who they were or where they came from – not even their nationality. Inevitably, in a county as superstitious and as given to rumour as Cornwall is, countless legends grew up about them. Daphne du Maurier tells one in her poetically reminiscent book *Vanishing Cornwall*. There are two Bronze Age rock carvings in a ruined mill also in the valley.

BOSCASTLE

The Norman de Bottreaux family built their castle here and gave the place its name. The name and a grassy mound over the ruins of their Great House is the only trace they left. There was already a harbour here in the 14th century, exporting slate, grain, and oak bark for tanning leather, but it was repeatedly wrecked by the weather. Sir Richard Grenville, of H.M.S. Revenge, rebuilt it in 1584 and it owes its present condition to restoration by the National Trust in 1962.

The National Trust owns much of Boscastle and much of the surrounding land. Forrabury Common, due south of Boscastle, is a rare example of stitchmeal, a uniquely Cornish form of Celtic land tenure. Each stitch, or strip of land is separated from its neighbour by a low bank or a furrow, and the National Trust owns 34 stitches of the total 42.

St Merteriana, the Parish Church of Boscastle, is 2 kilometres east of the town and was built on the site of the ancient Priory of St Sergius. The priory has disappeared but the church may once have been its chapel, although Victorian 'improvements' make it hard to tell.

There are three interesting buildings in the land between St Nectan's Kieve and Boscastle. Trewitten has one of the oldest farmhouses in North Cornwall, two storeys of two rooms each built before the 14th century.

Redivallen is an E-shaped Manor House with mullioned windows and a notable porch.

Trehane Barton is another farm, dating from the 14th century, although it has 18th-century additions.

Ten hectares of the northern side of Valency valley near Boscastle were given to the National Trust in 1971 as a memorial to Thomas Hardy and his wife Emma by one of his descendants. Emma (Giffard) came from St Juliot and was courted by the novelist whilst he was working as an architect on her brother-in-law's church, in 1871. He was an architect before becoming a writer. They married four years later and, although never a very happy affair, the marriage lasted until her death 30 years later. Only one of Hardy's novels *A Pair of Blue Eyes* is set in Cornwall.

Boscastle has a Museum of Witchcraft which is open from Easter to September, which may account for some of the more mystifying people you see in the town. The prettiest part of the town is around the harbour, where the houses are well maintained and development is restrained. The town has all the facilities of a modern resort.

Hotel:	Bottreaux House; Tel. Boscastle (08405) 231
B&B:	Bridge House, The Harbour, Tel. Boscastle (08405) 477
YHA:	Palace Stables; Tel. Boscastle (08405) 287
Early closing:	Thursday
Buses:	Tintagel, Plymouth, Bude, Bodmin

TREVIGUE FARM AND THE SAMPHIRE ROCK

Trevigue is a really solid 16th-century Cornish farmhouse standing isolated in its own farmland and now the property of the National Trust. Although you can persuade yourself that you are there for architectural advancement, you should try the real farmhouse teas or the light lunches prepared by the ladies of the house. They are quite delicious.

Samphire, the name comes from the French 'St Pierre', is an aromatic plant whose fleshy salty leaves were much prized in pickles. It grows in difficult places like on the rock, and the Samphire collectors lot is not an easy one. Shakespeare puts it vividly 'Halfe way down hangs one that gathers Samphire: dreadful trade'.

CRACKINGTON HAVEN

Great plans were laid in 1836 for 'Victoria', a brave new town with a modern harbour on the bay at Tremoutha Haven. The plans came to nothing, and Crackington Haven remains a sleepy little resort offering bathing and surfing to the few holiday makers that know of it. There is an unconsecrated graveyard in the village, where shipwreck victims were buried before the Church mended its ways and accepted them in consecrated ground. The village has a shop, a public house and, in season, the Coombe Barton Hotel; Tel. (084 03) 345.

ST GENNYS

A kilometre inland from the Haven the church of St Genesius is mainly Norman, but the top of the tower is 20th-century 'medieval'. The square font is made of Purbeck Marble, which is quite rare in Cornwall. In season you can find accommodation at White Lodge; Tel. St Genny's (084 03) 528.

WEEK ST MARY

The history of this village, 10 kilometres inland of the path east of Dizzard Point reads like a fairy story. Tomasine Bonaventura was a shepherd's daughter. In 1463, at the age of 13, a London merchant riding through the village took her off to London as a servant for his wife and himself. His wife died three years later and he married the girl. Two years later he died, leaving his considerable fortune to his 18-year-old wife. She then married another wealthy merchant, who died leaving her a second fortune when she was only 30. John Percivall, her next husband, became Lord Mayor of London in 1499, was knighted, and she was made a Dame – and then he died leaving her, at 50, an extremely wealthy, childless widow. So she returned to Week St Mary and lavished all her fortune on the village, founding a chantry and a school. The old school-house is now a farmhouse, and the Church of the Nativity of St Mary is 14th- and 15th-century.

POUNDSTOCK

Is not far from the path, south east of Millook Haven. Near it, Penfound Manor is one of the oldest continuously inhabited manors in the country. The house is Tudor but was built around a large medieval hall and the latest additions are 17th century, made in Stuart times. In the town the 14th-century guildhall and the church are both interesting. The two-storeyed guildhall joins the church at right-angles. The church of St Neot is Norman, added to in the 15th century and spruced up a little in the 19th century. The font is 13th century; the original pulpit is Jacobean; and there are some rather faded wall paintings which it is quite fun to try to decipher.

BUDE

Bude is not really famous for anything. It is a comparatively modern town, and the two things which distinguished it both date from the 19th century and are both largely forgotten. Sir Goldsworthy Gurney (1793–1875) the engineer and inventor lived here. He invented the oxy-hydrogen limelight, called Bude Light, which was used for lighthouses. He also developed a means for building solidly on sand. His home, The Castle, now Bude Council Offices was built this way – and is still standing.

The other thing worth noting in Bude is the canal. It used to run from Bude to Launceston but now only 3½ kilometres are navigable. It carried lime-rich shell sand and coal inland, slate and corn out. Opened in 1825 it was ingenious because it had no locks. Instead it used a series of inclined planes. The loaded boats were pulled up on rails by a complicated system of buckets filled with water which were sunk into deep shafts in the ground. The weight of the boats going down pulled the buckets up again. The canal was closed in 1891.

Stratton, really part of Bude today, is much older than its big neighbour, and used to be more important. It stands on the site of the Roman town of Musidunum, but was already Stratone when recorded in the Domesday Book in 1086. St Andrew's Church was built in 1348 and has 15th century additions. It has a Norman font and a Jacobean pulpit.

Ebbingford Manor in Bude is medieval but was restored in 1758. Both house and grounds are open to the public.

At Stamford Hill just north of Stratton, Sir Bevil Grenville led the King's Forces to victory over the parliamentary troops in 1643. Sir Bevil used the Tree Inn as his headquarters during the Battle, but you will find it somewhat changed today. Bude has all services.

Hotel:	Hotel Penarvor; Tel. Bude (0288) 2036
B&B:	Wellcome, 14 Burn View; Tel. Bude (0288) 2289
Early closing:	Thursday
Tourist Information:	Tel. Bude (0288) 4240
Buses:	Bideford, Exeter, Newquay, Plymouth, St Ives, Boscastle, Morwenstow

15

Bude to Barnstaple

All who have travelled through the delicious scenery of North Devon, must needs know the little white town of Bideford, which slopes upwards from its broad tide-river paved with yellow sands, and many-arched old bridge where salmon wait for autumn floods, towards the pleasant upland on the west. Above the town the hills close in, cushioned with deep oak woods, through which juts here and there a crag of fern-fringed slate; below, they lower, and open more and more in softly-rounded knolls, and fertile squares of red and green, till they sink into the wide expanse of hazy flats, rich salt marshes, and rolling sand-hills, where Torridge joins her sister Taw, and both together flow quietly toward the broad surges of the bar, and the ever-lasting thunder of the long Atlantic swell. Pleasantly the old town stands there, beneath its soft Italian sky, fanned day and night by the fresh ocean breeze, which forbids alike the keen winter frosts, and the fierce thunder heats of the midland;. and pleasantly it has stood there for now, perhaps, eight hundred years, since the first Grenville, cousin of the Conqueror, returning from the conquest of South Wales, drew round him trusty Saxon serfs, and free Norse rovers with their golden curls, and dark Silurian Britons from the Swansea shore, and all the mingled blood which still gives to the seaward folk of the next county their strength and intellect, and, even in these levelling days, their peculiar beauty of face and form.

KINGSLEY, Charles (1819–75). Historian and novelist. Opening paragraph of *Westward Ho!* (1855).

Introduction

Striking scenery and savage slopes provide variety and

challenge on this leg. From Bude there is some gentle cliff walking for the first 10 kilometres or so over rounded, down-like cliffs. After Stanbury Mouth the ground gets steeper, and between here and Welcombe Mouth there are five fairly daunting coombs to climb; the two steepest just after crossing into Devon at Marsland Mouth. These are followed by 5 kilometres of good level cliff walking and then a succession of climbs interspersed with level ground until you reach Mouth-Mill.

From Mouth-Mill to Clovelly the path winds through woods and the delightful park of Clovelly Court, and after Clovelly through tall woods on the Hobby Drive. Then the path is fairly mixed until just after Bucks Mills, where it enters the Portledge Estate and keeps to open cliffs and well kept farm-land almost until Westward Ho! You then have the choice of a trudge round the estuary and a ferry, or a bus direct to Barnstaple.

The coastal structure is still the Upper and Lower Carboniferous, sandstone and shales, which we first met at Boscastle and which takes us now almost to Barnstaple. Just before the town it switches back to Middle Devonian. One small exception to this is the area around Peppercombe, where the cliffs are red sandstone – Triassic Marls. The coast-line is varied: from Bude to Hartland Point there is a series of sharp headlands of harder rock which have resisted attack by the elements over the ages. Ridges with flat grass-covered tops often stretch inland from these headlands, leaving a succession of valleys to be crossed by the coastal walker. The coast here slices at right-angles through the folded and con-torted strata showing us an almost perfect cross-section of the earth's crust. Beyond Hartland Point the cliffs and their hinterland have something of the character of rocky downland sliced off to the sea. These north-facing cliffs with their abundant vegetation give the scenery a less abrupt character. The desolate unspoilt nature of parts of this stretch has also allowed wild life to develop undisturbed. Butterflies and birds are plentiful and varied here.

There are plenty of legends here too. It is a coast which has claimed many lives, especially in the stretch from Trevose Head to Hartland Point. At Longpeak, the twisted, rusting iron on the cliff top and on the rocks below is a substantial reminder that around that point alone over 130 ships met their fate in only a couple of centuries. Relics of ancient civiliza-tions exist in the castles of Embury Beacon and Peppercombe, and Hartland Quay and Barnstaple show signs of erstwhile commercial prosperity. Clovelly is certainly the jewel set in this part of the coast. But other places, like Morwenstow, also deserve attention.

Guide

Cross the bridge over the river and head off along the coast. The path leaves Bude up a road marked 'Private' leading past the last houses of Bude at Wrangle Point. Cross over a stile by the National Trust sign for Maer Cliff and keep to the edge of the cliff right through this area. At its northern limit, go landward around the large chalet, to avoid a landslip, and out of National Trust land. Just beyond the chalet follow signs back on to the cliff edge. Drop down into Northcott Mouth, where you cross over the stream by some concrete anti-invasion debris and climb sharply up on to the cliffs again.

You will then pass disused brick buildings, more reminders of the Second World War, and more farmland, hanging on to the cliff edge before descending into Sandy-Mouth. Cross the stream and climb back on to the cliffs on the far side. Continue along the high path past a disused coastguard look-out and down into Warren Gutter, where jagged slate ridges project vertically out into the sea. Up again over the hill and down steeply to **Duckpool.** Cross over, seaward of the pool, and climb steeply up Steeple Point. You are now almost upon the huge white dish aerials of the satellite tracking station, which you have watched growing larger for some time. Leaving them to landward, follow the path through gorse, close to the cliff edge, down to Lower Sharpnose Point. Double back up, towards the station once more and, crossing some rough estate roads, head off north again (left) along the coast.

The path now starts to descend, following the cliff edge, beside farmland down around Rane Point, to cross a stream on a footbridge at Stanbury Mouth. Then, after some more brief climbs it again crosses a stream to pass **Higher Sharpnose Point**. Here you descend to cross another stream. It is important to keep seaward on this stretch as there is a confusion of tracks which could cause you a detour uselessly inland. Once across the stream in the valley by Higher Sharpnose Point and you will climb up past Hawker's Hut – now National Trust property – which is just below the path to

STAGE	CUMUL.	TIME	BUDE TO BARNSTAPLE	TELEPHONE	TRAIN	BUS	FERRY	SHOPS	CAMPING	ACCOMMODATION	REFRESHMENT	CUMUL. DIST. KMS
			BUDE	x				x	x	x	x	731
3¼	3¼		SANDY MOUTH								x	734¼
5½	8¾	1:25	MORWENSTOW	x						x	x	739¾
11¼	20	2:50	HARTLAND QUAY	x					x	x	x	751
(1)		(:15)	(STOKE)									
5	25	1:15	WEST TITCHBERRY						x	x		756
11¼	36¼	2:50	CLOVELLY	x		x				x	x	767¼
4¾	41	1:10	WALLAND CARY	x				x		x	x	772
1½	42½	:25	BUCK'S MILLS	x					x			773½
(1)		(:15)	(PORTLEDGE HOTEL)							x		
11¼	53¼	2:50	WESTWARD HO!	x		x		x	x	x	x	784¾
6	59¾	1:30	APPLEDORE	x		x	x		x	x	x	790¾
(5)		(1:15)	(BIDEFORD)	x		x	x		x	x	x	
			INSTOW			x	x					
10	69¾	2:30	BARNSTAPLE	x	x	x		x	x	x	x	800¾

TIMES ARE BASED ON AVERAGE WALKER LIGHTLY LADEN.

NB.
1. STAGE: is the distance between that point and the preceding point.
2. CUMUL.: is the cumulative distance from the beginning of the chapter.
3. TIME: is the time for the stage (between that point and the preceding one) calculated at 4 kilometres per hour – the rate for a lightly loaded person walking without halt.
4. Brackets enclose places not on the Path but easily reached from it, together with distances and times from the Path.
5. CUMULATIVE DISTANCE: is the total distance from South Haven Point.

seaward when you arrive on top of Vicarage Cliff. A short way farther on, as you cross a dry stone wall, a path leads on to **Morwenstow**, of which Hawker of the Hut was vicar and whose church tower is plainly visible. The coastal path continues around the cliff and drops steeply into the valley to cross a stream by Lucky Hole, before rising almost as steeply on the other side on to Henna Cliff.

Now go down to cross a stream before Gull Rock and up, by well made steps, on to Marsland Cliffs, past a seat dedicated to

Harold Ford. Here Cornwall bids you a sad farewell with an extremely bad piece of path, difficult to follow, badly signed and very uneven. It leads down across the face of the cliff and round into Marsland Mouth.

You enter Devon, cross over the stream on a good bridge and climb up, behind a small hut which looks out to sea, on to the cliff above Marsland Mouth and down almost immediately to Welcombe Mouth with its unwelcome car park and people. Climb straight up the other side through gorse to reach a fine, level, grassy cliff-top path. This takes you past worked agricultural land, past Chisel Ridge, Knaps Longpeak and seaward around Embury Beacon – after which you can see the farm buildings of South Hole just inland.

Continue along the cliffs until, just beyond South Hole, you reach a sign taking you inland, along the north side of a stone wall with hedging, to the road. Turn left along the road for about 1 kilometre until you reach a road junction by some bungalows. A finger post directs you over a good stile and back on to the coast path. This follows the line of the coast, slightly inland of it at first before regaining the crumbly cliff edge. It sticks to the edge around Elmscott Beach, over Mansley Cliff, past Gunpath Rock (from which a sign points inland to the youth hostel at Elmscott) and past the rusting remains of hoisting gear and salvage relating to the Green Ranger wrecked in the cove near Hole Rock in 1962.

Shortly after this the path continues along Swansford Hill, with a stream running in the valley below to landward, until it descends itself to landward to cross the stream by a good bridge. Turn left along the road for 50 metres and climb up over the cliff. Descend behind St Catherine's Tor to ford the stream, cross the field and walk up above **Hartland Quay** on to the Stoke – Hartland Quay Road.

Turn inland up the road to the Rocket House, where waymark signs direct you north along the coast again. Climb up to the cliff top and go along the edge past arable land, seaward of a fine old ruined tower, along the Warren, above Broad Beach and down opposite the Point called Dyer's Lookout. Go inland a little through gorse to cross Abbey River on a good footbridge before turning seaward again by a cottage on the valley floor.

The path leads up on to the cliff on the far side then sharply down to another footbridge before climbing up and out towards Damehole Point. It is worth following the path right out on to the point. The South West Way Association consider it to be 'one of the most dramatic pieces of definitive right of way in the whole country'. Then come back to climb over a shoulder, turning slightly inland and crossing another well made footbridge over a stream by a permanently sited (and quite unsightly) caravan. Cross the field towards the sea and climb up, over a stile, on to Upright Cliff. The path now keeps to the cliff edge right up to Hartland Point (whose coastguard station and lighthouse are plainly visible) passing just seaward of the cultivated land.

When you reach the Point, pass inland of the look-out and, between the base of its hill and the stone wall of its garage below, you emerge through a latch gate on to the road. Turn right and follow the road up to the car park where the path leads up to the left on to the cliffs again. The path takes you around the R.A.F. radar installations, between the decaying perimeter fence and the sometimes fragile cliff edge. Leaving the fence behind, you cross a series of stiles on cliff-top arable land and come to the National Trust property above Shipload Bay. There is a steep path down to the beach for those who wish to bathe.

On the far (eastern) edge of the bay, the path leads on along the cliffs to a seat at Eldern Point, and continues along beside farmland on Gawlish Cliff. Undulating along the cliff edge, through fields, you pass a triangulation point above Chapman Rock, but it is difficult to see the Rock itself. The path continues over Exmansworthy Cliff, around above Beckland Bay and Windbury Point. There it goes out along the Ridge and then back inland to cut down through woods and cross a footbridge before climbing up out of the coomb and the woods, over the hill and, in the seaward corner of the next field, turning down left through woods to Mouth Mill.

Emerging by a cottage and a ruined kiln the path turns right to cross the stream on the grey stone beach and climbs up inland on a good estate road. This is the Clovelly Estate. The path is well marked through the rhododendron-filled woods. It takes you along the high cliff edge, through forest, on good woodland roads and tracks. Past Gallantry Bower then, just inland of the Angel's Wings shelter, through a very tall iron Kissing Gate, with clear views across well kept parkland to Clovelly Court. (You see the house but do not approach it.) You continue along the seaward edge of the park of Clovelly Court, finally swinging around, slightly uphill, to the right, to go out of the park through a large green gate on to the road.

Turn right and then immediately left. On the right is a car

park and cafe, on your left 800 metres of steep cobbled street leading down through **Clovelly**; straight ahead, through a gate, you will see Hobby Drive – nearly 5 kilometres of wooded estate road.

Take the stony, foot-breaking **Hobby Drive**, which winds interminably up through the fine forest until, just before the toll gate off the A39, you turn left on a path down into a gully, which you cross by footbridge. The path climbs up out of the gully and continues along the cliff edge over stiles, between farmland and rough vegetation on the cliff top, until it dips down and inland around the head of a pretty coomb unfortunately filled with refuse. Go right around the coomb, keeping seaward around the large field and cross the bridge-type stile on to a dirt road. Turn right and you come to a metalled road. This is the holiday village of **Walland Cary**. Turn right and immediately left to go down through the village, past buildings and chalets, at first on the metalled road and then on the track leading on through trees, across a field and, passing between two sheds, down a long windy track through woods to **Buck's Mills**.

Turn right up the main street and left up a path by the telephone box. This leads steeply up on to the cliffs again, seaward of a coastguard look-out and along a good cliff-top track, between high banks, to the road. Just before the road the path goes off to the left, down over three stiles, on to a track which undulates through woods until finally turning down to Peppercombe.

Turn right over the bridge, by a cottage, and left across a stile into a field. The cliffs are now very red. The path climbs a little and then leads around seaward on the low cliffs. Undulating, it crosses a bridge by a small white hut and climbs past the track leading inland to the **Portledge Hotel** (a good halt for those in search of refined comfort for their weary limbs, and reasonable fare for their hunger). When it reaches the cliffs through rich pastureland which stretches all along the coast to Westward Ho! go over the hill and down steeply through trees, till you find yourself in Babbacombe Mouth. Here you will take a flight of steps, cross two streams, the latter by a ruined kiln, and walk on through pastures till you reach the line of the old railway track which takes you around past Rock Nose and Mermaids' Pool into the rather unattractive resort of Westward Ho! There it is best to walk along the front to the bus stop, on the inland side of the Bowling Green, if you want to avoid a rather boring walk.

In season a ferry operates between Appledore and Instow. Walk on along the coast from Westward Ho! on the pebble ridge, past Goosey Pool and Sandymere – both inlands on Northam Burrows. Then go on around the golf course, and past the coastguard look-out on the point to join first the track and then the road into **Appledore**. There you can walk around the front past the life-boat station, to the ferry point and thus to **Instow**, or on, following the banks of the Torridge Estuary to **Bideford**. You can pick up the bus to Barnstaple in either Instow or Bideford.

Gazetteer

STOWE BARTON

This is the house Sir Richard Grenville left from when he sailed the gallant little Revenge to the Azores for the last time. That house has gone, gone too is the house John Grenville, Earl of Bath built to replace it in 1591. That mighty mansion was called 'The Noblest in the West of England' by Borlase, and Pevsner spent much ink on its eleven-bay façade, its seven-bay depth, its two stories and its two wings. It was pulled down in 1739 and much of the material was used to build Penstowe, the present house. Only the stables of the original house remain.

KILKHAMPTON

Further inland, due east of Stowe Barton, Kilkhampton is the Manor in which Stowe Barton stands. The Grenvilles owned it from 1066 until 1711 when it passed to the Bath family. The Church, originally Norman, was considerably altered by the Rev. John Grenville who was Rector from 1524 to 1580. There are many Grenville monuments in the Church, including one to Sir Bevil Grenville who led the King's forces to victory in the Battle of Stamford Hill.

Between Kilkhampton and the path are the motte and bailey of a Norman Castle belonging to the National Trust.

HIGHER SHARPNOSE POINT

About a kilometre east up the Tidna Valley is the 16th-century manor house of Tonacombe. This Tudor-shaped house with its great hall and secret rooms was built in 1585 and is unfortunately not open to the public.

MORWENSTOW

The Reverend Robert Stephen Hawker might be a little surprised were he to return to his hut on Vicarage Cliff to find his landscape dominated by the huge white saucers of the Satellite Tracking Station on Lower Sharpnose Point just to the south, but then he would probably compose a poem to them.

Hawker was vicar of Morwenstow from 1834 to 1874. He was a poet, a Man of God, and an eccentric. He was intensely patriotic and pathologically preoccupied by the fate of shipwreck victims, many of whom were buried in his churchyard, their graves marked by a ship's figurehead. It was his fear of the supernatural and ghosts that gave him such concern: he was afraid that the tortured souls might come to torment him. He built his hut out of shipwreck timbers and spent long hours looking out from it for ships in trouble or writing his poems and legends. The hut belongs to the National Trust now. Hawker even managed to stamp out the plundering of shipwrecks by his parishioners, which had long been considered a right, if not a duty.

He built his vicarage, or had it built, in a very original manner. Each chimney is a model of the tower of a church or of an Oxford college with which he was associated. He restored the church while he was vicar but did not introduce any gimmicks. It is one of the more complete Norman churches in Cornwall. The porch and some of the arches inside the church are decorated with primitive heads of men and animals, and there are some early English and some medieval additions. The font is a very primitive Norman egg-shape, and there are faint tracings of a wall painting of St Morwenna on the north wall of the chancel.

His best known poem was the 'Song of the Western Men' commonly known as 'and shall Trelawny die'.

> And shall Trelawny die?
> Here's twenty thousand Cornish men
> Will know the reason why!

The song became very popular and Hawker commented with unaccustomed bitterness 'all those years the song has been bought and sold, set to music and applauded, while I have lived on among these faraway rocks unprofited, unpraised and unknown. This is the epitome of my whole life.'

At the age of 19 Hawker married his first wife, a lady of 40. When she died 40 years later he took a new wife, a girl of 20, who bore him 3 daughters. He also introduced the institution of the annual Harvest Festival into the Anglican Church. At least four books have been written about him, the latest, *Hawker of Morwenstow* by Piers Brendon in 1975.

Morwenstow has facilities for refreshment and accommodation.

B&B: Old Rectory Farm; Tel. Morwenstow (028 883) 251
           Villa Rosa. Shop; Tel. Morwenstow (028 883) 228

Buses: Bude, Holsworthy

Devon

WELCOMBE

This is about 1 kilometre up the valley from Welcombe Mouth. The church is early and has an unbuttressed tower and no aisles. Its timber screen – probably Saxon – is one of the earliest in Devon, and the Jacobean lectern is also quite rare. The village has a fine old Devon farm and a blacksmith's shop which has been turned into an inn called the Old Smithy. Accommodation is available.

B&B: The Hermitage, Welcombe Mouth; Tel. Morwenstow (028 883) 258

EMBURY BEACON

The promontory fort here is Iron Age, but is interesting because its ramparts are particularly wide spaced. There has been quite a lot of learned debate as to the reason for this, but no one seems to have considered the possibility that it was simply an Iron Age error.

GUNPATH ROCK

The rusting derricks and scrap iron on the cliff and down

below have become something of a landmark. They belong to the wreck of the Royal Fleet Auxiliary tanker Green Ranger, cast on to the rocks in a force 8 gale on 17 November 1962. Despite filthy weather conditions and difficult terrain all of the crew were taken off by breeches buoy, although it took nearly 12 hours to hoist the seven to safety. The path to Elmscott Youth Hostel is signed inland just south of the scrap iron.

YHA: Youth Hostel, School House, Elmscott; Tel. Hartland (02374) 367

MILFORD

This is about 1 kilometre inland behind Longpeak. Farmers here have found a novel use for a medieval chapel – they have turned it into a tractor shed.

ST CATHERINE'S TOR

There used to be a Roman building on the top of this 85 metre tor and there was a massive wall connecting it to the high points close to it. Later there was a medieval chapel. Today you need a lot of patience and imagination to find evidence of these.

HARTLAND QUAY

The original harbour was built here in the 14th century by the monks of Hartland Abbey, and Parliament granted authority to improve it in 1566. The very illustrious trio of Sir Walter Raleigh, Sir Francis Drake and Sir John Hawkins had the Act passed. The harbour imported coal, lime, and general merchandise and shipped out corn and malt from the Abbey farms. Lead for the roof of Stoke church was brought in here in 1616, for example. In summer there is a shop in the group of buildings on the quay, and refreshment and accommodation are available.

Hotel: Hartland Quay Hotel; Tel. Hartland (02374) 371

STOKE

The little stone hut in the road just outside Hartland Quay is the 'Rocket House'. This is where Henry Trengrouse's Rocket Apparatus and other life-saving gear was stored for use in emergencies. A kilometre along this road is Stoke, with St Nectan's, the Parish Church of Hartland. The church is so grand that it has been called the Cathedral of North Devon; its 40 metre pinnacled tower is the tallest in the county. The church is partly Norman, partly 14th century and partly 15th century. The north east chancel chapel has finely worked Belgian flamboyant tracery panels and there is a 'Pope's Room', over the north porch, where a priest used to live. The solid oak beam above the screen came from H.M.S. Revenge, one of the last wooden battleships. The church was built on the site of the Celtic Shrine of St Nectan who, after being beheaded carried his dripping head to Stoke. A foxglove grew where each drop of blood had fallen; a phenomenon commemorated on each St Nectan's day, 17th June, by children carrying foxgloves to the church.

HARTLAND ABBEY

King Harold's mother, Gytha, wife of the Earl of Godwin founded the Abbey in the 11th century as a college of secular canons. She did it to thank St Nectan for saving her son from shipwreck. A Belgian, Geoffrey de Dinant, turned it into an Augustinian Abbey in 1189 and when Henry VIII confiscated the church lands he gave Hartland to the Keeper of the King's Cellar, Sir William Abbott. Abbott converted it into a mansion, and possibly part of that building survives in the present house, although none of the earlier buildings survive. The present house was built for Paul Orchard in 1779 and includes material from the original Abbey Cloisters, but even this house was tampered with in the 19th century. It remains a private house today.

THE WARREN

This tower on the cliffs above Hartland Quay is something of a conundrum. It is the kind of ruin that makes sensitive travellers spend the next few kilometres planning how to convert it into an isolated country retreat, with huge fires, books, music, a bed of everlasting softness and what the

French call 'every comfort'. However it ends up, it was either built in the 17th century as a look-out for the Barbary Pirates who infested the Bristol Channel, or in the 18th century as a folly or summer house for the owner of the Abbey. Now it is simply an enigmatic ruin.

BLEGBERRY

Behind dramatic Damehole Point, a few hundred metres inland, there is further evidence of the menace of Barbary Pirates, whose activities were not confined to the seas. Even isolated houses near the coast had to protect themselves. Blegberry Farm is one of the best and most complete examples of a fortified 16th-century farm to have survived the ravages of 'improving' owners or of neglect.

HARTLAND POINT

If you are ever leafing through a copy of Ptolemy's *Guide to Geography* (published in Florence 1400 A.D.) this is the 'Promontory of Herculeas' he refers to with such diffidence. The lighthouse, built in 1874, is open to the public on weekday afternoons, and Tichberry Farm, which is just east of the point and is owned by the National Trust, has a very ancient farmhouse and out-buildings. Accommodation is available at West Tichberry Farm; Tel. Hartland (02374) 287.

BROWNSHAM

Just before going down to Mouth Mill and into the Clovelly Estate there are signs to the two Brownsham Farms. Both farms are ancient and both belong to the National Trust. The Higher Brownsham farmhouse is of particular interest as it has a late Tudor ornamented plaster ceiling. The area is also a 28 hectare Nature Reserve.

CLOVELLY COURT

Clovelly Court was built in 1740 by Zachary Hamlyn, who had acquired the Manor from the Cary family in 1730. Its fine park provides charming contrast to the wild cliff scenery for those walkers who are doing several days of continuous coast. Gallantry Bower is named after an incident of gallantry which took place there in the 19th century; an incident of such a subtle nature that Victorian modesty prevented a record of the details being kept and handed down. Angel's Wings is more obvious: the canopy which protects these seats for weary walkers is supported by four powerful carved angels' wings, whilst others decorate the frieze. The shelter was built in 1826.

CLOVELLY

A photographer's dream; the most picturesque village in England; a gem; a jewel – perhaps it is all of these things. It is certainly pretty, well preserved, old and clogged with tourists at weekends and throughout the increasing number of 'seasons' the West Country enjoys. There is one main cobbled street which descends steeply to the harbour and 14th-century pier. It is lined with spick and span cottages and neatly laundered gardens. For those who can't quite manage the walk, there is a Land Rover service from the top and the bottom. No cars are allowed in the village.

Clovelly used to be a fishing port and relied on the herring catch for a time. Now it is tourists and care of the estate that provide the local livelihood. In common with churches on many estates graced with generous landlords, All Saints' is something of a stylistic sampler. The early church was Norman and traces still remain in the south porch. The tower is early medieval and the remainder of the structure is Perpendicular. The font is Norman and the pulpit Jacobean, built of black oak and presented by William Cary, then Lord of the Manor, in 1634. Charles Kingsley's father was Rector there from 1830 to 1836 and, although Kingsley himself was only 11 when he arrived, several of the scenes in *Westward Ho!* were set in the village.

Many of the cottages in the village were restored by Mrs C.L. Hamlyn when she was owner of Clovelly earlier in the 20th century and bear the mark C.H. In 1921 she gave Mount Pleasant, just above the village, to the National Trust as a memorial to the men of Clovelly who died in the First World War.

The Hobby Drive, 5 kilometres of lovely woodland, with good views back to the village and down to the sea, can be very tiring for the walker. It was built early in the 19th century by Sir James Hamlyn as a scenic nature drive. Whether it was built by Clovelly men to give them employment in depressed times or by Napoleonic Prisoners of War is immaterial, whoever carried out the work had little thought for those who might be called upon to walk it.

There are telephones and facilities for refreshment in the car parks above the village and in the village as well; there is also accommodation.

Hotel: Red Lion; Tel. Clovelly (02373) 237
B&B: The Old Smithy, Higher Clovelly; Tel. Clovelly (02373) 202
Buses: Hartland, Farm Cross, Bideford

CLOVELLY DYKES

Off the path, where the B3237 from Clovelly meets the A39, these fortifications may be Roman, although some authorities say that they are Iron Age. There are three concentric rings of banks and ditches, with banks from 4.5 to 7.6 metres high and ditches from 15 to 20 metres wide.

WALLAND CARY

This is unashamedly a holiday village with happy little hutch-like houses and bingo halls. There are also shops and public telephones.

BUCK'S MILLS

This is a tiny hamlet which earned its living burning lime from Pembrokeshire, which was used to neutralize the acid soil. Modern artificial fertilizers and stabilizers have made this practice obsolete. The two lime kilns still stand, however. There is a public telephone box.

WOOLFARDISWORTHY

The 'West Town' of Woolfardisworthy, 4 kilometres inland of the path, has a Norman church with a centrally placed octagonal stair turret in the west tower. This is unusual in North Devon churches although fairly common in the South. The square Norman font is undecorated and mounted on five shafts of blue stone. If you look for the village be sure to pronounce it 'Woolsery', otherwise the natives will not understand you.

PORTLEDGE HOTEL

Soon after the hamlet of Peppercombe an unmade road leads inland, by a ruined hut, to this fine old Tudor House. The manor has been owned by the same family for over 800 years, and Colonel Pine-Coffin now runs the house as an hotel. A comfortable, intresting halt; Tel. (02375) 262.

A bus from its gates serves Clovelly, Hartland and Bideford.

GREEN CLIFF AND ABBOTSHAM

The lime kilns at Green Cliff and the one near Cornborough are interesting because in 1805 they were fired by anthracite from a seam on the face of Green Cliff itself.

Abbotsham, as its name suggests, used to belong to the Abbey of Tavistock. Its 13th-century church of St Helen is unusual because the nave is higher than the chancel and there are no aisles. The circular font is Norman and probably original.

Kenwith Castle, whose ruins can be seen 1 kilometre north east of Abbotsham, is said by some to be the scene of Odun, Earl of Devon's victory over the Danes in 878 A.D.

WESTWARD HO!

It is always a little difficult to remember that the town was named after Charles Kingsley's novel, published in 1855, and not vice versa. Indeed, the town was created as a Victorian purpose-built resort and the developers thought that naming it after the novel would be an excellent promotion stunt. Today it is rather seedy and it is hard to believe that it was ever anything else.

Rudyard Kipling was at the United Services College in the town from 1878 to 1882 and his novel *Stalky & Co* was based on the resort. He describes his school days there in *Something of myself for my friends known and unknown*, which was published in 1937.

When the resort was being built they found flint instruments and reindeer bones on the site but, like most modern developers, they must have quickly concealed all evidence of historic occupation because no trace remains. It is still a resort today and the town has most modern facilities.

Hotel:	Buckleigh Grange, Buckleigh Road; Tel. Bideford (02372) 4468
B&B:	Vaggers, 1 Nelson Terrace; Tel. Bideford (02372) 5140
Buses:	To Barnstaple, Braunton and Ilfracombe
Early closing:	Wednesday

APPLEDORE

Hubba the Dane landed here in 878 and went on to lose his battle at Kenwith Castle near Abbotsham. Appledore was a fishing village and a port, and Charters Folly was built in 1800 by one of the town's merchants so that he could watch his ships come in. Appledore's boatbuilding yards were very well-known, and today Hinks Shipyard is the last in England capable of building large ships in wood. Its customers nowadays are often film producers looking for historical replicas. There are some pretty Georgian cottages down by the quay, and as a resort it has a great deal more charm than some of its neighbours. It has all facilities.

Hotel:	Seagate Hotel, The Quay; Tel Bideford (02372) 2589
Buses:	To Barnstaple, Westward Ho!, Braunton and Ilfracombe
Early closing:	Wednesday

BIDEFORD

The Manor of Bideford was given to Richard de Granville in 1066 at the time of the Norman Conquest and stayed with his descendants until 1750, when it was sold by the 3rd Earl of Bath's heir. The bridge, which is over 206 metres long and has 24 arches, was built by Sir Theobald Grenville in the 14th century but has of course been widened since. The Parliamentarians fortified the town on both sides of the river during the Civil War, which does not seem to have done much good because the town fell to the King in 1643. The Plague struck in 1646 and continued to take its deadly toll until 1680. A plague of witches then took over, and three were burnt in the town in 1682.

The town was an important commercial port – the third in England in the 16th century – as the several noble merchants' houses indicate. These date mainly from the 17th century when Bideford was growing fat on its share of American colonial trade. It was the first British port to import tobacco on a large scale, but by the mid 18th century the trade had moved to Bristol, chased away by French privateers who found the pickings so rich and so easy that they renamed the area 'Golden Bay'. The port sent five ships against the Armada in 1588 and there is an Armada Cannon in Victoria park.

The Church of St Mary, originally 13th century, was so extensively rebuilt in 1864 that it is of little architectural interest today. The west tower with its polygonal stair turret is original, as is the large square Norman font. Ford Farm on the A388 in the south of the town is a good example of a stone medieval farmhouse. The great hall with its screen and part of its roof as well as one of the barns are all original. The house is open to the public.

Today Bideford is a small commercial town. Its port still works a little, importing fertilizer, timber, coal and salt for the roads, and shipping ball clay out to the potteries. The town is also a resort and has all facilities for the visitor.

Hotel: Durrant House Hotel, Heyward Road, Northam; Tel. Bideford (02372) 2361
B&B: Rosskery, Orchard Hill, Bideford; Tel. Bideford (02372) 2872
Bus: To Barnstaple

INSTOW

Nowadays this village is best known as a sailing resort, and when conditions are clear there is a good view from it across to Lundy Island. The Church of St John the Baptist is probably 13th century in origin but most of it now dates from the 16th century. Tapley Park House is a Georgian mansion which was humiliatingly gothicized in 1885. However, it has very fine plaster work ceilings and a good collection of china and furniture on display. Its gardens, in the Italian Style, are also unusually good. At Yelland nearby, Michael Leach (son of Bernard Leach of St Ives) has a pottery, and if you have the time and a taste for good souvenirs, that too is worth a visit.

YHA: Youth Hostel, Worlington House; Tel. Instow
              (0271) 860394

BARNSTAPLE

The Ancient Britons knew it as Tunge Attertawe, the Saxons
as Berdenestaple, but by 873 A.D. people were familiarly
calling it Barum. It was Barnstaple in 930 when King
Athelstan (925–940) granted it one of the first recorded
charters (the town claims that it is the first). It was granted
others in 1189, 1201 and 1273. Athelstan also granted the town
the right to mint money, and founded Pilton Priory on the
outskirts of the town. Barnstaple Priory was not founded until
1107 by Judheal of Totnes, and to supplement this religious
might Athelstan built a castle which was reinforced by the
Normans when they arrived in 1066, but of which nothing
remains today.

The Long Bridge is the oldest construction in the town. It
dates from the 13th century, and is 158 metres long with 16
stone arches, three of which had to be replaced in 1589. The
town was an important market town for wool and woollen
manufactures.

The Church of St Peter and St Paul was originally 13th-
century but was considerably restored in the 1860s by Gilbert
Scott. Its tower is 13th century and it is unusual in that it is
attached to the Church asymetrically. The south end of the
chancel dates from the same period, although the two aisles
are Perpendicular. St Anne's Chapel, in the churchyard to the
east of the parish church, is a 14th-century chantry chapel
which was later used as a grammar school. Penrose's Almshouses in Lichdon Street were founded in 1627; Horwood's
Almshouses and school in Church Lane were founded in 1674
and 1679; and the Salem Almshouses in 1834. The Guildhall
was built by Lee in 1824.

Queen Anne's Walk, crowned by the Queen herself, was
built as a commercial exchange in 1708 and is very ornate. The
mushroom-shaped stone in the colonnade is the Tome Stone
where merchants would seal transactions in front of a witness
by placing money on it: the contract then became legally
binding.

St Mary's Church in Pilton, on the Braunton Road on the
outskirts of town, was founded as a priory in the 10th century
by King Athelstan and the roof-line of the old monastic
building can be seen on the north side. The tower is very early

but was considerably tampered with during the restoration work in 1696. There are several monuments in the church to ancestors of Sir Francis Chichester, the round-the-world yachtsman. John Gay, who wrote the *Beggar's Opera*, was born in Barnstaple in 1685, went to the grammar school there, and was apprenticed to a draper in the town before becoming a poet.

Today Barnstaple is still the principal market town for North Devon, and no industrial development has destroyed its quiet Georgian charm. The observant visitor is constantly rewarded by glimpses of interesting buildings or intriguing architectural detail as he walks around the town.

Hotel:	Imperial Hotel, Taw Vale Parade; Tel. Barnstaple (0271) 5861
	Downdrew House, Bishops Tawton (outside town); Tel. Barnstaple (0271) 2497
Bus:	To Ilfracombe, Braunton and Westward Ho!
Trains:	To Exeter and London
Early closing:	Wednesday

16

Barnstaple to Lynmouth

He had walked there many times before, and knew what was to be seen in clear air — the Welsh coast to the north, Lundy and the Atlantic to the west, and Dartmoor to the south; he knew every flower, bird, fern, grass, rock, animal, bush; and the vain and empty sky over all . . .

He came to the end of the down, to ground unbroken by plough or mattock, and rough with fern and bramble; and the sun came up, spreading its first pale gold on the ruined grasses, and laying long shadows behind the furze. In a brighter and more open air he began to hope again as he looked at the scene of those happy summer days now ended. The land dropped away below his feet — the estuary and the Branton pill were filled with shining sea; the Great Field, shorn of its Joseph's coat of summer corn-colours, lay serene and autumnal; the heave and waste of the sandhills, with their yellowing grasses; the level sands bearing round Aery Point, the sea wrinkled like an elephant's hide, but shining; the long blue length of land that stretched into that sea, anciently called Hercules Promontory.

WILLIAMSON, Henry (1895–1977). Description of dawn on downs above Braunton Burrows. From *The Pathway*, fourth and final volume of the tetralogy 'The Flax of Dream', and first published in 1929 after *Tarka the Otter* and before *Salar the Salmon*.

Introduction

The first part of the path, from Barnstaple to Saunton, is not entirely straightforward. The best solution is to walk the whole way along the Taw estuary and up to Saunton Sands, which gives a great opportunity to enjoy the prolific wild life on Braunton Burrows and, for most of the way, it is a pleasant, easy walk. The path around Croyde is not exciting but it is followed by an easy cliff walk and a walk through the dunes or along sands to Woolacombe. Woolacombe to Ilfracombe is a fine section of path but there is then too much road walking as far as Combe Martin. After Combe Martin the path takes to some wild and beautiful country, climbing up over Great Hangman and on round to Woody Bay, where an unfortunately long section on roads to the Valley of the Rocks can be wearing on tired feet, although it is through attractive country. Then there is the unspoilt cliff walk down to Lynton and Lynmouth, which Shelley used to enjoy. There are some steep slopes on the way but they are tiring rather than testing.

The general geological picture is clear. Apart from Braunton Burrows (Millstone Grit and Culm Measures) the coast is composed of Middle and Upper Devonian rock through to Combe Martin and of Lower Devonian to Lynmouth and beyond. However, these bare facts conceal a rather more complex structure, and geologists have much to interest them in this area. The 1,000 hectares of dunes at Braunton Burrows is a phenomenon in itself, as is the Valley of the Rocks and the famous Shell Beach at Barricane, where shells are washed ashore having been carried there on warm currents from the Caribbean.

Morte Point is like a slice of layered cake showing clearly where Middle Devonian slates rest on Morte Beds and the Morte Beds rest on Ilfracombe Beds. The 213 metres of Highveer Point are composed of Hangman Grits, while Wringcliff Bay and Lee Bay possess unusual quantities of mica and quartz in their rocks. The effect of all this is to give a varied coastline, from the low sands of Braunton and Woolacombe, to the austere High moorland of Great Hangman and Holdstone Down and the vegetation-covered cliffs around Watermouth, Woody Bay and Lynton.

Naturalists will not be disappointed here. The nature reserve, indeed the whole area of Braunton Burrows, is a rewarding hunting ground. Plants, insects, animals and birds are found in both quantity and quality. Some species, such as short-eared owls or merlins, French Toadflux or Water Germander are rare examples of birds and plants. Baggy Point and Morte Point are good observation points for viewing birds, as is Blackstone Point where great colonies of sea birds live. In the Valley of the Rocks a herd of wild goats still roams free, as it has done for centuries.

There are no unspoilt picture-book villages to visit on the path. Ilfracombe has a certain charm, Lynmouth and Lynton too. There are several churches of interest but the main attraction on this part of the path is the scenic beauty of its unspoilt stretches.

Guide

You have to get from Barnstaple to Braunton; it is possible to do so by bus, indeed the bus from Westward Ho! to Ilfracombe will take you there without the need to change. Better, however, is to walk along the route which may in time become the official path and which has the additional advantage of allowing you to observe the natural wealth of Braunton Burrows.

Make for the Barnstaple R.F.C., go down Rolle Quay and turn right into Mill Lane. Turn left down a narrow lane, which brings you past industrial works on your left, to the R.F.C. ground. Opposite the grandstand, a decrepit gate gives you access to the disused railway line. Turn right along the line which takes you, following the shore of the Taw estuary, past Heanton Court, to the airfield at R.A.F. Chivenor. Here you go inland from the estuary to skirt the airfield on its landward perimeter, still keeping to the line of the disused railway.

At Velator, you leave the railway line, turning left at the head of the creek, to go down its western bank, around Horsey Island, back onto the estuary. You now have another decision to make.

If the tide is out, continue on past the White House across the neck of Crow Point, watching out for red flags on the range danger area, and back on to the coast by the disused lighthouse. Then continue all the way up Saunton Sands to pick up the official path at the Saunton Sands Hotel, a distance of some 6 kilometres.

If the tide is high, turn right at the White House and, 500 metres further on, right again to go due north alongside a range and then a golf course, both seaward of the path. Swing north-west along the limit of the golf course into **Saunton** and due west to the Saunton Sands hotel.

| DISTANCE | | | | TELEPHONE | TRAIN | BUS | FERRY | SHOPS | CAMPING | ACCOMMODATION | REFRESHMENT | CUMUL. DIST. KMS |
STAGE	CUMUL.	TIME	BARNSTAPLE TO LYNMOUTH									
			BARNSTAPLE	x	x	x		x	x	x	x	800¾
(1)		(:15)	(BRAUNTON)	x		x		x	x	x		
17	17	4:15	SAUNTON			x				x		817¾
1½	18½	:25	CROYDE					x		x	x	819¼
8	26½	2:	WOOLACOMBE	x		x		x	x	x	x	827¼
2	28½	:30	MORTEHOE	x				x	x	x	x	829¼
5	33½	1:15	LEE			x				x	x	834¼
5	38½	1:15	ILFRACOMBE	x		x		x	x	x	x	839¼
6½	45	1:40	COMBE MARTIN	x		x		x	x	x	x	845¾
12	57	3:	TRENTISHOE								x	857¾
1	58	:15	HUNTER'S INN							x	x	858¾
3¼	61¼	:50	WOODY BAY							x	x	862
2	63¼	:30	LEE ABBEY									864
3	66¼	:45	LYNTON	x		x		x	x	x	x	867
¼	66½	:10	LYNMOUTH	x		x		x	x	x	x	867¼

TIMES ARE BASED ON AVERAGE WALKER LIGHTLY LADEN.

NB.

1. *STAGE: is the distance between that point and the preceding point.*
2. *CUMUL.: is the cumulative distance from the beginning of the chapter.*
3. *TIME: is the time for the stage (between that point and the preceding one) calculated at 4 kilometres per hour – the rate for a lightly loaded person walking without halt.*
4. *Brackets enclose places not on the Path but easily reached from it, together with distances and times from the Path.*
5. *CUMULATIVE DISTANCE: is the total distance from South Haven Point.*

Go along the inland (eastern) side of the hotel and pass behind it on the road, which you follow west along the coast to the outskirts of **Croyde**. Leave the road where it bends inland to Croyde, and continue along the coast, crossing the stream in the centre of Croyde Bay by bridge. On the far side of the bay, you are obliged to take to the road again for about 500 metres and then, just after crossing the stile by the National Trust collecting box, fork left on to the lower path and round to Baggy Point. Go up across the point and continue along the cliff path, past Long Bar, to the elbow of Morte Bay.

The official path goes straight on for 300 metres to join the main road from Putsborough to Vention. Better is another footpath which swings down to the left, quite steeply, into Vention. This path takes you into a caravan site. You can either drop down on to the beach and walk 3 kilometres or so along the sands, or you can cross the caravan site and follow the road along behind the beach, into **Woolacombe**. A bridle path exists from the car park on Woolacombe Down, left down through the dunes into Woolacombe, but it is not easy to find. However, you cannot get very lost between road and sea.

Keep to the sea front through Woolacombe, leaving it by Barricane Beach, and keeping to the coast out to Morte Point, a dramatically rugged point with the sea boiling about it even in calm conditions. Double back east on the high cliff path, past Whiting Cove, down over a stream (after which a path leads 400 metres inland to **Mortehoe**), up above Rockham Bay. Dip down to cross another stream above Rockham Beach and then go over the neck of a small point, down past Bull Point lighthouse. Be sure to take the path which continues over Bull Point and down to cross the coomb above Damaghue Rock. It climbs steeply out of the coomb and goes down to cross another above Pensport Rock and continues down to the road which takes you through **Lee**.

Go through Lee on the road and take the first lane you come to on the left after leaving the sea front. You now have an easy 5 kilometre walk to Ilfracombe. The hedge-lined lane takes you up to the gate, leading into the National Trust property of Flat Point above Shag Point. The path continues as a good open cliff-top walk, passing out of the Flat Point property into Torrs Park and so down to **Ilfracombe**.

Turn left down Torrs Walk Avenue and then along Granville Road, which brings you to the Victoria pavilion. Cut in front of this, along St James' Place, turn right into Broad Street, which leads to the attractive harbour. Walk around the harbour and turn left up the well-tended slopes of Hillsborough, past a number of outdoor leisure activities, to the line of vegetation higher up the slope, where you turn right on to a path marked 'coast path'. This takes you around the hill, on its inland side, back towards the coast and down into Hele. Turn right and walk up to the main A399. Then left, climbing up the road until you reach a pronounced right-hand bend, where a coast path sign sends you down in front of coastguard cottages, around the point and back on to the main road again. It is hoped that the path will soon continue around

Widmouth Head. At present you must follow the road for about 1 kilometre, then look out for a stile on the left which takes you on to a pleasant woodland track – just below the road – along the natural harbour of Water Mouth. At low tide, you can continue right down to the shore itself, leaving the harbour by the sailing club entrance. Otherwise, a three-branch fingerpost takes you back on to the road and left into Water Mouth.

Outside the sailing club, a particularly sinister stretch of path takes you narrowly between barbed wire fences along-side the road. This starts almost opposite the entrance to **Watermouth Castle**, which has been converted into a pleasure palace. You emerge from the barbed wire to walk a few unfenced metres along the road, before turning left across Napp's camp site and through woods for about 800 metres. You then come to the road again, along a track which leads up past the Sandy Cove Hotel.

Turn left on to the main road which bends right, then left and, at its next bend right, you continue straight on, down a narrow tarmac road which avoids a short stretch of the main road. It turns left at the bottom of a short, steep hill, and then right to re-join the main road through **Combe Martin**.

Turn left along the main road and then left behind the little cove on which the village stands. Cross the car park and take the path which leaves it marked 'coast path' and Great Hangman. You are now entering the Exmoor National Park, whose 58 kilometres of path constitute the best maintained and the best signed continuous stretch on the whole of the South West Peninsula.

The path climbs up past houses, up above Sandy Bay and then over Lester Cliff. It turns north-east to pass landward under Little Hangman (218 metres) on Hangman Point, and east over meadows to the rough stone cairn which marks the austere summit of Great Hangman (318 metres).

Now the path bends inland and down to cross the head of Sherrycombe and up, quite steeply (look out for this path on your way down) to head through pastures back towards the cliff tops. Go well over towards the sea on the top and you will find a well-defined farm track leading right along the cliff top by Holdstone Down.

Opposite the rocks known as the Mare and Colt the path turns inland once more, still following the farm track, up to some cottages, where it turns left along a road for a few metres. Just before a National Trust car park, it turns left again, going obliquely back to the coast above Elwill Bay. The path now continues as a mountain track, parallel to the coast, generally seaward of the fenced land, until it reaches the steep slopes of Heddon's Cleave, above Heddon's Mouth Beach. Here it swings inland and follows high above the valley before turning west, almost back on its main course, to slope down towards the road just below **Trentishoe**.

To the right is the hamlet with its church. You turn left down the road and left again until you come to the bridge over Heddon's River. Cross it and ahead of you lies Hunter's Inn at **Heddon's Mouth**.

Beyond the inn, a good wide track leads off along the side of the valley, up through woods, towards the sea. Take this and very soon you will find yourself on a high, grassy cliff path. Stay on this, inland of Highveer Point, past the Cow and Calf rocks and the Roman signal station (occupied from 50 A.D. to 70 A.D.), through the trees above **Woody Bay** to the National Trust car park.

The next four kilometres are on the road through **Woody Bay**, past the Woody Bay Hotel, down to Lee Bay with its beach and car park. The path then climbs up past **Lee Abbey**, leaving the estate by the top lodge, to the roundabout at the entrance to the **Valley of Rocks**.

Here you leave the road, turning left onto a path which climbs up seaward around the headland above Yellow Stone. You are now on a good cliff path, which takes you high above the sea, below the brow of the cliffs until you encounter the first houses above **Lynton**. The path leads directly on to a metalled road and shortly to a path which descends steeply, by a series of hairpin bends, passing under the cliff railway to **Lynmouth**.

Gazetteer

ASHFORD

The church of St Peter is 19th century but incorporates a spire of its medieval predecessor in the North Tower. Its only interest lies in the fact that it is a scaled-down replica of St Peter and St Paul in Barnstaple.

HEANTON PUNCHARDON

The church of St Augustine is Perpendicular in style. It has a
good peal of bells and as fine a Perpendicular monument,
dated 1523, to Richard Coffin. The late 18th-century Heanton
Court down by the estuary is now an hotel, and there is an
almost rectangular stone, expertly fashioned by some pre-
historic mason, buried in the second hedge below Wratton
House.

BRAUNTON

St Brannock came from Calabria in 300 A.D. to build the first
church here. He gave his name to the village (then Brannock's
Town), and was buried in Braunton. The present church,
whose airy size shows what an important place Braunton was,
is a bit of a mixture. The earliest part, the tower, is Norman
and so is the font which has finely carved 13th-century tracery.
The woodwork is particularly good; all of the solid chestnut
pews have carved bench ends, which is rare. The gilded wood
panelling in the chancel is Jacobean and the reredos is dated
1563. A brass to Lady Elizabeth Bowcer in the Lady Chapel
has the bust of a mailed knight on the reverse.

Braunton Great Field is one of the few remaining examples
of open strip cultivation left in England. Although 200 of the
original 700 strips remain in their original plan, it is easy to
imagine the others – grouped together now for ease of
working – as they were in Saxon times. Each strip used to be
separated by 30 centimetres of unploughed land and, many
retain their old names or have names which are clear corrup-
tions of them.

Braunton Burrows, beyond the field, is a huge 1,000
hectares of static sand dunes whose erosion has been stemmed
by the planting of marram grass. In spite of, or perhaps
because of, the presence of military ranges, the area is a
favoured one for the free development of wild life, and
naturalist walkers might find their average speed dropping
through the dunes. There is a nature reserve at the southern
end.

Braunton has all facilities including shops, accommodation
and refreshment.

| B&B: | The Laurels; Tel. Braunton (0271) 812872 |
| Bus: | To Barnstaple, Westward Ho! and Ilfracombe |

SAUNTON AND SAUNTON SANDS

A holiday resort of little interest. There is a bus stop at Saunton for buses to Ilfracombe, Barnstaple and Westward Ho!, and you may stay at the Saunton Sands Hotel, (Tel. (0271) 812872).

CROYDE

This village is a mixture of country-charming and modern-muddled. There is a 12th-century chapel at the east end of St Helen's Cottage, and just behind the village, inland, lies Georgeham, which is full of pretty thatched cottages. Otherwise Croyde has shops and refreshments and The Baggy Point Hotel (Tel. Croyde (0271) 890204). Early closing is on Wednesday.

WOOLACOMBE

Five kilometres of golden sand have prompted the growth of a tiny agriculture community into a still-growing holiday resort. The sands are its only positive asset but it does have facilities for shopping, accommodation and refreshment.

Hotel:	Narracot Grand Hotel; Tel. Woolacombe (0271) 870418
B&B:	Glenside; Tel. Woolacombe
Bus:	To Barnstaple, Westward Ho! and Ilfracombe
Early closing:	Wednesday and Saturday

MORTEHOE

Sir William De Tracy retired here after his part in the murder of Archbishop Thomas à Becket in Canterbury Cathedral in 1170. He founded the church of St Mary Magdalene, which has some Norman features and a 13th-century tower. There is an impressive tomb to his descendent, William De Tracy, vicar of the church until his death in 1322. The tomb may well include that of his ancestor. Morte Point derived its name from the Normans who lost ships and men with distressing regularity on its rocks. The Bull Point Lighthouse was not built, however, until 1879.

Local lore says that any man who is master of his wife has

power to remove Morte Stone from the point; it remains unmoved. Mortehoe has shopping, refreshments and accommodation.

Hotel:	Rockham Bay Hotel, Mortehoe; Tel. Woolacombe (027187) 347
B&B:	Sunnycliffe Hotel, Mortehoe; Tel. Woolacombe (027187) 597

LEE BAY

A small resort at the mouth of the Borough Valley. The bay has a hotel, and the village has a pub which serves food. There is also a tea-shop among the village's thatched cottages.

Hotel:	Lee Bay Hotel, Lee; Tel. Ilfracombe (0271) 63503
B&B:	Drummetts, Lee; Tel. Ilfracombe (0271) 62794
Bus:	To Ilfracombe

ILFRACOMBE

Ilfracombe can never live down the part it played in that most despicable affair, the invasion of Ireland. Not only did the town allow King John (1199–1216) to assemble his fleet there for the scurrilous attack, but it allowed Henry III (1261–1227) to do so too.

Ilfracombe existed before that; the Saxons knew it as Alfrincombe, Ilfridscome and Ilfordcombe, whence the modern name. Edward I granted it the right to hold a market and an annual fair from 1278. In 1346, the town sent six ships and 82 men around Land's End to join the Siege of Calais. During the Civil War, Ilfracombe started out being defended by the Parliamentarians, but the King's forces recovered it in 1644. The women of the town showed what they were made of in 1797 – there was hardly a man in Ilfracombe that year when four French ships threatened it, so the women stood on the cliffs and draped their red petticoats over their shoulders. The French took them to be a strong garrison of British infantry and sailed away.

The town really consisted of just one street until the train and fashion brought the tourists, and the tourists brought Victorian developers to Ilfracombe. Holy Trinity church is Norman, but was added to in 1321 and in the 15th century. Its roof is sumptuously decorated and quite majestic. St Nicholas' church on Lantern Hill was a pilgrim's chapel as early as the 13th century, but because of its height above sea level was turned into a lighthouse at the time of the Dissolution in the 16th century. It was recently restored as a chapel by the Rotarians, but a light is kept burning. Chambercombe Farm is 15th-century and is set in a pretty, wooded valley 1½ kilometres south-east of the town; however, most of the houses in Ilfracombe are late Victorian and even the harbour dates mainly from this period.

The Museum has a strong maritime flavour and has many early photographs, paintings and models associated with the sea. Ilfracombe has all the facilities one would expect in a popular resort town.

Hotel:	Royal Britannia Hotel, The Harbour; Tel. Ilfracombe (0271) 62939
B&B:	Georgian House Hotel, 10 Montpelier Terrace; Tel. Ilfracombe (0271) 63341
YHA:	Ashmour House, 1 Hillsborough Terrace; Tel. Ilfracombe (0271)
Bus:	To Barnstaple, Westward Ho! and Lynmouth
Early closing:	Thursday
Tourist Information:	Tel. Ilfracombe (0271) 63001

WATERMOUTH CASTLE

Although this castle was probably built on the site of a 14th-century battlemented castle, it is a Disney-like Victorian extravaganza. Built in 1825 it has distractions and attractions of all kinds in its pleasant grounds.

BERRYNARBOUR

If you follow the water of Water Mouth inland for about 2 kilometres, you come to this pretty old village. Its church was Norman and has 13th- and 15th-century additions. The Squire's Pew was built with a fire-place, mantelpiece and fire irons and the church contains some impressive monuments, particularly to Richard Berry, 1645, and Jane Spence, 1815. John Jewel, Bishop of Salisbury under Elizabeth I, was born at Bowden farmhouse nearby in 1522. He wrote the Apology for The English Church (*Apologia Ecclesiae Anglicana*), which was ordered to be chained alongside the chained bible in every church in the country when it was published in 1562.

COMBE MARTIN

The village excites enthusiasm mainly for its situation, which is extremely pretty. This was a market town in 1264, but was thriving before that because of its silver mines. The Phoenicians probably traded here for silver, and silver from its mines paid for the battles of Crécy (1346), Poitiers (1356) and Agincourt (1415). The mines were very productive in Edward I's time (1272–1307), and the yield of 20–168 ounces of silver per ton of ore, though a broad spread, was a good one. Two tankards still used by the City of London Corporation were made in 1731 from Combe Martin silver, taken from a tankard dated 1370 which had been presented to the Lord Mayor of London by Elizabeth I.

Today the village is no longer a market but is something of a market garden for the neighbouring towns and villages, growing strawberries, flowers and vegetables on its sheltered valley slopes.

The church of St Peter Ad Vincula has the only surviving example in north Devon of wainscoting with painted figures on it. The tower and the 13th-century chancel are also fine pieces of architecture and the church was extensively rebuilt in the 18th century. The only other building of interest (perhaps it should not be sharing room with a church) is the Pack of Cards Inn, built by a 17th-century gambler with the fruits of his trade. The four floors represent the four suits; the 13 doors on each floor, the cards; and the 52 windows, the total of the pack itself. Unlike the house in the child's game it was built to imitate, this house has remained standing for quite some time. It contains a large table which opens to allow two men to lie full length inside, indispensable for those inn-keepers who wished to save their customers from the press gang seeking sailors for the Royal Navy.

Combe Martin has facilities for shopping, refreshment and accommodation.

Hotel: Higher Leigh Hotel; Tel. Combe Martin (027188) 2486

B&B: Hill View Guest House, Woodlands; Tel. Combe Martin (027188) 3455

Bus: To Ilfracombe and Lynmouth
Early
closing: Wednesday

TRENTISHOE

The isolated hamlet tucked away at the head of the coomb, yet close to the sea, was a centre for smuggling in the 17th and 18th centuries. The church, St Peter's, is quite ancient but was rebuilt in 1861. It has no aisles but there are two intriguing features of the musicians' gallery of 1771: a hole cut in the woodwork to accommodate the bow of the bass viol and a 'neck' of corn carved in the wood. A local custom had the youngest harvester run to the barn with the first sheaf of corn while the others tried to throw water over it. If they succeeded the harvest would be wet, if not it would be dry. The custom was only recently abandoned and the carving is a reminder of it.

HUNTER'S INN

The original old thatched inn was burnt down in the 19th century and the present version is a romantic idea of what such an inn should look like. It is superbly sited, a fine place to quench both hunger and thirst.

HEDDON'S MOUTH

The lime kiln on the beach suggests that it was once a port but there is no evidence of this. It is certain that it was a smuggler's haven. On a night in 1801, the sloop Hope landed 96, 8-gallon casks of brandy here before going on to unload its legitimate cargo. Poetic justice had her sink with her cargo and hands before reaching Water Mouth, her final destination. In 1827 revenue men found £1,180 worth of brandy in John Hoyle's stables. Hoyle escaped, but support for him ran so high amongst the locals, that the brandy was removed to Barnstaple for safety. Hoyle was never recaptured.

MARTINHOE

The path crosses the site of a Roman fort near Martinhoe Beacon. It was built between 50 and 70 A.D. after a similar fort at Old Barrow, further along the coast, had been abandoned. The fortifications were quite impressive – accommodation for 60 to 80 soldiers was protected by two strong ramparts separated by a 20-metre ditch. Traces were found of field oxen, an armourer's forge and other paraphernalia.

WOODY BAY

This delightful, wooded bay was acquired by the National Trust in 1965. The bay had resisted 19th-century attempts to turn it into a resort, and its acquisition by the Trust suggests that it will now be safe from undesirable development. There is a lime kiln on the beach at Woody Bay. There is also The Woody Bay Hotel, right on the path. (Tel. Parracombe (05983) 264.)

CROCK POINT

There used to be clay pits here, where clay was worked for Dutch potters.

LEE ABBEY

This was never an abbey. It was the home of the De Wichehalse family who fled to England from Holland in 1570 and settled here from 1628 to 1730. Their house, Lee Manor, was destroyed and the present house was built in the 1840s. The Anglican Church bought it in 1945 and founded the Lee Abbey Community. The house is now used for conferences and retreats.

VALLEY OF ROCKS

This is magnificent Ice Age debris left here over 10,000 years ago – a rock-strewn corridor 14 kilometres long and 100 metres wide. It is barren, desolate and eerie. The Victorians called it The Valley of the Stones and prized it highly as one of the greatest wonders in the West of England, the very bones and skeleton of the earth. In the 1830s a walk was cut from Lynton around the seaward side of the cliffs to the western end of the valley, a considerable feat of engineering for the time. Shelley, Wordsworth and Coleridge all walked to the Valley, Shelley using the 1830 path on many occasions.

LYNTON AND LYNMOUTH

These two towns are really one – an accident of geography has separated them and an ingenious cliff railway has united them. Lynmouth has become the more important town. It has the port and it is on the A39 Trunk Road; Lynton used to have the railway, indeed it was really created as the railhead for its much older companion down the hill.

The cliff railway is unique and was the steepest railway in the world when it was built in 1890. It is 900 metres long, rises 140 metres and has a gradient of 1 in 1.75. It cost £8,000 and was a gift to the town by Sir George Newnes, the publisher. The railway is driven by gravity; two cars are connected by a looped cable; each has a 3 ton water tank beneath it which is filled at the top and emptied at the bottom. Very simple when someone else has thought of it!

Lynmouth used to be a fishing port and a small general port, but most of it was destroyed by a huge tidal surge in 1607. In a way, history repeated itself with the Lynmouth Flood Disaster in 1952. On the night of 15 August 1952, following weeks of very heavy rain on Exmoor, a further 25.4 cms. fell (3,200 million gallons). That was too much; the rivers broke carrying everything in their path down on to Lynmouth. The town was almost completely destroyed and 34 people died. It has now been rebuilt, as close to the original architecture as possible.

In January 1899, the Lynmouth lifeboat made a spectacular rescue. It was taken 20 kilometres overland across the moors to launch from Porlock Weir and it went on to save the 1800 ton Forest Hall.

Lynmouth was a favourite resort for the poets, Coleridge, Wordsworth, Southey and Shelley. Southey called it the finest spot he ever saw except Cintra and the Arrabida; Shelley spent his honeymoon here with his 16-year old bride, Harriet Westbrook, and wrote Queen Mab on a visit in 1812.

Hotel:	Tors Hotel, Lynmouth; Tel. Lynton (05985) 3236
	Lynton Cottage Hotel, Lynton; Tel. Lynton (05985) 2342
B&B:	Oakleigh, 4 Torrs Road, Lynmouth; Tel. Lynton (05985) 2220
	Neubia House Hotel, Lydgate Lane, Lynton; Tel. Lynton (05985) 2309

YHA: Youth Hostel, Lynbridge, Lynton; Tel. Lynton (05985) 3237

Bus: Minehead and Barnstaple

Early
closing: Thursday

17

Lynmouth to Minehead

One of the pleasantest things in the world is going a journey; but I like to go by myself. I can enjoy society in a room; but out-of-doors, nature is company enough for me. I am then never less alone than when alone.

'The fields his study, nature was his book.'

I cannot see the wit of walking and talking at the same time. When I am in the country, I wish to vegetate like the country. I am not for criticising hedge-rows and black cattle. I go out of town in order to forget the town and all that is in it. There are those who for this purpose go to watering-places, and carry the metropolis with them. I like more elbow-room, and fewer encumbrances. I like solitude, when I give myself up to it, for the sake of solitude; nor do I ask for

'a friend in my retreat,
Whom I may whisper solitude is sweet'.

The soul of a journey is liberty, perfect liberty, to think, feel, do just as one pleases. We go a journey chiefly to be free of all impediments and of all inconveniences; to leave ourselves behind, much more to get rid of others. It is because I want a little breathing-space to muse on indifferent matters, where Contemplation

'May plume her feathers and let grow her wings,
That in the various bustle of resort
Were all too ruffled, and sometimes impair'd',

that I absent myself from the town for awhile, without feeling at a loss the moment I am left by myself. Instead of a friend in a post-chaise or in a tilbury, to exchange good things with, and vary the same stale topics over again, for once let me have a truce with impertinence. Give me the clear blue sky over my head, and the green turf beneath my feet, a winding road before me, and a three hours' march to dinner — and then to thinking!

HAZLITT, William (1778–1830). Essayist. Walked a great deal with Coleridge and Wordsworth in the Lynmouth area when staying with them at Nether Stowey (1797–8). Extract from the essay 'On going on a Journey' (1821).

Introduction

This final stretch is one of good, varied walking and fine views. After the climb out of Lynmouth you walk along high cliffs until just before you reach County Gate; then the path runs inland for a while, along ancient country roads unaltered in modern times. These roads lead between banks and hedges across good farm land. The path then takes to forest tracks, crosses the beach at Porlock and climbs nearly 300 metres from sea level to finish with a few kilometres of good high, exposed moorland walking before the final descent to Minehead.

The rocks are Lower Devonian. From Lynmouth to Blackhead Point (just before Foreland Point) it is slate of the Lynton Beds, from Blackhead Point onwards Old Red Sandstone predominates. The terrain produced is one of rounded, steep, grass-covered hogs-back cliffs.

Buzzards, kestrels, gulls and cormorants are among the numerous birds which remain with you faithfully to the end. Rocky cliffs, open moorland, spinney, stream and wood provide habitat for a variety of birds. Exmoor ponies appear at random and you may also see red deer, the last great herd of which survives on neighbouring Exmoor. After Foreland Point there are clumps of sessile oak, which also grow in the company of holly, conifers and sycamore in Culver Wood, while Culbone Wood is fine old English oak. Halliday planted a number of rare trees in the woods that he created at Glenthorne.

Once again it is a stretch on which natural beauty predominates. However, Lynmouth is worthy of attention not only for the beauty of its setting, but because man has succeeded in repairing the destruction Nature wreaked upon the town in the disastrous floods of 1952. The town has been rebuilt and is again an important seaside resort. Above it, Countisbury is the site of a famous 9th-century battle, and displays the remains of an Iron Age Promontory Fort. Culbone, with its tiny Chapel and artistic pottery lies directly on the path, and the woods about it have a fascinating history as a sort of West Country Siberia to which successive groups of social outcasts have been banished. Porlock Weir and Bossington are villages of great charm, and Selworthy, just off the path, is reputed to be the most beautiful village in England.

Guide

Turn right at the bottom of the path which has brought you down to Lynmouth, on to the sea front. Cross the first bridge over the River Lyn, into the Municipal Park. Walk to the far (eastern) end of the park and take the path which leads from behind the pavilion – up the wooded hillside to join the main A39 road. Turn left and follow the road for 200 metres before turning left again, off it, across open cliff land. Passing close to the hamlet of **Countisbury**, the path contours Countisbury Hill to seaward, and continues out towards Foreland Point and the lighthouse.

A path does go all the way to the lighthouse, but the coast path cuts across the headland and dips down, beside Caddow Combe, to a road coming from the lighthouse. Turning to cross the bridge over the stream, the path continues along the road for a short distance and then goes on, below the brow of the cliffs, as a high cliff path. It carries on like this for almost 3 kilometres, crossing streams, sometimes in trees more often in the open, around Countisbury Cove, past Sir Robert's Chair until, emerging from a wood, the path turns inland, picking up a track which leads to the A39 Road just east of the hamlet of Wingate.

The path turns left and follows the A39 on a fenced track, just inland of it, for about 800 metres, then it bends further inland, over a low hill, for a further 800 metres before arriving at the car park and the Exmoor National Park Office at **County Gate**. Here the path crosses the A39 once more, this time into Somerset, and goes seawards on a well-made track.

DISTANCE STAGE	DISTANCE CUMUL.	TIME	LYMOUTH TO MINEHEAD	TELEPHONE	TRAIN	BUS	FERRY	SHOPS	CAMPING	ACCOMMODATION	REFRESHMENT	CUMUL. DIST. KMS
			LYNMOUTH	x		x		x	x	x	x	867¼
3	3	:45	COUNTISBURY						x	x	x	870¼
6	9	1:30	COUNTY GATE			x						876¼
8	17	2:	PORLOCK WEIR	x						x	x	884¼
(2½)		(:40)	(PORLOCK)	x		x				x	x	
5	22	1:15	BOSSINGTON	x					x		x	889¼
(2½)		(:40)	(SELWORTHY)									
8½	30½	2:10	MINEHEAD	x		x		x	x	x	x	897¾

TIMES ARE BASED ON AVERAGE WALKER LIGHTLY LADEN.

NB.
1. *STAGE: is the distance between that point and the preceding point.*
2. *CUMUL.: is the cumulative distance from the beginning of the chapter.*
3. *TIME: is the time for the stage (between that point and the preceding one) calculated at 4 kilometres per hour – the rate for a lightly loaded person walking without halt.*
4. *Brackets enclose places not on the Path but easily reached from it, together with distances and times from the Path.*
5. *CUMULATIVE DISTANCE: is the total distance from South Haven Point.*

It continues inland of, but parallel to, the coast on excellent unmade roads, between low banks and hedges, with little in the way of views. These were the roads the Doones used as they roamed this country in *Lorna Doone.* You first pass an unnamed farm, where you turn left, then go down past Yenworthy Farm and, later, through Broomstreet Farmyard, over a couple of streams and on to Silcombe Farm before descending through woods to **Culbone**.

From Culbone the path climbs up through Yearnor Wood on a recently made forest road and then falls quite steeply, along the slope of the cliffs, down to Worthy. The path comes out through a white gate by the lodge at Worthy. (This also serves as a toll booth for the road through Worthy Estate, cutting out the formidable Porlock Hill). Continue along the public road for 300 metres and the coast path turns off to the left, through fields down to **Porlock Weir**.

Go out of Porlock Weir on the road until it swings inland,

away from Porlock Beach. The path takes off to the left, down steps on to the beach. It then continues along the edge of the fields, just inland of the shingle. After about 3¼ kilometres the path strikes inland along a narrow road to **Bossington**.

Take the first turning left in the village of Bossington, over a stream, and out along a Farm track through a wood towards Hurlstone Point and the Sea again. Before reaching the Point the path is way-marked right. It climbs steeply round under the summit of Bossington Hill and on, by way of farm tracks, to pass beneath the summit of Selworthy Beacon, 308 metres. (Those who make short sharp detours to visit Hurlstone Point and the summits of both hills will be rewarded by fine views). Continue now over the open moorland, eastwards on a good level path. Just before Grexy Combe, seaward of the path, lie the remains of the Iron Age Settlement of **Furzebury Brake**. About 1 kilometre further on, under North Hill, the path turns sharp left, seaward down the eastern side of a combe (if you carry straight on down the combe you will come to the **Burgundy Chapel**) and then right to continue its descent through the woods above Greenaleigh Farm. Finally the route follows a good path through Culver Cliff Woods, descends to Minehead, where it emerges, down steps, from between two cottages on the Quay at **Minehead**, less than 100 metres from the Red Lion Public House.

Gazetteer

COUNTISBURY

Countisbury, or Shorebury Camp, is an Iron Age Promontory Fort with a ditch 1½ metres deep and ramparts 8.8 metres high. This site vies with Kenwith Castle as the place where Odun defeated the Danes in 878. It is said that the defenders became the attackers – leaving the fort and chasing Hubba and 800 of his men downhill to annihilate the whole force. You will have to make your own choice between the two.

The little Church of St John the Evangelist is mainly 18th century. It contains an unusual, well-carved screen dating from about 1700. Look out for the chained swan carved on a bench end in the chancel, which is also unusual.

The stone buildings next to the Blue Ball Inn have been converted into the National Trust's base camp for Exmoor, and are used by young people and adults for working holidays.

Foreland Point Lighthouse, built in 1900, is open to the public. Old Barrow Hill, a little further east, has a Roman signal station similar to the two at Martinhoe. It was occupied in the 1st century A.D. as part of the protection against threats from the tribes of Wales, which were finally conquered towards the end of that century.

COUNTY GATE

County Gate forms part of the border between Devon and Cornwall and is the gateway east into Lorna Doone Country. Indeed, it is easy to conjure up images of the Doones as you walk along ancient narrow roads. Between high banks and hedges unchanged for centuries, past the working farms of Yenworthy, Broomstreet, and Silcombe. The Doones are fictitious. The roads are real. R.D. Blackmore's book, published in 1869, tells the story of a feud between John Ridd and the Doones, a family of robbers and murderers. Ridd loves Lorna Doone, whose father murdered Ridd's father. Ridd rescues her from her family and discovers that she is the daughter of a Scottish nobleman and not a Doone at all and that she was stolen from her parents by the Doones. They marry. Many places between County Gate and Minehead are associated with the story. Blackmore wrote much of the book at Parsonage Farm, Oare, and had Ridd and Lorna marry at Oare Church. Yenworthy Farm, Porlock Hill and the Valley of Rocks are also featured in the Book.

A nature trail leads 5 kilometres from County Gate to Glenthorne Beach. You can get full details of it – included in an informative leaflet and a map – from The Exmoor Park Office at County Gate.

CULBONE CHURCH

St Culbone's is the smallest complete medieval church in regular use in Britain. The Church is 10.7 metres long and 3.7 metres wide and sits 122 metres above sea level, in the un-spoiled woods of Culbone. Notice the early rood screen, and the remains of an anchorite's or hermit's cell on the north side. The spire is slate.

The only other building which remains is used as a pottery. Its products, known as Culbone Pottery, are artistically and stylishly made in ceramic and stoneware and since you are almost at the end of your journey it's worth trying to find room for a piece as a souvenir of your visit. A romantic visitor to this out-of-the-way community was Coleridge (1772–1834) who stayed in a farmhouse at Culbone, where he wrote his dream poem 'Kubla Khan'.

Culbone was the home of England's last fern gatherers who cut ferns in Culbone and Yearnor Woods and sent them to Billingsgate where they were sold to decorate fishmonger's slabs.

PORLOCK WEIR

You can get some feel of the charming port this used to be if you stand in the little square by the Ship Inn. The port was a bustle of activity, unloading coal from stout coasters in from Wales, loading pit props cut in Culbone and Yearnor Woods and being sent to Wales to prop up tunnels, shafts and galleries in the fast developing pits. Today sailing boats and pleasure craft replace those old sea work-horses of yesterday and sun-brushed holidaymakers replace those weather-beaten men whose livelihood was wrenched by toil and labour from the sea. Only a little of the charm remains.

Hotel: Anchor; Tel. Porlock (0643) 862636
B&B: Gore Point; Tel. Porlock (0643) 862409

PORLOCK

The town is 2½ kilometres inland of the path from Porlock Weir. Since the invention of motor travel, it has been the starting point of stress and heartache for motorists about to climb the hellish gradient of Porlock Hill. Modern motors cope quite well with slopes, so it is those that tow caravans that now come to grief in two's and ten's on Porlock Hill through-out the year. The town itself is old. The Saxon's called it Porteloca and it was probably a seat for Saxon Kings. The Danes attacked it in 918; King Harold burnt it in 1052.

The Church is dedicated to St Dubricius, the 7th-century Celtic saint who married King Arthur and the lovely Guinevere. The Church was built in the 13th century, and the shingled spire, the nave, chancel, east vestry, south aisle and the effigy of a cross-legged knight in the south wall are all part of the original, although two fragments of a decorated Saxon cross-shaft on the west wall suggest that there was an earlier church on the site or nearby. The five bay arcade is 14th century, and the 15th-century porch was touched up in the 1800s.

The County Library Reading Room is part of 15th century Doverhay Manor House. Its three-light windows resemble those of the 16th-century chapel at Lynch, north east of Porlock, which belonged to one of the Sydenham's Manor Houses. At Allerford, also not far east of Porlock, there is a pretty two-arch pack horse bridge.

Porlock has all facilities for shopping, refreshment and accommodation.

Hotel:	The Castle; Tel. Porlock (0643) 862504
B&B:	Hurlstone, Sparkhayes Lane; Tel. Porlock (0643) 862650
Bus:	To Minehead and Lynmouth

SELWORTHY

King Harold's sister Eadgyth was lady of this manor in 1052. How wise she was, for this is one of the prettiest villages in England. Its setting – just behind Selworthy Beacon south of the path – is beautiful. The village is unspoiled and its owners, the National Trust, care well for its handful of thatched houses and their gardens.

A solid 14th-century stone tithe barn stands near the church. Look for the window arch with a pig, a sheep and a sheaf of corn carved on its wood, showing clearly the barn's intended purpose. All Saint's Church is of the same period. The tower and chancel are 14th century and the south aisle, although contemporary with them, was rebuilt at the end of the 15th century and is splendid. The south door is the original door, with linenfold panels, and the pulpit has 16th-century panels. There is a delightful 19th-century gothic squire's pew in the south porch and another chained book in the church: *A Defence of Bishop Jewel's Apology of the Church of England*, dated 1609. Elizabeth I had ordered the apology itself to be chained into Churches in 1562, but it appears to have run into a spot of bother and needed a defence.

BURY CASTLE

This Iron Age camp to the north of Selworthy is almost square – 64 metres by 46 metres – with rounded corners and solid ramparts. Further north still, on the southern slopes of

Selworthy Beacon, is a 'Memorial Hut'. Sir Thomas Dyke Acland (1787–1871) owned the land between here and Minehead, and he walked to this spot with his children every Sunday morning. The hut is a memorial to him and a shelter for walkers.

Most of the land from Porlock to Minehead and from Dunkery Beacon to the coast, belongs to the National Trust. The farms, villages and hamlets, as well as 5000 hectares of Exmoor and various round barrows, stone circles, bridges, cottages and quoits have all been acquired and protected by the Trust.

FURZEBURY BRAKE

You can just trace the ditch and stone ramparts of this Iron Age hill fort: there is no more of it visible.

BURGUNDY CHAPEL

The remains of this chapel are not really worth the scramble down the hill and up again you have to make to see them. No one knows how it got its name or why it was built in this isolated spot.

MINEHEAD

William the Conqueror took Minehead from Edgar, Earl of Mercia and gave it to his friend William de Mohun of Dunster, who was still its owner when it was recorded as 'Mahved' in the Domesday Book 1086. You can only debate whether the modern name is a contraction of 'Mohun' and 'heved', the Saxon name for 'head', or a corruption of 'mynYdd', the Welsh name for mountain. The answer will not be found today. Minehead stands on its bay between two headlands, in the shadow of a hill and is composed of three communities: Quay Town, Lower Town and Upper Town. Quay Town gives a clue to the town's creation. It started as a harbour in the 12th century, although it probably operated as a port before that. In the 17th and 18th century the town was prosperous, trading with Wales, Ireland and the West Indies and the New World, but its life as a trading port had practically died by the middle of the 19th century because of the development of deep-water ports more strategically sited than Minehead. A charter granted in 1558 was revoked in 1604, and the town was handed back to the Luttrel family owners since the 15th century. They remained owners of the Port until 1951 when they sold it to the local Council for £2.

Lower Town grew up behind the thriving port. Its principal development came in the 18th century, but little remains earlier than 1791, when a fire destroyed the town. A row of Almshouses built in 1630 survives in Market Street.

Higher Town became joined to its lower neighbours for administrative convenience and as a result of the fluid nature of 19th- and 20th-century development. Some of its old thatched houses remain and Church Steps is a picturesque little passage which gives a little of the former flavour of the old town. The 15th-century Church of St Michael is in Higher Town, the figure of St Michael commanding a fine view from its niche in the tower. Furniture inside the church illustrates different periods in its use: the font is original, dating from the 15th century, the communion table in the north chapel is Elizabethan, the pulpit is Jacobean, and the tombs span many ages. A tomb chest in the church is possibly of Henry de Bracton (1216–1272), a judge under Henry III and resident of Bratton Court, 1 kilometre west of the town. Nothing remains of Bracton's house but the ruins of the 15th-century house and chapel which replaced it are there, as well as the massive oak gate at the gate house. Queen Anne's alabaster statue was in the church until at least 1873. It was presented to the town in 1719 by Sir Jacob Bancks, a Swede who married into the Luttrell family and was Member of Parliament for Minehead for 16 years. The statue now stands in Wellington Square, sheltered by a late Victorian Canopy.

Like Padstow, Minehead has its annual fertility rite dating back to the Middle Ages. Each May Day a hobby horse dances through the streets of Quay Town with helpful hints and odd demonstrations for any woman not yet with child. Inevitably this is a great excuse for municipal festivities: drinking, dancing, singing, eating and laughter. Try to finish your walk on the 30 April if you want to see it, but you will need a good night's rest before the fun.

Hotel:	Northfield Hotel, Northfield Road; Tel. Minehead (0643) 2864
B&B:	Rivington, 22 The Parks; Tel. Minehead (0643) 3174
YHA:	Youth Hostel, Alcombe Combe; Tel. Minehead (0643) 2595

The South West Way

Bus:	To Taunton, Lynmouth and Exeter
Trains:	To Taunton
Early closing:	Wednesday
Tourist Information:	Tel. Minehead (0643) 2624

Bibliography

A History of Dorset	Cecil N. Cullingford (1980)
The Buildings of England–Dorset	John Newman & Nikolaus Pevsner (1972)
City–County Histories–Dorset	J.H. Bettey (1974)
Dorset through History	Peta Whaley (1977)
The Making of the English Landscape	Christopher Taylor (1970)
Buildings of Britain 1550–1750 SW England	Patrick Brown (1981)
Rural Life in Wessex	J.H. Bettey (1977)
West Country Shipwrecks	John Behanna (1974)
Companion Guide to the Coast of SW England	J. Seymour (1974)
Devon	A. Jellico & R. Mayne (1975)
The South West Peninsula	R. Millward & A. Robinson (1971)
The Buildings of England–South Devon	N. Pevsner (1952)
Cornwall and its People	A.K. Hamilton Jenkin (1970 Ed.)
Cornish Shipwrecks	R. Larn & C. Carter
Vanishing Cornwall	Daphne du Maurier (1967)
Buildings of England–Cornwall	N. Pevsner
The Naturalist in Devon and Cornwall	R. Burrows (1971)
A Cornish Anthology	A.L. Rowse (1968)
A West Country Anthology	S.H. Burton (1975)
Buildings of England–North Devon	N. Pevsner (1952)
Buildings of England–SW Somerset	N. Pevsner (1958)

Useful Addresses

SOUTH WEST WAY ASSOCIATION

Mrs M. Macleod, 1 Orchard Drive, Kinkerswell, Newton Abbot, Devon. (08047) 3061

WESTERN NATIONAL

National House, Queen Street, Exeter EX4 3TF. (0392) 74191

WEST COUNTRY TOURIST BOARD

West Country Tourist Board, Trinity Court, 37 Southernhay East, Exeter, EX1 1QS. (0392) 76351

RAMBLERS ASSOCIATION

Ramblers Association, 1/5 Wandsworth Road, London SW18 2LJ

YOUTH HOSTELS ASSOCIATION

Youth Hostels Association, (England and Wales), St. Albans, Herts, AL1 2DY. (0727) 55215

Other useful addresses, including ferry services and the Lulworth Range Officer, are shown under the relevant sections of the Gazetteer.

Index

NB. Page references in bold refer to Gazetteer entries.

Index of Gazetteer headings